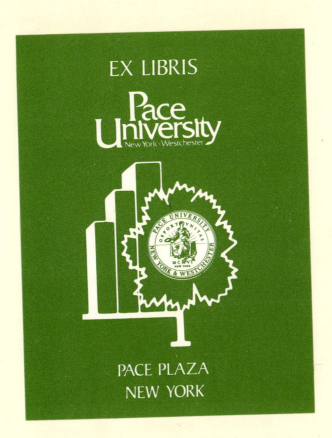

Ruth Suckow:

A Critical Study of Her Fiction

by
Margaret Stewart Omrcanin

DORRANCE & COMPANY
Philadelphia

PREFACE

Only a few American women novelists and short story writers have achieved and preserved a position among the foremost of American authors. Ruth Suckow in the twenties appeared to be destined for such distinction. But in the decades that followed this role seemed to become less secure as writers and readers responded to changing moods and forces in America.

Between the years 1921 and 1959 she published twelve volumes, of which eight are novels, two are collections of short stories, one a collection reprinting two novels and selected stories, and a volume containing a memoir and seven short stories.

Cherishing the common and universal in her fiction, she shunned the critics' term of regionalist as a misinterpretation of her intent. An examination of her entire work leads us to accept Ruth Suckow's sense of the enduring in the rural life styles of her narratives and the folkways of her people. For the 1970s her "folks" thesis as the basis of American civilization has particular interest.

For this study neither a biographical nor chronological method was basically satisfactory. Her stories and novels do not seem to grow out of events occurring progressively in her own life, or from social-historical events, but from a few particular phases of her life and environment which she re-examines throughout all of her fiction. While some extension of her material and development of techniques can be noted, the chronological order of publication does not reveal any significant advance in subject matter, theme, or method. Thus it was most useful to consider her writing in its entirety with reference to particular elements examined in each chapter. The study is then primarily an analysis of the fiction of Ruth Suckow utilizing, in addition to her creative work, her own autobiographical statement and her few statements about her own writing method.

Following an introductory review of the Iowa literary scene before Miss Suckow's writing and a summary of publication facts and critical judgments, this book examines in Chapter II the author's use of her native Iowa and the kind of physical and cultural scene she presents. Chapters III and IV consider the range of significance beyond this regional portrait by examining those universal values of thought and feeling to be found in her themes and characters. Chapter III, in particular, examines her themes and characters that are of social significance, and Chapter IV turns to her characterization and understanding of human experience. Her narrative method and technique in the short story is the subject of Chapter V followed by summary and conclusion in Chapter VI.

The appendices include a biographical chronology and a bibliography of all her published work.

Chapter I

CRITICAL CONFRONTATIONS

Ruth Suckow's first contribution to American fiction was a short story about Iowa people in an Iowa locale.[1] It appeared in a journal[2] established as a publication outlet for native writers at a time when the national consciousness was acutely aware of its component parts and when American literature had a strong regional flavor.

For the next three years Miss Suckow published other stories and short novels of the Iowa scene in periodicals until the novel, *Country People,* appeared in 1924, first serially in *The Century Magazine* and as a book issued later in the year by Knopf (May, 1924). She established her position as a painter of Iowa life in these and in successive stories and novels which were said to be "among the most authentic and veracious of all records of Middle Western life."[3] In her native state, which hitherto had few literary spokesmen, she became what Allan Nevins has called "one of the best, because one of the truest, of all the literary voices of the Union."[4]

Before the decade in which Ruth Suckow began to write there was a paucity of Iowa literature. A sense of cultural exile and a timorous attitude of Iowans toward themselves and their state, along with their sense of aesthetic meagerness and sterility, tended to inhibit and delay literary expression. Intellectually and spiritually awake later than any of its neighbors, Iowa lagged noticeably in literary activity. In the period of the nineties which marked a definite beginning of a recognized movement of middlewestern literature, some few voices were heard that called attention to the Iowa scene. After this beginning, however, there was a lapse for more than a decade. Iowa's loss of colonial complex did not become really apparent in its literature until after 1920.

In the three decades prior to Miss Suckow's publication, a few writers did utilize the Iowa locale in their fiction. Hamlin

Garland was the first to use successfully the contemporary Iowa scene in his fiction. He is the outstanding product of the period in which Johnson Brigham's *Midland Monthly,* established in 1890 and published for five years, gave impetus to the movement of middlewestern literature. Encouraged by his eastern associates Garland wrote with authentic response to the Iowa farm scene he had known in some of his stories in *Main Travelled Roads* (1891), *Prairie Folks* (1895), and later in *A Son of the Middle Border* (1917).

Stories appearing in *The Midland Monthly,* which published much fiction that was rich in regional detail, added little besides Garland's to the literature of Iowa. In a search of *The Midland Monthly* for stories with Iowa material, John T. Frederick found little genuine faithfulness to the Iowa scene. The first story in Volume I was by Octave Thanet (Alice French) of Davenport, then Iowa's most distinguished writer. While the scene of the story is an Iowa town, he observed no single detail to localize its setting and he reported that still another story by Miss French with an Iowa setting but similarly lacking in specific background appeared in Volume III. Other volumes revealed no stories except Hamlin Garland's that could be said to impart with validity the life or scene of Iowa, although there were stories of other places rich in regional detail.[5] While Garland was the first to make use of the Iowa farm, Miss French's portrayal of "Fairport," the locale of her *Stories of a Western Town* (1893), is cited by Frederick as being "the most sustained and penetrating fictional study of a small Midwestern city, in Iowa or elsewhere, before the First World War."[6]

Wallace Stegner in his article, "The Trail of the Hawkeye,"[7] noted a group of writers all born in Davenport within a ten-year period who were later to become distinguished. Among these were George Cram Cook, Susan Glaspell, Arthur Davison Ficke, and Harry Hansen. Others came to Davenport from elsewhere. Floyd Dell came from Barry, Illinois; Cornelia Meigs from Bryn Mawr, and Alice French was brought to Davenport when she was five years old. By 1908 most of these writers had left the state to live elsewhere, and except in the stories of Alice French their fiction had made little significant use of the Iowa scene.

2

By the second decade of the new century the awakening to the values of local material for literature had in other middle-western states produced vigorous and significant expression. Yet with the exception of Garland, no writer in Iowa attempted to use local subject matter with faithfulness to the scene until some time after a distinct literary movement was well established in other middlewestern states. Before any significant volume of Iowa fiction was published, the literature of the Middle West included: Theodore Dreiser's *Sister Carrie* (1900) and *Jennie Gerhardt* (1911); Willa Cather's *O Pioneers!* (1913) and *My Antonia* (1918); Edgar Lee Masters's *Spoon River Anthology* (1914); Carl Sandburg's *Chicago Poems* (1916); Sherwood Anderson's *Winesburg, Ohio* (1919); and Sinclair Lewis's *Main Street* (1920).

In Iowa the postwar generation of writers was the first willing to live in the state and to regard the materials of local environment as fit for literary subjects. Iowa City and Des Moines became the centers for literary figures as Davenport had been before that time. Stimulated by the efforts of John T. Frederick, through his publication *The Midland,* and of Louis Worthington Smith, a professor at Drake University, the younger generation really began to create a literature of Iowa. To this group, Ruth Suckow, Phil Stong, Tom Duncan, Paul Engle, Winifred Van Etten, James Hearst, Jay C. Sigmund, Mackinlay Kantor, and Marquis Childs, Iowa is indebted for a literature which truly portrays the state. This literary movement, gaining force in the twenties with Miss Suckow the outrider, continued into the thirties and forties, gathering in many new writers whose literary efforts were both revealing and substantial.

Originally, regional literature followed two directions. First came the rediscovery of the pioneer and the power and drama of the historical West. Naturally fiction of this type tended to be romantic and to place more emphasis on the melodramatics of the pioneer struggle than on veracious details.

The second tendency was more widespread and concerned with immediacies. The attitude was increasingly contemptuous and hostile. The authors, now more sophisticated, often wrote

3

from a distance and regarded with scorn, humor, or satire the materialistic emphasis and the barrenness of aesthetics and intellectual accomplishment.

Iowa writers responded to both attitudes. The fiction of Herbert Quick belongs to that tradition which celebrates the heroic and dramatic in American rural life. In his trilogy of *Vandemark's Folly* (1922), *The Hawkeye* (1923), and *The Invisible Woman* (1924), Quick used pioneer history and the native scene. Other creditable novels in the pioneer tradition are Margaret Wilson's *The Able McLaughlins* (1922) and Josephine Donovan's *Black Soil* (1930), begun as a requisite for a master's degree.

The scorn of the hostile critic who did not care to live in Iowa but used its material for satire is evident in Carl Van Vechten, whose Maple Valley of *The Tattooed Countess* (1924) has been cited as a close imitation of Sinclair Lewis's Zenith and Gopher Prairie in its caricatures of local figures, their boastful pride in local projects, the aesthetic pretensions of the youthful Gareth Johns, and its use of exotic words. The novel pictures the Cedar Rapids of 1897 and exposes the frustrated and narrow lives, the aesthetic sterility and deadly conformity of the town.

Even in the early twenties there was no conspicuous flowering of Iowa literature. Only a few names are worthy of being put beside Miss Suckow's. After Quick, Van Vechten and Margaret Wilson, there are three other writers whose work began to show an interest in Iowa's towns and plain people. Not as thorough or as objective in their treatment as Miss Suckow's fiction, the novels of Roger L. Sergel, Josephine Herbst, and Bess Streeter Aldrich yet mark the beginnings of this emergence.

In his first novel, *Arlie Gelston* (1923), Sergel presented the Iowa landscape and the town of Coon Falls in which he gives what Frederick called a "firm and accurate"[8] impression of place. Miss Aldrich, who in the next decade was to give in *Miss Bishop* (1933) a portrait of a midwestern college in the town of Cedar Falls (Oak River in the novel), published *The Cutters* (1926) in which she writes of a family in a small town in a sentimental and humorous manner. Josephine Herbst's *Nothing*

Is Sacred (1928) deals with a family in an Iowa town, but contributes nothing to the building of character or place. These books broadly use the regional materials that Miss Suckow's fiction presents with care and understanding. Writers who came after her are, on the other hand, more significant interpreters of Iowa than any who preceded her. In the literary history of the state she occupies the role of a pioneer in creating recognizable portrayals of the Iowa scene.

Before her first short story appeared in *The Midland,* Miss Suckow had contributed a number of short poems to literary magazines. The August, 1918, issue of *Touchstone* included a poem entitled "An Old Woman in a Garden"; a second poem, "Song in October," appeared in *The Midland* for September-October of the same year; and in *Poetry* of June, 1921, there appeared her last poems to be published. Under the title, "By Hill and Dale," are four short reflections: "Prayer at Timberline"; "Beauty"; "The Old Ones"; and "Grampa Schuler."

This slight body of poetry attempts no large themes or intense avowals. Its subjects and themes are those extended in her fiction: the quiet beauties of nature, small griefs and sadness, the eccentricities of the old, the clash of youth and the aged, expressed with the same clarity and sympathy that distinguish her longer work.

In the quatrain, "Song in October," expressing the assuagement from private pain in the beauties of nature, her imagery is delicate and sharp with something of the oblique approach of Frost, e.g., "As mist along the stubble rye,/As silver rain across the sky."

The reflections of "Hill and Dale," all personal, are on the relation of people, nature and things. The epigrammatic characterizations of Grampa Schuler and his grandson have something of the laconic quality of Robinson and Masters.

The longer poem, "An Old Woman in a Garden," written in free verse, is a portrait of a lonely woman who finds compensation in her kinship with the "strong pushing life" of earth, rain, and flowers. It has the poignancy of the unrequited and the sadness of the unrealized. Its colloquialism has the naturalness of Frost's poetry.

Encouraged first by John T. Frederick and later by H. L.

Mencken, Ruth Suckow began her publication of fiction in 1921, and from then until 1936 she was a frequent contributor to magazines concerned with contemporary literature. During that period, in addition to the contributions to periodicals, Miss Suckow also published six of her eight novels, two collections of short stories, and a volume of collected stories and reprints of two novels.[9] Her longest novel, *The Folks,* was published in 1934, and was the selection of the Literary Guild for October of that year. From 1936 to 1959, the year of her last published book, she was less productive. In 1942 the novel *New Hope* was published; in 1952 a collection of stories and a memoir entitled *Some Others and Myself* appeared; and in 1959 the novel *The John Wood Case* was published.

Five of Miss Suckow's novels and one volume of short stories have had publication and distribution outside the United States. Her publisher, Rinehart & Company, has recorded agreements with Jonathan Cape, Ltd., of London, and Messrs. Some & Company, of Oslo, Norway. Contracts were made with Jonathan Cape for *Country People* and *The Odyssey of a Nice Girl* on February 6, 1926; and for *The Bonney Family,* January 27, 1928. The agreements with Some & Company are for *Cora,* November 20, 1930, and *The Bonney Family,* October 12, 1932. *The Folks* was published as *Fergusons* by P. A. Norstedt & Company, Stockholm, in 1936, and by Gyldendal Nordisk, Copenhagen, as *Ungerne Flyver Af Reden* (The Birds Fly Out of the Nest). The English edition of *Iowa Interiors* was published by Jonathan Cape, Ltd., as *People and Houses,* 1927.

It was John T. Frederick, the editor of *The Midland,* who accepted her first story, "Uprooted," for publication. During the winter of 1921-1922, at the invitation of Frederick, Miss Suckow went to Iowa City to serve as editorial assistant on *The Midland.* At Frederick's suggestion she submitted some stories to H. L. Mencken who "became immediately and effectively enthusiastic, buying her work generously, nine stories in one year."[10] From 1921 to 1923, *Smart Set* published all stories purchased from Ruth Suckow. In 1924, when Mencken gave up the editorship of *Smart Set* to edit *The American Mercury,* Miss Suckow got a new outlet for publication. From that year until 1929 *The Mercury* continued to publish her stories. By that time she was well-established as a short story writer and had published six of her twelve books. In Frederick's opinion it was Mencken who was a great help in bringing about her book publication by Knopf.

Since he was eminent and influential and was able to pay for her work, his interest meant a great deal to her in the way of encouragement and help.[11]

In addition to *Smart Set, The American Mercury,* and *The Midland,* other magazines which published her stories and articles were: *The Century Magazine, Good Housekeeping, Harper's Monthly Magazine, Pictorial Review,* and *Scribner's Magazine.* Most of these contributions were later reprinted in one of her collections. Fiction published in periodicals which was not reprinted included the three following short novels: "The Best of the Lot," in *Smart Set* (November, 1922), "Other People's Ambitions," in *Smart Set* (March, 1923), and "A Part of the Institution," in *Smart Set* (October, 1923). Only three of her published stories were not reprinted. They were: "Strong As a Man," in *Harper's* (April, 1929); "Visiting," in *Pictorial Review* (July, 1929); "Three Counting the Cat," in *Good Housekeeping* (February, 1935).

During her lifetime the author kept in her own possession most of her original manuscripts. After her death in 1960 the majority of her papers were given to the State University of Iowa, Special Collections Department. The publisher's copy of *The John Wood Case,* with a few changes and deletions made jointly by the author and editor, Mr. Pascal Covici, is in the Emma Mills Collection of the New York Public Library.

More than two hundred letters that span a forty-two year correspondence are in the collection of Suckow Papers presented to the University of Iowa Libraries by Ferner Nuhn.

Walter P. Salefski, Decatur, Illinois, is a collector of Miss Suckow's published work. He has the manuscript of "Golden Wedding," written in pencil on the back of pages from an old ledger. The front had been used by her father for sermon notes. It was probably written in the latter part of 1924, in Earlville, Iowa. Mr. Salefski has a number of letters and copies of all her books published in the United States.

Ruth Suckow published few statements about herself or her writing. In the sketch, "A German Grandfather," in *The American Mercury* (November, 1927) she included some autobiographical facts as well as her impression of her paternal grandparent. The volume *Some Others and Myself* included "A Memoir" which supplied some biographical details although it deals primarily with her religious heritage and the development of her own beliefs. Her father, William John Suckow, records more of the family data in his autobiography, "Seventy Years in Retrospect." This account, however, has not been published.

Always somewhat reticent on the subject of her craft, she published only a few statements on subjects related to her fiction. In two magazine articles she expressed some views about the subject which becomes the material for her fiction. One article, entitled, "Iowa," in *The American Mercury* for August, 1926, examined some of the pertinent facts about her native state. In the essay "The Folk Idea in American Life" in *Scribner's Magazine* for September, 1930, she made a testament concerning what she believed to be the basis of American life and civilization. More specifically related to her literary intent and method is the preface, called "Comments and Addenda," in the volume *Carry-Over.* An unpublished manuscript, "Development of a Story," is the substance of a talk given at Indiana University and elsewhere to writers' groups. Opinions about the role of the middlewestern writer are stated in the essay "Middle Western Literature," published in *The English Journal* (March, 1932). Additional observations on the craft of writing appear in "The Short Story," in *The Saturday Review of Literature* (November 19, 1927) and "I Could Write If Only—," in *The Outlook* (March 21, 1928).

In the remaining published essays she expressed herself on a variety of topics related to literature: "Literary Soubrettes," in *The Bookman* (July, 1926): "Elsie Dinsmore: A Study in Perfection," in *The Bookman* (October, 1927); "Hollywood Gods and Goddesses," in *Harper's* (July, 1936); "An Almost Lost American Classic," in *The English Journal* (March, 1953); "Friends and Fiction," in *Friends Intelligencer* (February,

1955); "Robert Elsmere Reviewed by Ruth Suckow," in *The Georgia Review* (Fall, 1955); and "The Surprising Anthony Trollope," in *The Georgia Review* (Winter, 1958).

Critical comment about Ruth Suckow is also limited. While most of the books on twentieth century fiction mention Miss Suckow, they include few discussions or interpretations of great length. Until 1969, when a critical biography by Leedice McAnelly Kissane was published by Twayne, no book-length study of Ruth Suckow was in print. Other extended critical studies are limited to those by Joseph E. Baker,[12] John T. Frederick,[13] and Frank Luther Mott.[14] Books devoted to some special consideration such as Howard Odum's *American Regionalism,* Ima Herron's *The Small Town in American Literature,* and Harry Bernard's *Le Roman Regionaliste Aux Etats-Unis* recognize her contribution.

Reviewers expressed more interest in the early publications than in later ones. While *Country People* in 1924 and *Iowa Interiors* in 1926 were greeted as realistic fiction of the farm and small town in the tradition of the main stream of American literature in the twenties, the publication of the last novel, *The John Wood Case,* in 1959, was not heralded as a history-making literary event.

In the period from 1921 to 1959 the response of critics was varied: markedly favorable, hostile, and indifferent. Praise is the dominant note of the earlier reviews, while a rather uniform complaint of dullness and tediousness marks the later reviews. A few judgments can be cited to indicate the critical attitudes most frequently taken toward Miss Suckow's fiction.

While not all of the early reviewers were as absolute in their judgments as H. L. Mencken, who wrote of her as "unquestionably the most remarkable woman now writing short stories in the Republic,"[15] most critics saw a particular significance in her work as a contribution to middlewestern literature during the first half of the twentieth century, especially of the twenties and thirties.

As interpreter of Iowa she achieved, in the opinion of Allan Nevins, a significance not held by any previous author. Frank Luther Mott, in regarding her as "pre-eminently the interpreter of Iowa Life," supported the judgment by Nevins.

I think Miss Suckow has produced the strongest and most significant stories written by an Iowan writer since Hamlin Garland's stories of the nineties. As a novelist she is in my judgment, Mr. Garland's superior.[16]

A major portion of her fiction had been published when Carl Van Doren considered it not only a valid interpretation of Iowa life but of all rural America.

Ruth Suckow, beginning with *Country People,* studied contemporary life with honest realism, and in her long *The Folks* (1934) came nearer than any other writer has done to representing the whole of American life on farms and in small towns.[17]

In more than one discussion Miss Suckow was placed among writers who set the tone and trend of American fiction during the thirties and was named among such literary figures as these:

Dreiser, Lewis, Anderson, Sandburg, Masters, Dell, with younger writers like Ruth Suckow and James T. Farrell, have produced the most original, the most vigorous, the most outspoken literature in the nation; their novels and short stories, their verse and autobiographies, have been the models and examples for several literary generations.[18]

Disparaging criticism, where it has appeared, is generally in accord with the opinion expressed by Joseph Warren Beach.

I have puzzled a good deal over the work of writers, like Ruth Suckow, who seem to have all the materials for significant fiction—character, background, feeling and understanding, seriousness and industry—and yet somehow just fail to ring the bell. It cannot fail to interest those acquainted with these localities and these conditions of living, which are in many respects most typical American conditions. The stuff is all there, and there is also in the author the sympathy and insight we should wish for the interpretation of this human data. Yet somehow it fails to take strong hold on the imagination . . . and the farther one reads the more troubled one grows that matter so interesting, presented so faithfully, should prove so wanting in fascination. . . .

It is very hard to say just what is wrong. Perhaps one thing that is wanting is rigorous selection of matter. And yet there are plenty of books that are equally crowded with intimate detail which never make this impression of tediousness. It is not so much selection itself that is wanting as a principle of selection. And the principle of selection, which would affect both the style itself and the subject matter presented, would be, I think, some coloring of the mind (beyond mere honesty and goodwill) which would give a more special turn to all that is said.[19]

To the reader returning to her stories and novels Ruth Suckow's distinction lies in her unfailing observation which captures a scene with all its fullness of meaning and in her intense sympathy and compassion for all human travail.

As she records the world of farms and villages in a passing era of American life her fond intimacy and memory indeed bring charm to her remembrances of things past. Aware of the uncertainty that follows a changing era, however, she perceives the characteristic pattern in American society to be in its fresh beginnings without reliance on old patterns. In such only are youthfulness and simplicity, equality and freedom and the New Testament tenets of love and peace cherished by Ruth Suckow. This trust in fresh beginnings is her particular coloring of mind.

11

Chapter II

PORTRAYER OF THE IOWA SCENE

Like Willa Cather who stressed the importance of a writer's first fifteen years in acquiring thematic material, Ruth Suckow can mark her early years as the most significanct in her preparation for writing. Sensitive from childhood to the natural beauty of the Iowa countryside and gifted with unusual powers of observation and memory, Miss Suckow nurtured her native talents with an intimate knowledge of Iowa towns and a compassionate understanding of its people.

She rarely abandons the scene familiar to her from childhood. In some of her novels, the characters make wide excursions. At the close of the narrative they may plan to leave or may have left; but always they are of Iowa, their makeup indelibly determined by it. Her recurrent scene is the Iowa of farms and towns populated with immigrant and native-born rural folk. With an eye for minutiae she has used delicate brushes to fix and catch the moods and meanings of her own inescapable country—a country bounded by meadows and brooks, woods and towns. The people and things that move in it are as plain as the ginghamed figures of a Grant Wood painting; the colors are the colors of the earth and of things close to the earth.

Perhaps no single statement stands so well to show her feeling for her local scene as the one relating to Fred Bonney, the minister, unhappy in his work of raising funds for a college. Giving up the idea of resigning in order to return to his small-town pastorate, he recognizes with sadness that, "For good and all, he must accept the college and put away the church—give up the personal satisfaction from the thing small enough to touch every part of it with his own hands and savour every detail."[1] In his first surge of loneliness in the new surroundings he yearned for the intimacies of his life in Morning Sun, "knowing all the little personal things about people, entering deeper

12

and deeper into the life of a small community."[2] The reader of Miss Suckow's fiction feels that she likewise savors every detail with affection and purposely limits the scene in order to enter more deeply into the life of the small community. As exact as Dreiser in her compulsion to search out every revealing detail, she differs from him in the ineffable quality of tenderness with which she cherishes her scene.

The state that furnishes the raw materials of Miss Suckow's fiction occupies a central position in the Middle West; it combines the qualities of half a dozen states, and hence often has seemed undistinguished to its own people and to others. Physically and culturally, Iowa possesses many of the qualities of its neighbors.

Its northern corner borders on Minnesota, and is windy and sloughy, with numerous lakes and Scandinavian towns. The beautiful northeastern portion is like an extension of the woods and dells of Wisconsin. The southern part is tinged with the softness, laxness and provincialism of Missouri and Arkansas. Much of the west is flat, windy, harsh, like Kansas, Nebraska or the Dakotas. The central portion is the very heart of the prairie region—smooth, plain, simple, fresh and prosperous. All these differing elements, however, are smoothed down with a touch of gentleness into that lovely, open pastoral quality which is peculiarly Iowan after all.[3]

Despite the variety of pastoral setting, with its profusion of woodlands and pastures, lakes, brooks, and river valleys, cornfields and barns, Allan Nevins has observed that Iowa is the last state we associate with beauty.[4] Its beauty lies in familiarity—those aspects of the earth so often overlooked because they are unspectacular.

The region, largely covering the fertile peninsula formed by the two largest rivers of the country, contains a greater total acreage of grade-one agricultural land than any other state. This immense farmland is the Iowa known to most Americans.

Here are the corn and wheat fields, the characteristic white houses, big red barns and tall silos; and, at regular intervals, grain elevators and church spires dominating the little towns. It is from this area largely that the State's agricultural prestige is derived.[5]

While this Grant Wood richness is characteristic of much of Iowa, there is another picture—that of a wide and lonely prairie where the land lies flat and bare as a table top and even the people take on a measure of its monotonous regularity.

Ruralism, far more than urban industrial life, has influenced the stability and conservatism of a society where people have lived in the same way for several generations, marked by the qualities of individualism, self-reliance, common sense, practical materialism, and isolationism, the prerequisites of pioneer culture. The farm element, like the rich soil, seems to Miss Suckow to retain many of the pioneer virtues of sturdiness, independence, and freshness.

Among what are too often regarded as the plodding traits of this region and this people, Miss Suckow has discerned something rare and distinctive—an "authentic" quality which she has strived to incorporate in her own fiction.

That something is, at its worst, timid, deprecating, wishy-washy, colorless, and idealistic in a mild, fruitless way. At its best it is innocently ingenuous, fresh and sincere, unpretentious, and essentially ample, with a certain quality of pure loveliness—held together and strengthened by the simplicity and severity of its hardworking farmer people.[6]

Lying close to its farmland are the small towns that grew in the center of farming populations, near a grist mill or a railroad station. The importance of the railroad in the settlement of these towns is evident in the fact there is no place in the state farther than twelve miles from a railroad.

The railroad often determined the town site on the prairie, loaded a tiny depot on a flat car and brought it to the spot. Next came the freight house for supplies and a stock

14

pen for loading cattle; then a tiny grain elevator, a general store; a doctor, a lawyer, and a newspaper—a new town in Iowa.[7]

Such towns were well known to Miss Suckow. As the daughter of a Congregational minister, she experienced frequent changes in residence. By the time she was fifteen years old she had lived in five Iowan communities: Hawarden, LeMars, Algona, Fort Dodge, and Manchester. All of them except Fort Dodge were small towns, although three were county seats.[8] It is from the small towns known in her girlhood that she most frequently draws her beloved picture.

Although Ruth Suckow never lived on a farm, she spent a part of nearly every summer in visiting her grandfather on his farm in Hancock County.[9] Her father's pastorates were frequently in villages and towns close to farmlands. As a child she accompanied him often on his country calls, riding in a little wooden seat he had made for her on the handle bars of his bicycle.[10] From these rides she acquired very early a love of the country and a deep-welling familiarity with country sights and sounds.

That was when I came to know the deep brown loessal soil of that semi-Western prairie region as my native earth—when the wild roses became my "favorite flower," and the meadow larks nesting along the bare roadsides my "favorite bird." The whole impression of this great open, rolling region on the edge of the West was of breadth and freedom under the immensity of the blue sky.[11]

From her visits in the homes of church members she stored up innumerable details of farm houses and of domestic rural life. Her sensitive response to these early experiences was perhaps her best equipment for writing. To these early impressions she later added a mature appreciation and a philosophy and method of writing.

In turning to local materials Miss Suckow was in unison with the literary trend of her era. She was, however, directed more by her own temperament and artistic motives than by any adherence to a group or movement. Joseph E. Baker has described her work in this connection as "Definitely a product of our growing regional consciousness, yet not consciously a part of the regionalist movement."[12] With her own inclination to use the specific and the concrete as a medium of expressing an idea, presenting a character, or evoking an atmosphere, it was natural for her to turn to the familiar scenes of her native state. To her the advantage of examining regional materials lay in the intensified perceptiveness of the writer.

> What it did most was to awaken the sense of young artists to what actually was the nature of the country in which they lived—and so to themselves, and so to the larger aspects of their country, and so to the world.[13]

An awareness of the distinctive quality of the Middle West she believed to be essential for its artists.

> Things are all the same—but also, they are all different. Art, partially determined by time and place, catches in a frame what would otherwise be lost. What we have here in the Middle West, the particular way, the fresh way, in which the ancient stream of life manifests itself, colored and shaped by local conditions, has never been before and will never be again. We must catch it, or its essence is eternally lost. That is the deepest reason for a middle western literature.[14]

Along with this concept of the role of the middlewestern literature and the middlewestern artist is another basic idea central to all of Miss Suckow's writing. Sensitive to the contemporary search for "Fork Art" but not in sympathy with its retrospective emphasis, Miss Suckow perceived what she believed a more significant and a more genuinely American pattern in our culture and civilization. She has consistently tried to establish norms of regional values and to turn regional writing from the folk element to that of the "Folks." The writer should not, she says, expect to find the folk element in America expressed in just the same terms or with the same meaning as in other civilizations.

> To discover it in its broadest aspects, we must look for it among the people who do actually form the great mass basis of our particular civilization. They are the people who go by the name of "just common ordinary Americans." . . .
> The whole matter may be summed up in this: the folk idea in America has become the idea of "folks."[15]

This concept is interrelated with her use of regional materials and enters into her selection and portrayal of the rural scene. Her landscapes of farm and town cannot be separated from her people, or her people from them. The gatherings of the plain Americans within their own domestic circle, the enlarged group of churchgoers, or community celebrations and festivities are as much a part of the Iowa scene as its cowsheds and cornfields.

In presenting her Iowa scene with its interrelated physical and social elements Miss Suckow deals most frequently with the opening years of the century. There is no schematic arrangement of her fiction to present in sequential order the era of which she writes, but her stories and novels together reveal the Iowa scene across the changing hues of thirty years. Her work is a panorama of the native life of her period. With few exceptions the period covered is from the turn of the century to the decade or so following the First World War. Her scene is the Iowa of a time considerably later than the territorial period—the period of harsh and primitive existence. It is a period beginning not long after the unrest in the Middle West of the nineties and extending from about 1900 into the Hoover era, but not quite into the depression years. It is the time of her childhood and youth, an era that began with horse and buggy and closed with a brand new Model T Ford that could whisk the family to town and the movies in a hurry. The economic stress of the thirties is only foreshadowed in some of the stories.

Miss Suckow's thorough acquaintance with the different parts of the state makes her aware of the diversity and likeness of the Iowa scene and cognizant of that permeating quality she calls "authentic" which belongs to middlewestern life—a downright quality, a plainness, a simple freshness. With an accuracy of detail she can shift her fictional setting from one Iowa town to another.

While no single book or character is in its entirety autobiographical, all of the novels contain suggestions in scene, incident, or characters that reveal Miss Suckow's memory of her observations or experiences. In *Country People* she writes of farmers with German ancestry like her own who live in the same area of prairie and timber lands where her grandfather Suckow had settled. It is in the experiences of the main character of *The Odyssey of a Nice Girl* that the book bears the closest resemblance to her own life. In *The Bonney Family* the portrayal of a minister's family in the parsonage of a small town and later in a college town uses environment and character from her own experience. In *The Kramer Girls* the type of town she knew as a girl rather than a specific town provides the scene. In *Cora* as in *Country People* she again makes use of the German element in Iowa people and creates one character who embodies many of the personal characteristics she has described in her grandfather. The novel *The Folks,* while true to the social scene she knows so well, does not present as many specific parallels to her own life as other books. In *New Hope,* a late novel, she draws the most specific and the most extensive parallels to an actual place in this fictional portrait of her birthplace, Hawarden. The last novel, *The John Wood Case,* utilizes an incident involving the misuse of funds similar to an occurrence she recalls.

Throughout her fiction memories and observations fuse with her creative talents in her portrayal of her native state. An examination of her fictional settings reveals how extensively she used the actual local scene.

For her first novel as well as for her first stories Miss Suckow drew on her knowledge of the farm and of farming people. *Country People* is actually the only one which deals primarily with the Iowa farm. For its setting she went to the open prairies of Hancock County where her grandfather had settled. In this novel the farm and farm life are treated more fully than in any other. She recounts the story of three generations of a farming family—and does it with a hardness and tightness of style in keeping with their narrow lives.

The farmland near Turkey Creek and Richland Township, the two towns in the Wapsipinicon County of her novel, is the locale for this book. In 1850 the elder Kaetterhenrys of the novel came as German immigrants to the Turkey Creek region. Miss Suckow's own immigrant grandparents had moved from Albany, New York, to Elkport, Clayton County, Iowa in 1869. In 1874 they occupied a farm on the Turkey Creek River six miles from Elkport. In Albany they had united with the Dutch Reformed Church but were later converted to Methodism by the evangelist, Peter Cartwright.[16] Her father records that a Mr. Rudolph Fiegenbaum, a retired minister "functioning as a land agent," had established a large colony of German Methodists on the unbroken prairie of Hancock County, near Klemme—"The section in which are located most of the scenes described by my daughter Ruth in her novel."[17]

The large German Methodist community of the novel had a similar beginning. Henry Baumgartner, a convert to German Methodism, had started the community of Turkey Creek in the interests of both riches and religion. "He had sent back to Prussia and got a dozen families to come and settle on his land, promising them help in getting started on the condition that they should all become German Methodists. . . . Other Germans had begun coming in until the region was full of them."[18]

Turkey Creek, fifteen miles north of Richland in timber country, was a backwoods town with no railroad. In 1850 it had a few stores and houses and a town hall of yellow limestone at the end of the main street. While not actually a pioneer town, it was years behind the times—a hilly region of tall timber and bottom land. The younger Kaetterhenry, ambitious to own land and become a prosperous farmer, moved from the timber to the prairie land of Richland Township area where the fertile farms lay in "some of the best land in the country" that "didn't give the farmers much chance for complaint." This was a rolling country of neat, plain farms set off in square fields; the buildings and machinery were kept in good repair and sleek cattle grazed in pastures "that sloped down, emerald green, turfy,

19

almost mossy to the edges of the creek."

Men who kept an eye out for land deals noted shrewdly how well the buildings and barbed-wire fences were kept up, the red barns and silos, the prim white houses, square or with an ell, some of them with front yards enclosed in fences, and rose or snowball bushes growing.[19]

The Richland Township area was in many ways ahead of Turkey Creek. There was more prairie and less timber. Eleven miles from Wapsie, the county seat, it was connected with Chicago by the Illinois Central Railroad. Here it was easier to market crops. With the coming of the automobile, the road to Richland in front of August Kaetterhenry's farm became Primary Road 5, widened, ditched, and graveled for auto traffic. When the Ford replaced the two-seated buggy there came also new farm machinery, run by electricity, and electric lights in the barn. August Kaetterhenry, starting with nothing but the money he had saved from hiring out, acquired one 250-acre farm for himself and another 200 acres for a son. August's farm was an especially well-kept one.

It was a neat, plain farm, two hundred and fifty acres, virtually all under cultivation. The house was set back at what was termed "a nice distance" from the road—a white house with pink trimmings and a narrow porch. . . . Tall summer lilies, orange with dark spots, grew near the front porch in a spreading patch. On the west of the house stood the wind-break—two rows of elms that were lofty now, rather thin, and close together. The lawn ended at their trunks in a ridge of high grass and feathery weeds that the boys could not keep cut. A barbed-wire fence, caught together in one place by a wooden staple, separated them from the cornfield. The lofty upper branches rustled and moved slightly against the blue sky. In the evening their outlines were blurred and there was a sadness in their dark leafiness, high and motionless.[20]

Suckow makes us aware of the patient struggle for

ownership. With money saved from years of hard work, August began to put a run-down farm in good condition. At first he paid for part of his stock and implements and went in debt for the rest. He meant to work without stopping until he paid for his farm.

> To have a farm free from encumbrances; to own "clear" the stock, the machinery, and the land, was what he was working for. All that he had or could make went into the farm.[21]

There may be emotional attachment to the land in August's desire to have his son, Carl, carry on as owner of the 400-acre farm with the promise of becoming as good a farmer as his father. But it appears to be more a sense of pride and security that his son should enjoy as much, if not greater, prosperity than he had. Naturally August and Emma regard their younger son Johnnie with a bit of suspicion because of his desire to become a mechanic and to own a garage instead of a farm.

The richness of this prairie soil meant no more to them than what it could, with unremitting effort, be made to produce. The novel fails to show a sense of intimacy of man with the earth, that identity with the qualities of growth and strength derived from the soil, or that sense of an inexorable fate pursuing man when pitted against the primal elements. The land does not inspire the heroic in its characters, nor does it produce any aesthetic reaction. It stands only as evidence of their acquisitiveness, and it has no overtones beyond this. Incidents follow the life cycle of birth, schooling, courtship, and marriage. With the new family come hard work before the eventual retirement, sickness, and death. Few incidents, if any, result from what Mary Austin in her discussion of regional literature has named the four great causatives: climate, housing, transportation, and employment.[22] There is a strong sense of movement of agricultural life in Iowa over a period of three generations, but this movement is one of social, technical, and economic change; changes brought about by the son's new way of doing things, the coming of the automobile, and the building of the primary road.

In conveying this sense of change, Miss Suckow weaves her regional scene into one of her central themes—that of social transition. This general movement typical of the middlewestern farm element is treated with more detail in *Country People* than in any of her other novels, but it becomes part of the general social background in her fiction and is fitted into the whole social pattern of the folks. While Miss Suckow has made no effort to continue or elaborate the history of a single family in her novels, as Paul Corey has done in his trilogy of the Mantz family,[23] many of her people seem to have had a similar origin and might have come from the same stock as the Kaetterhenrys.

While hard work and thrift set the dominant tone of *Country People*, the book is not without enthusiasm for the farm scene and activity. Threshing time, which climaxes the farmer's achievement and produces excitement and social interest as well as hard work, provides the narrator in farm fiction a departure from the drabness, monotony, and loneliness of work in the field. Hamlin Garland, who often reminisced about the toil, the sweat, and the mud of farm work, wrote pleasantly in both his stories and his autobiography of this phase of farm life. In *Country People,* she also beholds the rude joy of harvesting.

The threshers were at the Stilles' two days. It was in early September, dry, burning weather, when the bright new evergreens in the grove at the North of the house stood motionless and pointed against the blue sky. The men worked with their old horse-power thresher out in the fields, where the stubble was bright and harsh under their feet and the sun blazed on the yellow-gold straw-stacks that piled up behind the machine. . . .

He [August] pretended not to notice, but he saw the girls, standing there leaning against each other, half closing their eyes against the sun, which was bright on their black hair and flushed cheeks, the blue dresses against the blazing gold of the straw-stacks and the stubble out under the blue prairie-sky. The chaff filled the air, and the men turned to grin with a flash of white teeth in their blackened faces.[24]

Throughout the novel her feeling for country life is apparent. Whether she is describing the white barns, the silos, the neat square fields of oats and corn, or the high rolling pastures dotted with clover, her writing gives a sense of the solid and real.

The wide yard sloped east to the barns and sheds across "the drive." It was worn bare of grass about the buildings and scattered with chicken fluff and droppings. The geese ran squawking across it when teams drove in. The great barn stood at the end of the slope, raised on a high foundation, with an inclined platform of heavy planks that thundered and shook under the horses' hoofs.[25]

Nature itself provided the living drama of that countryside with its seasonal changes. More engaging than its picnickers was Richland Grove, the site of the Fourth of July celebration.

The grove had been well cleared of under-brush, and there were open spaces through which the sun shone golden-green. There were bur-oaks in clumps, larger oaks standing apart, full-leaved, casting a gracious shade. The ground lay in smooth, rounded slopes with long fine green grass that was full of little whirring things. It was sprinkled with wild gooseberry bushes, bitter-smelling white yarrow, clumps of catnip filled with black-bodied wild bees. The creek was dry, a narrow stream bed filled with hot white sand. Some children were running along it with bare feet.[26]

The peasantish courtship of August Kaetterhenry and Emma Stille following this picnic was neither dramatic nor colorful, and the reader learns little of what is felt or said as they ride to Wapsie to be married, but he does feel the scene.

It was late February, just before the last thaw. The road to "Wapsie" was a winter study in dull black and white. The snow, which had an opaque, thick look under the colour-less winter sky, drifted down the black earth of the slopes; the plumtrees in interlaced masses along the creek, low, spreading, done in smoky black . . . ; the creek half under thin greyish ice cracked and broken down in places; the road dead black, sifted over with fine snow. The buggy looked small on that great expanse of land, the hoofs of the horses on the hard wintry road made a lonesome sound.

The town had a closed-up winter look. The girls did not speak as they drove along the wintry street.[27]

Following the brief ceremony,

They drove back to the farm down the dim, chilly road, the bare bushes thin and small, the fields spreading out black and sprinkled with snow. There was a wintry red in the Western sky.[28]

Again the scene emphasizes setting more than action. When the first three boys from Richland Township left for service in World War I,

The little town was silent. Away from the station stretched pastures, the dew lying wet and heavy on red clover and tall weeds. The train came bearing down upon them, puffing out blackish smoke into the pale morning sky. It went black and big into the red prairie-sunrise. The fields were left silent again. The scattered group of people on the platform got into their battered cars and drove back home to the morning chores.[29]

Just as essential to the rural scenes as the fertile farms and green pastures are the pink frame schoolhouses on the side of the road, the scene of many country socials; the groves with their rich, thick cluster of oaks and hickories for the Sunday School picnics and the Fourth of July celebrations; the prairie houses like that of August Kaetterhenry, "white with pink trimmings, a narrow porch, a triangle of wooden lace under the peak in front"; the white frame church out in the country with its Sunday gatherings and social activities.

24

The country German Methodist Church attended by farmers of Turkey Creek and Richland was a familiar type in the Iowa countryside.

It was a plain white frame-building, bleak and small, a long hitching board in front of it, and behind it the sheds for the teams and the two tiny outhouses all standing stark on a great clearing. Church was held in the afternoon. The farmers drove there in lumber-wagons, tying their horses to the long hitching-board, or in bad weather putting them in the sheds. They stood about on the church-steps, talking, the men together and the women in another group, until the preacher drove up.[30]

Most of the farmers in the Turkey Creek area were German Methodists. They drove to church in lumber wagons and before and after services stood about on the church steps where the older folks talked about the weather and the crops; and the young men in their thick, dark best clothes, "stood about in abashed Sunday-constrained groups, pretending to talk to one another, but aware of the girls, whose eyes were aware of them." It was for this the young men came.

Weddings were made much of in the community. The celebration sometimes lasted three days. Yet there was more intoxication at the camp meetings held in the timber by the traveling Methodist evangelists. This religious debauch was about the only emotional outlet for the farmer committed to endless days of hard, grinding work. In the larger communities there were socials at the country schools, box suppers, bob rides and big country parties where they played old country games and kissing games.

Next to the church and school socials the outstanding events were the country fairs and the celebrations of national holidays. On blistering hot days farmers with their families drove to Fourth of July celebrations, carrying their dinner in big pasteboard boxes. They joined the other branches of the family to eat together on the grass and bought their ice cream from the Ladies Aid. To these outings came "family groups, old ladies sitting on cushions or in buggies, unattached boys going about hoping to find girls, men pitching horseshoes."[31] Entertainment consisted of singing and reciting patriotic songs and poems, band concerts, and usually an oratorical delivery by a state representative speaking from a stand draped in red, white, and blue bunting. In creating the atmosphere of these outings and gatherings, she catches the essential spirit of farm, church, street, and home.

In *Country People,* primarily a farm novel, the rural town geographically and culturally close to the country is a natural part of the setting. When it is time to retire and turn over the farm to the sons in the family, the Iowa farmer of Miss Suckow's fiction moves to a nearby town. The Richland Township of this novel lies close to the country scene. The little railroad station, which in winter stands bleak in the midst of frozen pastures that in the summer are wet with dew lying heavy on red clover and tall weeds, is a reminder of the nearness of the country. When August visits his new house being built in town, one is again aware of the short remove.

In the early summer evenings there was a kind of sadness and bareness in the new house, standing stark against the pale evening sky, the new boards around, the raw dirt, the tools thrown down whenever the men had happened to drop them, the vacant lots beyond, and then the pastures stretching away, damp and fresh with dew, and the slow-moving forms of cattle.[32]

Ruralism pervades these towns in which retired farmers, widows, and spinsters make their homes. The church and high school again become social centers for the women and children. The men's few business activities take them to the farmers' bank, the general store, the grocery, the post office, the barber shop or restaurant; and the *Richland Banner* or some other local paper will inform them in folksy paragraphs of illness, trips, funerals, and church socials.

In this first novel, Ruth Suckow is a sparse chronicler experimenting with subject matter and themes that recur in later fiction: the farmland itself; the nearby village; the farming people of immigrant ancestry; the pattern of family life and the community folkways; the social and economic transitions with the ensuing contrast and conflict between generations.

In the second novel, *The Odyssey of a Nice Girl* (1925), the scene shifts from farm to town. The farm element is only incidentally treated. Again it serves to emphasize the theme of transition and to point up a contrast between farm and town. But the town dominates the scene in this novel. Grampa Schoessel had never forgiven his son, Ed, for leaving the farm and abandoning certain ways of his parents.

> Ed had left the German Methodist Church. Grandpa always had to act a little grumbling and grudging, because Ed lived in town and kept a store, and because he was bringing up his children to be "so fine."[33]

In her aversion to the farm, Marjorie, the central character of the novel, points up the contrasts between the niceties and comforts of town and country crudities. Yet she was not insensitive to the appeal of things on the farm—things like the windmill and the best buggy, black and shining with its grainy leather top and stiff shiny whip, nor to the natural beauty of the country.

> Dimly she sensed a kind of beauty—the blue sky was in it, and the rustle of the corn, that spreading silence of the country. But she hated the sunbonnet.[34]

Her world of friends in town, her amusements and reading had made her a stranger to the country cousins and the rustic pleasures. She felt as foreign to the ways of her cousins as Patricia in "The Little Girl from Town." In her eyes Buena Vista, the county seat with its three thousand inhabitants, was greatly superior to Germantown where the farm of her grandparents was located.

Suckow did not in this novel continue the farm novel tradition that might have been intimated as her chosen field in *Country People*. The next three novels, *The Bonney Family* (1926), *Cora* (1929), and *The Kramer Girls* (1930), though partially occupied with a rural atmosphere, all have the town for their settings.

In *The Folks* the farm again takes its place in the total

scheme of the book, but it is not the main setting. Yet as she frequently does, she uses the farm to emphasize her themes or to highlight a character mood or trait. The farm is a real thing in the lives of Fred Ferguson's family although they live in Belmond. Neither Fred Ferguson nor his brothers had taken to farming. In the familiar middlewestern routine they had started out farming and then moved into town. But in times of stress the farm is a bulwark of strength and solace to various members of the family. When the son Carl was distressed with his own domestic problems and felt defeated in the knowledge of his own failures, he went to the farm where he could be alone and feel the "healing" quality of "its plain simplicity." When Fred Ferguson, Carl's father, a retired Belmond banker, is bewildered by the actions of his children and disturbed by the clouds threatening the social structure, he finds confirmation of his old faith and confidence in revisiting the family farm.

> Well, anyway, it was good land. His father hadn't made any mistake about that. It was good land, and they had owned it for a while, worked it, and received its benefits. This belief in the goodness of his native soil lay underneath the tottering structure of business faith, religious faith, everything. Whatever folks might do with it, the land was here. That was good. If folks treated it right, it would never let them starve.[35]

Usually the farm is something accepted in the way of life, and there are only a few occasions when the characters comment about it. In the novel *New Hope,* three characters express their feelings about the land. To the small town banker from a farming family, land was first of all an investment; to Mr. Greenwood, the idealistic young minister, it was "the richest endowment any people ever had given them," offering the possibility to "make anything of the country here if we go about it, make actual use of our opportunities." But to Andy Miller, the owner and operator of the farm, it is the place "where we live and are going to raise our crops." This last practical view is the motivating one among Miss Suckow's farmers.

Actually it is in her short stories, where she depicts with poignancy the futility, dullness, and drabness of the rural scene, that farm life receives its most penetrating treatment. Her reputation as the portrayer of the drab, the ugly, and the dull in the farm scene is based more on her stories in *Iowa Interiors* than on her longer fiction. She looks upon the poverty and toil of farm life and that impoverishment which is of the spirit. Treating her scene with more poignancy than in *Country People,* with an eye for specific observation, she records the sadder aspects of life among Iowa farmers, the emptiness of whose lives is a betrayal of their lifelong habit of toil. But even while she presents the pathos, barrenness, and helplessness in the lives of the characters in such stories as "A Start in Life," "Mame," "Uprooted," and "Renters," she is at the same time aware of the deep stabilities of country life intimated in the stories of "A Rural Community," "Retired," and "A Pilgrim and a Stranger."

The young girl in "A Start in Life," the initial story in *Iowa Interiors,* leaves a poor and impoverished farm place to become the hired girl in the home of a young couple in better circumstances. Her anticipation and excitement are turned into loneliness and unhappiness by the realization that comes in her first day at work—the meaning of hiring out. The pathos of her poverty and loneliness is emphasized early in the story by the dismal sight of her own home on the outskirts of town. The rain had left the roads a yellow mess with water lying in all the wheel ruts. The little road, we are told, had a "cold rainy loneliness." As the wheels of her employer's car spin in the thick, wet mud in the efforts to get away from the house, Daisy sees her own home in all of its poverty and cheerlessness.

In that moment, Daisy had a startled view of home—the small house standing on a rough rise of land, weathered to a dim colour that showed dark streaks from the rain; the narrow sloping front porch whose edge had a soaked gnawed look; the chickens, greyish-black, pecking at the wet ground; their playthings, stones, a wagon, some old pail covers littered about; a soaked, discoloured piece of underwear hanging on the line in the back yard. The yard was tussocky and overhung the road with shaggy long grass where the yellow bank was caved in under it. . . . She saw her mother's face—a thin, weak, loving face, drawn with neglected weeping, with its reddened eyes and poor teeth . . . in the old coat and heavy shoes and cleaning-cap, her work-worn hand with its big knuckles clutching at her coat. She saw the playthings they had used yesterday, and the old swing that hung from one of the trees, the ropes sodden, the seat in crooked. . . .[36]

The farm that is neglected and run down because money is lacking to keep it in repair is the scene of the story "Mame." For eleven years Mame Bussey with a blind and crippled husband had stayed on the farm at Karnak to care for "the old folks" but was unable to maintain it in good condition. The need for money to meet an increase in taxes is the occasion for a conclave of other sons and daughters. The more prosperous members of the family who have moved to town for business opportunities are smug and complacent in their own comforts. As they look out on the unkempt sight, they find it easier on the family conscience to attribute the poverty of the farm to Mame's shiftlessness rather than to circumstances

The house was painted a dingy, faded, darkened, hideous yellow, with a faint reminder of green on the border of shingles around it. Tall trees stood about it, bending their upper branches and rustling in the hot, dreary summer wind that was blowing. There was a fence of wire in loops at the top, rusted, bent down in one place as if something had trampled and run over it. The pump on the sloping platform back of the house, and a wooden washtub broken at the rim, an old broom, ancient bee ware boxes, broken flower pots, a mop with a stiff greyish cloth leaning against the wall. Old sheds, the empty barn, the outhouse absurdly trimmed like the house—under the fruit-trees an old decayed beehive, reminder of the days when Mame and Alick had "tried bees"; . . . a kitchen chair with no back out under the trees.[37]

A more prosperous farm is the scene of "Renters," but ironically it does not bring prosperity to the man who has made it thrive. Fred Mutchler learns the helplessness of the renter at the mercy of land holders.

"They expect a man to take care of it like it was his own, and then any time they can send him off."[38]

Like Haskins in "Under the Lion's Paw" by Hamlin Garland, Fred and his wife, Beth, toil unceasingly on the old Hunt Farm near Concordia, two hundred and fifty acres of rich, rolling land with its wide green pasture through which Soldier Creek ran under low hanging willows. It had been the showplace of Soldier Creek township. In the study of hopelessness of renters and the injustice of owners, Miss Suckow creates vividly the country scene. One sees, smells, and feels the summer heat as Beth Mutchler looks out on the farm, aware of their struggle and the hard work to make it productive.

She did not see Fred. She went around to the front of the house and stood on the porch, screened with the thick wild cucumber-vines. A still country morning, with the smell of coming heat scorching through the coolness. Dew heavy, like a gleaming crust on the long grass, on the freshly opened nasturtiums along the edge of the porch. She had planted those this spring. The evergreens in the grove were motionless, the drive to the road was mysterious and hushed. The sun was a fire-red ball, round, like a harvest moon, just above the sky-line in the east.[39]

Before the ominous call of the Hunt family to announce their plans to turn over the farm to a son-in-law known in the community to be worthless, Beth can feel a temporary satisfaction and hope after her earlier experience on harsh Dakota farms.

The place looked so pleasant. . . .
A mourning-dove called from the lonely over-wooded grove, making the stillness more still. A little light breeze

31

rattled among the glittering leaves of the big cottonwood at the end of the drive. The shining white chickens were all crouched in a snowy group in the hollows they had made in the dry bare earth beside the house. The big house across the drive stood in a hot mysterious silence, hollyhocks burning pink against the wall. Over the pasture-land at the west the blue of vervain seemed to hover, to waver and shimmer a little, like a haze in the heat. The baby, its plump, damp legs bare, crept around over the long grass near Beth's chair.[40]

Even to the retired farmer the seasonal changes strike an instinctive response and awaken a nostalgic desire for the active life of the country. Seth Patterson in the retirement he had worked for all his life could at times recognize that farm work had been getting "pretty hard," that he didn't want to keep farming all his life. But spring sights and sounds make him restive.

But getting toward spring—the farm, the red barn smelling of hay, the way the ground sloped to the pasture with low wet places in the path, the long groaning cry of the windmill, and the sound of the breeze in the willow grove at evening—[41]

An old man in "A Pilgrim and a Stranger," as far from his Iowa farm as Denver, cannot find adequate compensation for his familiar farm scene even in the beauty of the western mountains. Forced to leave his farm for a better climate, he is sad and homesick. On his way from town he pauses to compare the scene with the one in his mind's eye.

A gap in the buildings showed the chain of mountains, dim blue with faint streaks of silver. He looked dispassionately at them. He thought: "I'd give the lot of them for a real corn field."

... The corn would be ripe "back home" by now. They would be cutting and shocking and filling the silo. He had

32

never missed out on it the way he was doing now. It didn't seem like fall.[42]

To the farmer living in town the early signs of the winter thaws still appear as a prelude to the spring planting. As Seth Patterson made his aimless way to town he looked uneasily at the sky.

The sky was drowned deep in blue. The evergreens in the yard showed dark against it, the bleached boughs of the maple-trees seemed to be drinking it in. Little shining rivers, all current, ran down the cement sidewalk. The grass on the lawns was burned dry and pale-brown, but was wet and greenish underneath with raw watery places in the little hollows. Snow still formed a dingy crust on the shady side of the brick drug store he was passing.
It all made him say: "Won't be long now till the ground's ready."[43]

In many of Ruth Suckow's stories and novels her characters feel a tender affection and attachment for the home of their childhood. Pleasant memories are at times almost nostalgically recalled. In "A Rural Community," the situation is similar to the story "Up the Coulee" by Garland. In both cases a prosperous son returns for a visit to the old homestead. In Garland's story the return of Howard McLane, a successful actor, is not a happy success. Brought back by feelings of guilt for his mother's hard life and for his brother's hardships on the farm, he is at every turn confronted with the sullen and weary aspects of farm life.
In Miss Suckow's story, Ralph Chapin, a successful journalist who returns to his home and foster parents at Walnut, in the northeastern corner of Iowa, is fascinated by all the vague reminders of the old days. The entire story with its musing autumnal atmosphere is replete with memories brought to life as Ralph Chapin revisits his favorite scenes.

He looked from side to side—eager to recognize old landmarks, half amused when he discovered them, yet feeling all the time a tinge of sadness that was like the haunting of melancholy in this exquisite autumn day. This was the very street along which they used to drive when they came into town with a load or on Saturday nights. A wagon came along now—rattling slowly, an old man with a thick white beard hunched over on the seat, a bushel basket of apples and some gunny sacks full of nuts jolting about in the back. That—everything he saw—teased him with elusive memories. This old house had always stood here—a one-story house of dingy brick, plain, with square small-paned windows, an old-timer. The big oak-tree at the corner! Here were vague reminders of the old days—plain white houses with almost a New England air, fallen leaves half raked upon the lawns, some late petunias bordering white house walls, a rockery, a bed of pansies and withered sweet alyssum edged with white clam-shells from the Mississippi. Rope swings from the boughs of elm-trees, a boy with bare feet who stared after him, pumps with tin cups dangling, even one of those queer old hammocks made of slats! It was like going back into his past, in a kind of dream. There were memories that he could almost touch—but not quite—

He looked beyond the houses, at the line of low hills on the south. He stood still—almost caught his breath at the sudden stab of emotion. With a strange impulse he took off his cap, held it crushed in his hand. There they were still—the old eternal hills! How well he knew them, better than anything in the world. The "lay of the land"—something in that to stir the deepest feeling in a man. Low rolling hills, fold after fold, smooth brown and autumnal, some ploughed to soft earth-colour, some set with corn stalks of pale tarnished gold. Along the farther ones, the woods lay like a coloured cloud, brown, russet, red and purple-tinged. As he walked on, the houses grew fewer, everything dwindled into pasture land. The feeling of autumn grew more poignant. There was a scent of dust in the stubble. The trees grew in scattered russet groups. One slender young cottonwood, yellow as a goldfinch and as lyric in its quality, stood in a meadow, alone. Not even spring beauty was so aching and so transient—like music fading away. Yet, under everything, something abiding and eternal.

He came to the very edge of town, almost to the woods through which Honey Creek ran. A house stood at the turn of the road. Of all things he had seen, it was the most autumnal. It stood plain and white against the depths of blue sky. Its trees were turning to pale yellow, its yard scattered with dry leaves. On the back porch yellow seed corn hung by the bleached husks to dry. Hickory nuts and walnuts were spread out on a piece of rag carpet. On the fence posts, orange pumpkins were set in blue granite kettles to ripen. The corn in the small field was in the shock. The smell of apples came from somewhere.[44]

This passage is quoted at length because it expresses so well the feeling held by many of her farm people for the familiar country sights. Here is that sweet sadness that accompanies, for the sensitive, any return to old and loved places. Chapin beholds this lost world and sees in it the qualities of enchantment. It is all the sweeter to him while making a kind of last communion since it is irrecoverable. No aspect escapes his heightened sensitivity as he revisits the precincts of his past. A part of his being that has been so long somnolent springs suddenly alive, and he is overwhelmed by it. For him it is a thing beyond tears, beyond reflection even. It is a thing surrendered and gone, yet somehow kept, somehow retained in those recesses of the mind where things that often seem lost have been merely stored. He walked dreamlike in the world of his past, and every sight revived feelings that had enchanted a younger heart.

Unlike Howard McLane, who leaves his farm home with feelings of pity, bitterness, and sorrow, Chapin finds in his visit an affirmation of the country life which remains largely fixed in the face of change. The spreading countryside "over which changes passed like shadows of the clouds across the pasture" imparts a quietude and satisfaction because some place of which he is a part has retained its sameness.

The talk seemed to bring him certain country things—the bitter sappy smell of a new-felled tree, the scent of nuts in autumn woods, the tanging smell of cider in the October sun, the dry ghostly crackle of pale-gold corn stalks left standing in the fields. He began to feel a certain something about his foster-brothers that satisfied him, that curiously pleased some primitive depth in him. He began to be glad of their slow voices, their odd turns of speech, their rustic air. These things suggested the deep stabilities of country life—the slow inevitable progression of the seasons, the nearness to earth and sky and weather, the unchanging processes of birth and death, the going of the birds in the fall and their sure return in the spring, the coming, night after night, of the familiar stars to the wide country sky.[45]

The clinging to a place that symbolizes such stabilities as Chapin finds in his home at Walnut becomes a persistent theme in almost every story. In one of her sketches in the volume *Some Others and Myself,* Miss Suckow, as an adult, revisits a friend's home that aroused pleasant memories. Confronted with the realities of the poorness and plainness of a neglected site, she recoils from the evaluation of her adult eye and records, "I struggled for the charm of memory."[46]

In the stories of *Iowa Interiors* which give her most bleak and dismal portrayals of farm life there still lingers much of the charm of memory. There is, of course, recognition of the failure to fulfill the promise those memories once held, but the recollections of the physical details of place are sharp and often happily revived.

These details of the farm scene and of country things are profuse and specific. Almost every event relates to its natural setting amidst the seasonal changes and the activities so familiar to the farm.

No feature of Ruth Suckow's domestic scene is more characteristic than her minute descriptions of houses—both the buildings and the interiors. A social history of Iowa as well as the vicissitudes of many a life might be inferred from the furnishings alone. To record or even classify them would result in a history of items for collectors and curators. In her "Memoir" she records an interest as a child in visiting the houses of old ladies in the towns where she lived. On those visits no item seems to have escaped her eye. In her fiction the descriptions of houses, churches, and public buildings are detailed and specific; the interiors—the parlors, kitchens, and spare rooms, the churches, schools, stores, and depots—are fully furnished. A few examples will illustrate her penchant for such observations.

The tone of the story as well as the character of Summer Street in "A Homecoming" is indicated in her description of the residences:

The houses were of the older type, of white frame mostly, and looked as if they had been long lived in. The bushes had spread out; weather-beaten chairs and stools stood out under the big trees. One house had a little spiked iron fence on the roof, above a border of green-painted shingles. Another had trimmings of dingy brown. One had a great pine-tree growing in front of the door. One was of brick with Gothic windows and a little Gothic porch painted yellow, so that it looked like a small Presbyterian church. The lawns had old-fashioned flowers grown too thick—petunias by the front walls, close to the damp stone foundations, cosmos and zinnias—and fruit-trees in the back yards. One expected old couples whose children had gone, or widows, or spinsters, to be living in these houses.[47]

The atmosphere of deterioration and decadence that frustrates her youth and surrounds the story of "The Daughter" is due partly to the descriptions of the tyrannical invalid mother and partly to her surroundings.

She looked much more natural in the old sitting-room of her little house, where she had sat so long that the place belonged to her. Her chair caught the light from the west window. Her plants, which Mary tended for her, filled the other window. Her footstool—a box covered with the remnants of the red-flowered ingrain carpet—stood before her chair. Beside it, the little walnut table that held her spectacles, the chequered box in which she kept her pills, and the big soft rag that she held to her mouth when she coughed. She was in the air of the room—close, slightly stale, with an ancient smell that came from medicine, from the carpet, the painted woodwork warped and crackled with heat.[48]

The homes and rooms of old people, musty and unchanged for years like that of the Moshers in "Mame," appear frequently.

That old front room—was it possible that it still existed, just like that, was not a dream of his boyhood? That ancient organ, the ingrain carpet, those old, old chairs, the scroll-back horsehair lounge, the "God Bless Our Home" executed by Flo in "spatterwork."—That same old musty house smell that he associated with the place and all that had ever happened there. Plants on stands and in brackets by the front window. . . .[49]

The parlors of the old folks in the country bear much resemblance to each other:

The close musty air, thick with the smell of the carpet, told that it had not been opened for months. It had a dank chill, even in the clear warmth of the September afternoon. The enlarged pictures on the walls looked as if they had frozen into their silver frames. The closed organ, with its insertions of faded silk, was a tomb of wheezy melodies. The big illustrated Bible with its steel clasp lay beside the Life of Abraham Lincoln—which Art had peddled once—on the knitted lace doily of the stand. Knitted tidies were fastened with ribbons to the backs of chairs. A black memorial card on one of the little balconies of the organ stated in gold that John Luther Shafer had died at the age of thirty-two. . . . A large pink shell lay beside the door. A bunch of withered pampas grass stuck up from a blue-painted vase in the corner.[50]

And when the country folks came to town they brought the same possessions with them and kept the same kind of sepulchral parlors.

> The hallway was cold, and the front room that they kept shut off in winter. The front room had their best carpet, an organ, a golden-oak centre table with a knitted doily, chairs of various eras, and their own pictures in silver and red-plush frames. It was stiff, chill, proper. They almost never used it.
>
> He put back the red portieres and the folding doors, and went into the sitting-room.[51]

The domestic scene of the era is truly recorded in such household descriptions. The interiors of Miss Suckow's homes are not always dismal and gloomy. Her women seem happiest when, like Sarah Bonney, they sit in their kitchens made spic and span by their own efforts and enjoy the scent of nut bread baking and the beam of sunlight as it brightens the jelly glasses on the window sill; or like Marjorie Schoessel, home from the Boston School of Dramatics, who feels the essence of home in her crisp dotted swiss curtains and her white bedspread freshly laundered. "They were whiter than things had ever seemed to be at the association—a special kind of whiteness that meant home." Similarly Rose Kramer finds temporary assuagement of her anxiety over her husband's failure when she wakes in a sunlit room in his mother's home.

> Early in the morning, the long stretches of sunlight fell slanting across their bed, across the clean blue and white of the patchwork quilt, across the thin, faded, softened ingrain carpet on the pine-wood floor. All the room was sunshine . . . even the tall wardrobe, the little commode, the thick white crockery with its decorous adornment of pink crotchet.[52]

Whether she is describing the sepulchral parlors, the musty bedrooms where the old folks lived with a few possessions in sullen loneliness, or the homes of her middleclass housewives to whom good housekeeping and good cooking meant respectability; a furniture store, or a tailor shop; the dirty day coaches with red plush seats sprinkled with peanut shells, and floors covered with pink gum wrappers and sputum, or the dreary railroad stations with their dusty waiting rooms and Ladies Parlors, she fills her pages with minute observations that have the ring of truth.

The town scenes of her stories and novels have similarities and variations. Each of her towns is made distinct with abundant detail. All are vividly real. The settled small towns of Buena Vista and Valley Junction in *The Odyssey of a Nice Girl* and *The Kramer Girls* are both close to farming areas. Their monotony and dullness make their youth long to escape while their warmth and intimacy stir feelings of affection. The town of Morning Sun, the setting for part of *The Bonney Family,* had a "pastoral quality of a small town on an inland river."[53] It is viewed nostalgically in the midst of change as the old life there becomes a "legend irrecoverably pure in its simplicity bathed in a sadly beautiful light of remembrance."[54] Quite different are the two towns portrayed in the novel *Cora:* Warwick with its "young, fresh, crude, growing life of a polyglot little town on the western border of Iowa" where everything is cooked beneath the blue haze of the prairie sky; and Onawa, the next home of the Schwietert family, the one industrial town in her novels. In Onawa there are more jobs, more immigrants, and more poverty than in the other towns. Belmond, Iowa, in *The Folks* is the most modern and most prosperous town of the novels. Still another type of town is the fresh and youthful New Hope near the Dakota border. Rapid building and growth are the outstanding qualities of this community with only fifteen years of history. "Everywhere were the same smells—raw and fresh from weedy lots and new cut lumber." In the final novel, *The John Wood Case,* the time is the same as in *New Hope,* the early nineteen hundreds, but Fairview is an older town dating from before the Civil War. There is similarity in all of them and something singular in each one.

In the short stories the towns are usually deserted by all but the aged, the spinsters, and widows who are poor and ailing, while those with a better fate are changing from the status of country town to small city. Characteristic of the first type is the Karnak of the story "Mame." One could see from the station only the depot, a straggling, rutted road, a few stores, a brick bank with a Ford outside, and some elderly frame houses with evergreen trees. The only men with money there were the banker and the retired farmers. The younger men had moved on to the next town for better business opportunities.

The town of Shell Spring in "A Homecoming," also a community of retired farmers, was one of those slow, pretty, leafy towns beside a quiet river.

> The old settlers could sadly note changes here and there. In the last ten years it had been growing from a country town to a very small city. People had bridge parties instead of great suppers at the Grange. There was a new bank building with a Rest Room, a new Hotel, electroliers down Main Street; and gradually the two blocks of paving in the "business part" had lengthened out down East Street, down to where the houses began to straggle out and sweet clover to bank the roadsides. Building was chiefly on East Street. Square white houses with sleeping porches and stout white porch pillars. An occasional out-of-place bungalow, and a near-bungalow with the upper story painted yellow and the lower white. Here and there was a gaping wound in the earth where one of the old houses— low, painted dark, covered with wooden gingerbread—had been uprooted to make place for a new.
>
> Automobiles went down this pavement taking the Lincoln Highway to Golden Prairie.[55]

Coreville, in which Seth Patterson of the story, "Retired," leads a life typical of the retired farmers, is especially characteristic of the Iowa town of Suckow's stories. Here are the muddy streets, the general store where men wearing mackinaws and overalls tucked into reddish rubber boots lounge near the table covered with oilcloth, the post office where the smell of paper and tobacco smoke mixes with that of fresh mud on the

41

floor and the blue-striped mail bags are hunched in the corner for the rural carriers, and always some place for the men to gather and talk. In Coreville the place was the produce house.

> This was where the old fellows in Coreville always congregated. It was a big dingy room littered with slatted poultry boxes with chickens' heads poking through, and with egg cases piled up in the corner. The men had a place by the stove where they sat on a wooden settee and some battered kitchen chairs. There were five of them today, all white-haired, all rough and weather-stained like old furniture that has been left out in the weather. Most of them had on woolen caps and old coats and sweaters.[56]

Life depicted in such towns is much the same as that of the novels, but in the novels it is portrayed in more detail and on a larger canvas.

The setting for *The Odyssey of a Nice Girl* is the small rural town of Buena Vista. Seen from the train, Buena Vista is a "great spreading cluster of dark summer tree tops." It is a town of three thousand people and is the county seat. Most of the people living there engaged in small businesses. Opportunities for young people were limited. Young women out of high school or college who wished to earn money could sell homemade candy, take magazine subscriptions, or give private lessons in music or elocution. The social life, reminiscent of Gopher Prairie, was set and formal in a small way.

> People all seemed to do the same things—drive, shop in Wahseta, play cards, listen to victrolas, attend clubs and lodges. Nothing could go on without organization—as if people looked to one another cautiously before daring to venture even an amusement.[57]

There is the same social atmosphere at church and school gatherings that is present in other novels. Emphasis is on the familiar pattern of family life. The German grandparents and farm background are in this novel as are the intimate details of household life and the school activities of a young girl.

Buena Vista was not a distinctive town, although to Marjorie Schoessel as a child it was more impressive than Germantown, the home of her grandparents, because it had two blocks of brick paving, rows of brick buildings with trimmings of iron lace, wide streets, and big trees. Her father in his combination furniture store and undertaking establishment cultivated the same qualities important to other characters of her fiction. Life at the store meant contacts, intimacy, knowledge of people, and a sense of ownership. The school and its functions were more important in the social scheme than the church which had been the focal point of community life in *Country People*. There is still, however, a goodly share of church suppers, missionary society and lodge meetings. Incidents of sickness, deaths, and funerals viewed as community interests in *Country People* are treated with more emphasis on their relation to the central characters. More attention is focused on the responses to these events by the main characters.

The small town seems to have served its purpose in childhood, but is accepted with bitterness in maturity. The dullness of conformity and routine comes to Marjorie for the first time after graduation.

> The town . . . it was as if she had never realized what the town was like before. The brick-paved Main Street, the tree-lined roads, the red courthouse, the walk that led to the schoolhouse, had always been irradiated by a personal excitement and expectation. What was gone? For the first time, she seemed to realize the streets, the teams from the country, the slow rattle of drays across the brick pavements, the automobiles that were constantly growing more plentiful around the courthouse where the iron hitching-rails still stood. People lived here, just lived on and on, kept stores, waited on customers, went down town to buy things for supper. . . .[58]

The dullness, drabness, and routine of Miss Suckow's small town, however, are seldom unrelieved by affectionate feelings for the personal and intimate aspects of rural life. These feelings are indicative of the values inherent in the life of the folks with

43

whom she is always concerned. The fond associations of childhood memories and intimate things about home exercise their grasp. In a time of crisis when Marjorie's affections were divided between returning home and remaining in Boston, it was that "treacherous, clinging love of home, of lawn, the flowers, every piece of furniture," that pulled her back and held her. From the time of her childhood the old haunts—the snowball bushes, the cistern top and the barn, and her tree-house with its platform for play—her bench, and the steep wooden stairs had been the kind of things that held her affections.

Nostalgia recurs when Rose Kramer recalls her home in the town of Valley Junction, the setting for most of *The Kramer Girls*. Town and country are fused in her memory.

> She loved the way the road dipped down and then rose in the distance, with blue sky between and above thick trees. She loved the chance and unconsidered way in which little unnamed side-streets petered out and dwindled into the country. She loved being able to know that country was all around her and that at any moment she could reach it . . . go beyond the row of tall and gloomy evergreens that marked the furthest boundary of the last yard, and stand and let sunny silence sink into her whole being, not just into her mind. . . .[59]

No more distinctive than Buena Vista, Valley Junction had one unique feature—a little park in the center of town with its fountain that was like four great petunias, set into each other, each one smaller than the one beneath it. But Rose Kramer, like Marjorie Schoessel, liked best that feeling of familiarity in the small town.

> She could enjoy having everybody she met on the street speak to her; knowing people by their names, instead of just as—the laundress, the ice man, the paper boy, the janitor, the fruit stand man.[60]

In her portrayal of the small town of Morning Sun in *The Bonney Family*, she seems to achieve a more complete fusion of the physical details of the rural scene and the intimacies of human associations than in earlier books. She herself believed the charm of this book to be the manner with which it seems to "capture and hold something of the pastoral quality of a small town on an inland river."[61] The "summer light" on its pages comes not only from its natural beauties, but also from the simplicity and freshness of the way of life. Even after moving from Morning Sun, Mr. Bonney cherished the feeling that people there were more friendly and sincere ones than he ever met afterwards. They were the friends of his youth. In this town he had been at once helper, father, elder and brother of all his people. It was with affectionate memory that recollection of this pastorate took on a legendary quality for him and for his family.

In both *The Bonney Family* and *New Hope* she imparts an almost romantic glow to the idyllic pastoral scenes of her novels. True, her idyll is tempered by the realistic acceptance of the transitory nature of these ideal places. Nevertheless, both novels leave a strong impression of nostalgia in the portrayals of the towns of Morning Sun and New Hope. Both places have a similar appeal for her in their brightness, freshness, youthfulness, and simplicity.

Throughout *The Bonney Family*, Morning Sun is described in the terms of summer—the summer light, the summer river, the summer look of the church, summer leisure, the freshness of summer air, fragrance of summer flowers; while New Hope is characterized in terms of youthfulness, newness, and freshness.

Morning Sun is the setting for only part of *The Bonney Family*. The college town of Frampton to which the family moves suggests the Grinnell of Miss Suckow's high school and college days. The *Des Moines Register* in an article of April 20, 1930, said of Grinnell that it was a town of personal and intimate charm but not a place in which to look for eagerness of inquiry, youthful audacity of thought or action, or really stirring intellectual currents. Vincent College, located in Frampton, had an equally unstimulating environment. An absence of humanity and of aesthetic appreciation characterized the faculty of this college where students were under suspicion for reading Sherwood Anderson; the literature instructor "proudly out of touch with current American writing" declared that the *Spoon River Anthology* was not poetry; and the modern novel course stopped at Kipling. An "arrogant young man" from an eastern college who had come with iconoclastic views was quickly shaped to the mold: he married, bought a white colonial house with green shutters, attended the Episcopalian Church and "settled down in the faculty circle."

The novel *Cora* is unlike her other novels. It is the only story of a young woman's escape from the small town to a successful career. In this novel Cora's marriage, an unconventional one after a week's vacation in Yellowstone Park, is of short duration. Deserted by her husband, she returns home to resume her career and to live with her widowed mother and unmarried aunt. The novel opens with the familiar small town scene, but early in the narrative takes the family on to the larger town.

Economic necessity required the Schwietert family to move, but Cora's family held the same kind of affectionate memories for Warwick as the Bonney family cherished for Morning Sun. They recalled fondly the little frame house near the creek, the vacant lot behind their house, the hill where they went for wild flowers early in the spring, the long board walk, the iron bridge over the creek, the blinding brightness of the sun glittering on the water—the side street off Main Street, with the junk shop, the marble iron works and their father's tailor shop. The appearance of the tailor shop is as characteristic of Warwick and the Schwieterts' life there as any scene in the early part of the novel. It was a small frame building, dark and hot inside, smelling of grease and singed cloth.

> The shop had a side stoop, dating from the time when the old tailor had lived in the back room with his family. . . . A scraggly box elder tree gave a little shade to the stoop and dropped a fat green worm, with a slap, to the hard ground. Behind the shop was a rank tangle of sunflowers and weeds that used to be the old tailor's garden. It had a high board fence along the alley. This place was heaven to the children. Mr. Schwietert liked to have them play there, and gave them his tailor's shears for cutting, and little pieces of

ancient beeswax, and samples of woolen cloth with prinked edges.[62]

Family life in Warwick was pleasant, but did not bring a living. Their next move was to Onawa. From their arrival in Onawa at the dirty station, crowded with "hordes of immigrants," everything was different. It was a clanging city with hard pavements, looming buildings, and noisy street cars. After living in a double frame house, "grayish and flimsy," occupied on one side by a "colored" family, the Schwieterts moved to a better house, but to an unattractive street. Here Suckow gives one of her few descriptions of a poor city neighborhood. A sobered Cora, returning one evening from her job in a glove factory, walked down the little straggling street where their house stood.

It was like country out here beyond the bridge, except that the frame houses were almost uniform, set closer together than small town houses, and the walls and trees were blackened by smoke from the iron works. On one side of the road, in a weedy hollow, some Italian shanties clustered. In bright daylight they looked dreadful—tipsy things: some painted a dark red like freight cars, and the yards a mess of cans and old shoes with dingy washings hanging on ropes strung insecurely too near the ground . . . dirty little brown-faced children shouting out impudent taunts, that made Cora cringe and then grow furious.

But the soft March twilight gave the ramshackle settlement, with its busy scattering of débris, a smallness and a pathos, here on the great rough stretch of earth under the big gentle sadness of the sky . . . the voices of the children, of the squat dark women, the yelping of a dirty white dog, were only little sounds, brief and quickly fading, within the great enveloping softness, dispassionate and sustaining, of the evening air.[63]

Belmond, Iowa, setting for *The Folks,* is much the same as

other towns. It was a little town with a retired, old-fashioned look. Its white houses with wide lawns and big trees showed the New England influence. Beyond the residence streets was a shady ravine through which "the crick" ran that served Belmond as its only source of water. The feed store, the decaying livery stable, and the yellowish tower of the court-house rising above the trees were familiar buildings. Belmond, also near farming land, was larger and of a later period than most of the fictional localities. It supported two banks, movies, a library, and several churches, with the Presbyterian and Con-gregational churches rivals for prestige, a hotel that served a forty-cent lunch to businessmen and a weekly luncheon to Rotarians. More cars speeded on its asphalt roads. But family dinners on Sundays and holidays, parties, school events and graduation exercises, and church activities are still of the familiar homespun character.

Belmond was a town where in the twenties "life seemed to be running along its appointed way, only with natural prosperity and well-earned comforts added."[64] The home of Fred Ferguson, like other well-to-do homes in Belmond, had under-gone the same metamorphosis—with parlors and living rooms thrown into one, old furniture relegated to the attic, inside bathrooms and new fixtures added, and the barn made into a garage. Like all other middle class homes of the late twenties, it had a radio, a victrola, a piano nobody used any more, and an over-stuffed davenport. The contrast between country and town family members in their way of living was becoming greater. The Fergusons in town even employed a woman to help when Annie entertained the Ladies of the Monday Club. If hard times were around, they had not struck Belmond. In Belmond Fred Ferguson, banker, Republican, Rotarian, and Presbyterian, carried the responsibility for the farm and the "old folks" and the affairs of his bank and his church, and viewed with con-sternation, shock, and sadness any change in the status of either institution.

The locale of the novel, *New Hope,* has a particular interest for its similarities to her own birthplace in physical and social aspects. New Hope is not even a thinly disguised portrait of Hawarden. Only a change of names distinguishes it from the actual locality. The physical details, the newness of the town, and its spirit of friendliness, enterprise, and democracy identify the fictional town of New Hope.

Both Miss Suckow and her father have described the town of Hawarden. In William John Suckow's unpublished manuscript, "Seventy Years in Retrospect," he recorded many details of his first pastorate in the Congregational Church. His daughter repeated some of these descriptions in "A Memoir," and in her novel has given meaning and significance to the life there.

Hawarden, a small town on the northwest border of Iowa, is in Sioux County, thirty-five miles north of Sioux City. In 1889 its population was six hundred. Of its natural setting Mr. Suckow wrote that most of the town was down on the river bottom. On the east it climbed a gentle slope known as Gladstone Hill, named by an admirer of the celebrated British statesman.[65] The hill was the main residence portion of the town where the better class houses were built. The Dry Run Creek cut through the town separating "The Hill" from the business section. The parsonage was at the foot of the hill in the shallow gully made by the creek. To the west across its muddy western river, the Big Sioux, could be seen the low Dakota bluffs. Its great rolling countryside is described by Ruth Suckow as giving a feeling of openness and loftiness.

New Hope likewise was separated by its Dry Creek and had its hill section of the best residences. The Dave Millers, the most prominent family in the story, lived there on a street that sloped down to the bridge. Across the bridge was the lot where the church and parsonage stood. The town was a mile away from the river which marked the boundary between Iowa and Dakota. Of its farmland she writes in the novel:

All felt excited by the fertility that lay around them, in the smooth high billows of dark-brown loessal soil: the deep fresh fertility, for centuries undisturbed—waiting for their own plows, so Dave said—while across from the Dakotas blew the dry, pure, limitless air of the West.[66]

In 1889 Reverend Suckow accepted his first pastorate in a Congregational Church at Hawarden, a town not then ten years old. "It had grown up all of a sudden, as it were, to fit the needs of the railroad, the Chicago, Milwaukee and St. Paul, and was an offshoot of an earlier town, which the railroad by-passed, and which still remains as a not-wholly-assimilated portion of the newer town."[67] The names of parishioners to whom Mr. Suckow refers suggest English and German ancestry: Ball, Wood, Lynn, Stein, Seifert, Sutliff, Washburn. The town buildings included a two-story frame school house, a bank, several stores and shops and a "neat appearing" Congregational Church. Two other denominations, the Baptists and the Methodists, held services in an old school house. There were two weekly papers. Its residence streets were marked with frame houses and box elders.

Of the newness of the town, Miss Suckow writes that it was not a pioneer town, in the ordinary sense; the pioneering age in the northwest section of Iowa, the last part to be settled, was over. Its atmosphere was of youth and freshness rather than of primeval newness. "The town . . . lay as if in morning light. Everything seemed to be just starting up, just beginning."[68]

In accepting the "call" to New Hope, Reverend Greenwood, like Mr. Suckow, had left the church of his immigrant parents, and made his own choice of the Congregational Church.[69] New Hope had not been in existence then more than fifteen years and was one of the towns that existed because of the location of the railroad. When Dave Miller came, there had been nothing but the railroad. The town that he shows to Mr. Greenwood on his arrival had made progress in the short time. Its Main Street with red sandstone and frame, mostly frame, store buildings faced across a broad width of dusty road. The store in which Miller had started business and the bank he later established were on this street. Only three miles beyond the new town—far enough to have been left "high and dry" by the railroad was Canaan—an old community. Its location too far from the river and too far out in the countryside had been a mistake. Canaan had failed to survive two disasters: the location of the railroad, and a cyclone which had destroyed most buildings except a store and the post office. A few citizens of the Canaan community continued to live in their old residences and comprised an older element in contrast with the new.

50

The same atmosphere of newness and youth that had been felt in Hawarden also permeates the entire "morning world" of New Hope. Typical of this aura of youthfulness is the description of the minister's first day there.

> The morning air was bright with the sense of arrival. There was a feeling of newness all about, exhilarating, hopeful; it seemed to carry the scent of fresh-cut boards across the weedy roughness of the vacant lots.[70]

Of its primeval quality, Suckow writes of New Hope as of Hawarden, it "wasn't built upon ruins, . . . It started history here."[71] Even the cemetery looked new, bright, fresh, with its few clean shining granite stones. There wasn't even a Civil War monument, the town was so young.

In both towns the New England influence was apparent in the dominance of the church with a Puritan heritage and in the stock of the early settlers. However, this element is shown in the novel as elsewhere in her fictional towns to have been tempered by the western environment. Among the settlers there remained something of the communal conscience, the Puritan strictness, the rigor and fierce righteousness. In general these qualities were modified—in character and social institutions as well as in the religion which retained the simplicity, freedom, and community of action without the stern theology of Puritanism.

> The Puritan faith of New England, carried westward, had lost the narrow stringency of the mountain valleys and become diffused with the open prairie light.[72]

Both Ruth Suckow and her father write of Hawarden as one of the most pleasant of Reverend Suckow's pastorates. To Miss Suckow her most vital memory is its community spirit—its enterprise and democracy.

The spirit of enterprise everywhere present was felt in church and business affairs alike, Mr. Suckow reports. In this period "life teemed with all sorts of interests." One year he played in the band. He was a member of a male chorus. For a time he published a weekly paper called "The Dial" for which he obtained mailing privileges. The growth of the church was rapid. New families were constantly arriving and new houses were being erected. The church was the most satisfactory one he ever had. It had an excellent choir and a flourishing Endeavor Society. Cantatas, operettas, and debates always drew large crowds. The suppers, socials, community meetings, and entertainments were numerous.

In New Hope both the Dave Millers and the Greenwoods are busily absorbed in numerous town and church activities. Dave Miller in his business undertaking and his eagerness to get the country settled is representative of the community. "We don't want the land unoccupied," he had said. The spirit of enterprise in New Hope is summarized in a review of the minister's first year there.

All the winter activities went into full swing. The Relief Corps ladies held their bean supper in the Opera House; and once a month there were suppers at the church. The suppers were never so well attended; the congregations never so large. Business was growing; stores were full; A. D. Murdock figured so closely that he ran out of stock; town was packed with teams on Saturday nights. At six-fifteen the big flyer came through and the golden windows flashed on westward through the wintry dusk. New Hope increased its population by more than two hundred, counting babies born. Cass Story published a fine editorial calling New Hope the growing metropolis of the growing West.[73]

Of the democratic spirit that prevailed in Hawarden during her life there Miss Suckow wrote, "I had, not the very best imaginable, and yet an exceptionally fortunate experience of a real, acting democracy."[74] The special value of these years she notes is the good fortune to have shared in "that central experience of American life—the experience of a fresh beginning."[75] The democratic spirit that characterized both town and church affairs is best stated in a passage Miss Suckow quotes from her father's autobiography.

The church was young, and had worn no ruts, developed no hampering traditions. The people were amenable to any reasonable leadership and ready to give enthusiastic co-operation. No social cleavages had yet become noticeable in the community; it was more like one big family.[76]

Comparable qualities of democracy and community spirit are the distinguishing features of New Hope. "Everywhere there was a sense of natural comradeship, of being all together at the start and working together for the future."[77] The town had the atmosphere of freedom and equality that in some places became merely an academic idea. There was even the rawness of a new community where bedrock showed, where it hadn't been covered up yet by layers of classes and customs. "All trades were needed and folks could see that all were on something of an equality." As one character puts it: "That's what we need. That's the way to keep it. That's the way things ought to be."[78] Again Dave Miller sums up the feeling of the town. "We can get things done here as long as we all pull together."

In coming to the close of the novel one might say of it what Miss Suckow records of her move from Hawarden:

[it] closed the cover of the book upon the first golden period of youthful trust and "enthusiastic co-operation" and gave those few years in H_____almost the quality of a legend.[79]

In the last novel, Miss Suckow turns to another small town at the turn of the century. In contrast to New Hope, Fairview was an old town. It also had been settled by New England people and had kept what was called "an atmosphere of culture." At first only a trading center, it was in the early 1900s a thriving town of two thousand, but was still "fresh and youthful." Owning a surrey and a house with inside plumbing was indicative of the wealthier class. Fairview possessed a quality of innocence and simplicity that was symbolized in the John Wood family— an example of perfect harmony.

In both *New Hope* and *The John Wood Case,* Miss Suckow's central purpose is to reveal the community spirit of each locale.

In both instances the community is a major protagonist in the drama. The communities are unlike. The first novel treats of a raw new town of the early 1900s; the second deals with an old town of the same era that existed before the Civil War. The first deals with the happy participation in an early stage of development of a prairie town. The later novel deals with the sadness and indignation stirred by a community's betrayal. The existence of two such towns in the same era is explained by the history of Iowa's settlement. "The northwestern section of Iowa was the last part of the State to be settled; towns in the southeastern section were old, as age goes west of the Mississippi, when homesteading was taking place in the northwest."[80]

New Hope begins with preparations for welcoming the new minister, and closes with the departure of the minister a few years later. During the term of his pastorate a whole community and its citizenry are portrayed. The chapter headings suggest the folk emphais of this novel: "Arrival," "The Church," "The Town," "The Countryside," "The Parsonage," "Festivals," "The Big Crowd," "May Day," "The Turn of the Year," "Commemoration," "The Call," "Exodus."

In *The John Wood Case* the community temper provides the central motif. In its portrayal of the reaction to the dishonesty of a citizen, the novel is not unlike Martin Yoseloff's *The Family Members* (1948) in which he writes of a town's response to the illegitimate pregnancy of the daughter of the Y.W.C.A. secretary. But beyond this there is little to compare to Yoseloff's humorous and satiric novel. In Miss Suckow's story it is the indignation of the church members that causes the matter to be formally discussed. The familiar pattern of family, church, school, and community appears in the last novel. The church services, the meeting of the trustees, and the graduation exercises are the scenes for assembling the citizenry of Fairview who sit in judgment.

Against this setting of pastoral landscapes and small towns imbued with the atmosphere of the folks spirit, Suckow exhibits her gallery of Iowa portraits and family groups: farmers, widows, and spinsters; children and adolescents; ministers and teachers; small store owners and bankers. As Frank L. Mott observes, the people who crowd her canvas frequently are themselves background for action, appearing to be in the narrative not necessarily to forward any plot, but to form part of the setting itself.

The immigrant influence appears, but with little emphasis on old country ways. The second generation and their adaptation to a new world receives more attention. In her essay on Iowa, Ruth Suckow points out that in Iowa it was more customary for the recent immigrant to speak of the "old country" than the mother country. Those of German descent and those of English, whether from the eastern states or direct from England, are sharply contrasted. Some range in economic status exists among her characters, but in general she sees a great homogeneity which eliminates wide variance in her social and economic milieu. More contrast appears between generations of a family and between people of different national origins than between social levels in a community. Her people are the commonplace Americans familiar to the small towns of all the states. Her classic types are simple, naive, friendly, gregarious, well-meaning, God-fearing, hard-working, thrifty, unsuspecting, honest, and patriotic. They are seldom mean, suspicious, unchurchly, murderous, venal, or covetous.

Iowa's native stock and the people of Miss Suckow's fiction were largely Scotch and English who came originally from the South and New England; the immigrants were Germans, Hollanders, Scandinavians, Welshmen, Bohemians, and Irish. In her fiction Suckow presents the immigrant element and also the intermingling of nationalities. The most frequently represented are German and English. She portrays the German element most often in the older generation—the aged grandparents—and observes the sharp contrast between nationalities as the second generation of Germans marry into families of English ancestry. The old country ways soon become alien. The children in most cases assume the cultural pattern of the New England ancestry, which appears to be the element of social preferment not so much as a result of conflict but a natural consequence of being the first and strongest influence.

With her own heritage from German grandparents on both sides of her family one might expect her to have found a natural subject for her fiction in the immigrant's old country traditions and his life in a new country. Actually this German influence seems to have been slight in the development of her own personality and interests. In her sketch of her German grandfather she wrote that the "war was the first thing to make me realize that actually I came of German ancestry."[81] At that time Miss Suckow was twenty-five years old. She had spent summers with her grandparents in the German township, Liberty. But she, like the younger generation in her novels, felt more affinity with the intellectual and aesthetic influence of New England. Her grandfather was the oldest settler and was a member of the German Methodist Church he had helped to found. His singing of German songs and his story-telling were regarded more as a dramatic performance than as a foreign legacy. However, the old man in his late years—ninety, deaf, sitting alone singing German Methodist hymns and folksongs—is certainly the prototype of many of the German grandparents of her stories who in their last years retreat into a private world unknown to their grandchildren, sometimes even to their children. From her own ancestry she draws two types of German immigrants and both appear in her stories. The Suckows in this country were farmers and practical people; the Kluckhohns were of a different social class and better educated. Her grandfather Kluckhohn she describes as a "German pietist and visionary with mystical eyes."

In her fiction Ruth Suckow emphasizes the assimilation more than the isolation of the foreign element. After the story of August Kaetterhenry's family in *Country People*, she never returned to a full treatment of her German people, and August is more like his neighbor farmers than he is like his parents. In this one novel only is there recognition of any overt hostility between nationalities. During the War period boys on the street had yelled at August and painted on his barn in red letters, "Old Dutchy Kaetterhenry." After the war "August never felt quite the sense of home and security in Richland Township that he had felt before."[82]

In *Cora* Mr. Schwietert, Cora's father, is one of Miss Suckow's most delightful characters. He retains his German speech and German ways more than any other protagonist. And in one story, "Midwestern Primitive," the German mother, Mrs.

56

Hohenschus, is a main character. But with these exceptions, attention is not focused on the German element except among the older generation. Their children soon lose its distinguishing marks.

The New England influence actually dominates the Iowa scene and affects any group Miss Suckow depicts. It sets the standard of education, refinement, and social superiority. As a child she was attracted to personalities that reflected its quality.

My particular friends, when I was a child, in the various towns in which we lived, were old ladies of New England type and origin, whose white houses I visited. . . .

I admired the bright eyes of these old women, their decisive and sometimes caustic speech, their intellectual vigor, and their goodness.[83]

Particularly Miss Suckow notes this New England influence in the religious heritage of Puritanism as it was tempered by western environment, in the physical character of the church buildings, and in the characteristics of many of the people whose homes, manners, furnishings, and speech she depicts in detail.

The domestic scene provides the subject and focal point in her fiction. The family as a social structure with its racial origins, its changing mores, its relation to the community, and the interrelationships of its members persists as the subject matter of her fiction from the earliest to the latest of her stories and novels. Only within the domestic scene do characters and incidents acquire significance. More impelling than any individual character in a novel is the family. The narratives revolve about the Kaetterhenrys, the Schoessels, the Schwieterts, the Bonney family, the Wood family, the Dave Millers, and the Fred Fergusons. It is within these domestic groupings and gropings that the reader finds the kind of people who make up the Iowa scene.

Feminine and domestic affairs dominate the novels and stories. Even the farmers, the shopkeepers, the ministers, the bankers are seen largely in their domestic roles. The affairs of church or business furnish background more than motivation. Such emphasis upon the domestic scene limits the range of character types and the scope of their actions. This focus, almost entirely on human relations within the family or in relation to the institutions of a small community, eliminates characters whose lives are vitalized by any concern with a public life. So closely does she confine her interests to the family in home, church, and school that not even the country doctor or storekeeper, perennial rural types, ever become central characters. Within the rural families the pattern varies little. The daughters marry usually because there is nothing else for them, and the sons either continue on the farm or go to town to become auto mechanics or storekeepers; the more successful ultimately become bankers and their lives continue to center around folk institutions. Ralph Chapin on his return to his rural community perceived the fixity of the pattern—a pattern that is recurrent in Miss Suckow's fiction.

> A wife, a home, and a child—these things continued under all the seeming revolution in the lives of men. Eagerness and striving after other things—and then a sense of emptiness, and back to the old things again.[84]

In her novels and short stories Ruth Suckow turns repeatedly for character selection to the very young and to the aged. In her novels her youthful characters are more frequently portrayed with full analysis.

Of the sixteen stories in *Iowa Interiors,* ten are about old people: couples retired from the farm and living in town; old couples living on run-down farms that are no longer self-supporting; couples around whom center the family reunions and observances of anniversaries. Two of the stories deal with frustrated lives of daughters tyrannized over by invalid or dominating mothers. In two of the stories, characters who have left the Iowa towns have become successful.

In "The Top of the Ladder," a home town friend derives a vicarious pleasure in Joe Ramsay's incredible success and suffers disillusionment and defeat in Joe's inexplicable suicide. In "A Rural Community," the successful journalist who returns finds the life of the home folks an affirmation of the fixed way of living.

Another volume of fourteen stories, *Children and Older People,* includes as the title suggests, six stories of children: children in church festivals, neighborhood groups, school children, fragile, delicate, and favored children, and children who learn to suffer early. Women whose lives are lonely, frustrated, and disappointing—spinsters and married women—are the subject of six stories. This volume does not ignore the retired couple, in this instance a couple in California who find in their interdependence their greatest satisfaction in the strange and unconventional environment. Here also is "Midwestern Primitive," the only story to make significant narrative use of the German mother.

All of the stories or sketches in *Some Others and Myself* draw upon her memory of the old ladies of her childhood acquaintance whose strange ways hold something of "a picturesque but decaying charm." Of one household she writes:

The three women lived in that house with the frame tower, not like sleeping beauties waiting to be awakened, but in the dim and changeless after-enchantment of stillness when the prince has gone from their lives.[85]

In the house of another, in a story where she has oddly abandoned her Iowa scene for a Kentucky post-bellum town as setting, Miss Suckow "was tantalized by that fancy of a spell upon the place, the same feeling that the clocks were stopped and the whole household lived on in unmeaning timelessness after time was over."[86] A muted nostalgic tone indeed pervades the entire collection of vignettes.

Some range of economic prosperity occurs among her families, but all might be said to belong to middle class rural society with sufficient prosperity for each generation to have more comforts than the previous one. Except in *Cora* and to some extent *The Kramer Girls,* economic struggle is not a major theme in the novels. A frugality born of hard-earned security is a common quality of her characters, but economic concern is never as dominant as it becomes in Paul Corey's trilogy where mortgage-ridden farmers, living under the threat of sale, are in constant anxiety. August Kaetterhenry made his family live conservatively, but he prospered and left an estate. The Schoessels in *The Odyssey of a Nice Girl* make a sufficient living from the furniture store and undertaking business to indulge Marjorie's whim for the study of dramatics in Boston and to replace the horse-drawn hearse with an auto hearse when necessary. The Bonney family live modestly and are conscious that church members watch their spending. They take their summer vacations in the backyard and Mrs. Bonney remakes the children's clothes to cut expenses, but they are not conspicuously less fortunate than their townsmen and in time enjoy a larger income. In the novel *Cora,* the inability of her father is a source of embarrassment and resentment that breeds an urgent ambition for success in Cora herself. Rose Kramer disappoints her sisters' ambitions for her by marrying a hometown boy who is a builder. When he fails in business, Rose goes to work and manages to maintain a respectable position. The Fergusons in *The Folks* can be called prosperous. Mr. Ferguson presents each child with a thousand dollars at maturity. The Millers in *New Hope* were among the early settlers and were successful first in a store and later in the bank. They are prosperous in terms of a rural town of 1900. In *The John Wood Case* the protagonist is not driven by poverty to misuse funds. He worked for the wealthiest man in the town, was in line to inherit a part of the business, and had already benefitted from a small estate inherited by his wife.

Economic stress becomes more of a reality in the short stories. The farm renter and the minister share the fate of the migrant. Their livelihood depends in the first instance on the land-holder and in the second on the good will of the church members. The stories "A Start in Life" and "Man of the Family" show a similarity of situation. In both, the young member of the family is forced into employment and responsibilities. The emotional conflict, however, in each story is different. Modest living prevails in all of the stories and novels, but suffering and need are not a major quality in Suckow's scene.

In recording her scene, she is honest and temperate; she lacks both satire and sentimentality. She takes neither the romantic-historical tone nor the tone of social protest that marked Hamlin Garland's stories. She did not, she could not, look contemptuously with the mind of the East. But she strove to give a sure and total picture of the time and region. These pictures neither indict nor celebrate; they delineate.

Her response to both beauty and ugliness is what imparts distinction to her picture of the Iowa rural scene. She presents both sides of farm life, its limitations and advantages; she does not exalt farm life over the town and city or exploit peculiarities of character, but finds the essence of place in a deep-rooted and binding culture whose manners and codes she presents with an almost clairvoyant accuracy. Like Hamlin Garland she is conscious of the toil, the crudities, and the brutalizing effects of farm life, but she also sees an affirmation in the stabilities to be found in such a life.

The beauties of her scene differ from those beheld by Herbert Quick's J. T. Vandemark in 1855, when he gazed across the great expanse of unsettled prairie—an unbroken surface of a great sea of grass—but her sensitivity to the natural beauty of farm and countryside permeates all that she writes. She has seen the monotony, the complacency, and the conformity of the small town, but she has avoided the caricature and the satire to be found in Van Vechten's searing attitude. Her characters live a more sober life than those of Phil Stong's farms and villages. Among Miss Suckow's villagers there is nothing of the malice, adultery, and cruelty that exist among the twenty or so householders of Brunswick in *A Village Tale* or other characters of Stong's fiction. Stong's characters can be more joyous and happy as in *State Fair* and more energetic in business as in *The Long Lane*. Violence and crime are completely absent from the lives of her people. No recognition of racial antagonisms such as Edna Ferber remembers as part of her bitter childhood experience in Ottumwa, Iowa, can be found in any of Miss Suckow's stories. Her farmers also come to independence more easily than the Mantz family, whose endless struggle with mortgages, banks, sales, employment, and their ambition to escape the farm life occupy much of Paul Corey's trilogy.

Miss Suckow in her portrayal of the Iowa scene differs in subject, attitude, and method from her predecessors and contemporaries. Her preference for scene and character is the essence of her method and temper. She is more a pictorial than a dramatic writer.

The repetition of her picture of the early part of the century perhaps suggests a reluctance to relinquish it. With her commonplace characters and their uneventful lives she does not make as great appeal to the imagination as some other writers do, but she excels in communicating her intimate understanding of and compassion for these ordinary lives. Her fiction which extols the "just common ordinary Americans" in their plain churches, happy schools, neat farms, and "snug" towns and homes has its limitations as a rounded portrait of the Iowa scene. The absence of struggle in the economic and commercial scene as well as in the agricultural life, the neglect of the intellectual and creative, and the failure to show an articulate voice in the affairs of government restrict her scene.

Reading her fiction to view the Iowa scene is like looking through the old family photograph album that appears in her every parlor. The same people appear over and over again. Individuals, groups, landscapes, buildings, and events repeat themselves with certainty. But in her pictures, Miss Suckow, like a versatile photographer, varies her focus and lighting, her range and scope to catch traits or qualities that reveal special insight. From these the reader comes to know the appearance of the farms and towns; he is acquainted with their people and their homes, and feels the atmosphere that dominates the events and group life of the Iowa folks.

Chapter III

SOCIAL HISTORIAN

The social milieu in which Ruth Suckow like many of her fictional characters matured was that of the secure and serene years before 1917. Her own roots were in those prewar decades which clung to the nineteenth century optimism and confidence in the American ideal and conceived it a duty to achieve material prosperity as well as to pursue the life of the spirit. Henry Steele Commager has said in partial summary of that era:

> the two generations after 1890 witnessed a transition from certainty to uncertainty, from faith to doubt, from security to insecurity, from seeming order to ostentatious disorder.[1]

This uncertainty culminated in the postwar decade in which Suckow began her writing. Responses to the malady of the age varied from cynicism and iconoclasm, confusion, resignation, and rebellion to a retrospective view based on a trust in the past and the familiar.

The period which she has called "that almost windless interval when the small sound of the windmill could be heard"[2] saw the climax of material prosperity and at the same time the beginning of a cycle of stress described in one study of American literary thought as

> a testing period to determine whether the long-cherished ideals of democracy, progress, and opportunity will continue as the motivating forces in American life, or whether our destinies will henceforth be controlled by some new, uncharacteristic, and more frankly cynical system.[3]

Such a concept led her to examine her scene in order to reveal the decay or survival of these ideals in her contemporary society. In her novels she records middle class life in America in a changing period of national history. The institutions through which she makes her observations reveal a gradual breakdown of the ideals of domestic and religious life. At the beginning of the era depicted, migration and settlement of emigrant grandparents are matters of family history and legend; at the end, in a time of uncertainty, insecurity, and disorder, the family is disintegrating and its young are moving either east in search of culture and freedom or west in search of greater opportunity and happiness. In her record of the years included in this period she examines American life as it is affected by social changes, always mindful of the diverse elements of its culture. The American society she depicts ranges from that of early settlements when life was simple and free of social cleavages to more complex communities.

Neither a social reformer nor a propagandist, Ruth Suckow has maintained that her purpose was to observe and record; her fiction fulfills this intention. She was aware of social currents in the American scene, but she did not engage in controversy with satire or polemic. She had published most of her fiction by 1936 when *Carry-Over* appeared with the preface "Comments and Addenda." In this statement she said of the period in which her stories and novels were written, "the time was neither wrong nor right."[4]

In such an interval, it was possible to look down into the material as if into a well of water that was for the moment clear and undisturbed. The purpose was to discern; to catch a reflection; to hold and keep. In a period of storm, such contemplation is not often possible. But the effort to perceive, as far as possible without prejudice or partiality, has a value of its own.[5]

Apparent in all of her writing is the commitment to the belief that one function of the artist in America is to record the passing scene. In doing so she concerns herself with human aspects more than with political or economic issues. The institutions she portrays are largely social with little or no political or economic coloring. Her observations on the social structure of

American society and the forces that influence it, however, throw a shadow beyond the locality of the Iowa scene and suggest the larger American vista.

That America which draws her discerning eye is not static but is shifting constantly. Its transitions are her abiding subject matter and their effects on the life of family and community provide her recurrent themes. The chronicles encompassing several generations emphasize this theme in the novels, and in the short stories the incisive revelations of character and experience grow out of the same social pattern which the longer fiction depicts more fully.

In her essay, "The Folk Idea in American Life," she explained the pattern of the "folks" as essential in the structure of American society. Historically, she sees the origin of the "folks" spirit in the mingling of groups who found likeness in fortune and aim but not in blood. In the early days the people were not a folk; they were many—the folks—with ideas of variety and plurality bound firmly into a whole. She observes that it was the early necessity for an intensely communal life that gave to the word *community* a special meaning in this country, more important than town, village, or even state. The application of *folks* as a term applied to families also related to American beginnings. The idea of one big family was the essence of pioneer life. In a country where racial ties were weak, the family unit was the one everybody could understand. Miss Suckow sees an extension of the folks spirit of pioneer days, when the idea of family solidarity was the essence of pioneer life, into a later period when church, school, and family were the centers of community life. But, as she notes, the twentieth century witnessed an era of rebellious young who longed to break away from the folks. In her novels she presents the weakening of the folk values in that era of rebellion.

Primarily the social history of Miss Suckow's fiction is her presentation of life in her small towns and the social patterns of family and community existence over three decades. Their importance is in revealing the social temper and social values of the era rather than in recording political or economic events. The implications of these observations give them social significance. She is concerned with people as social beings and in treating them as such reveals certain fabrics of American life. In her treatment of towns and farms she notes changes in physical appearance, in population, and in social mores. In both farm and town families there is a departure from family patterns of language, church membership, and occupations, and a weakening of family ties.

She notes clearly the forces of change in their effects on human relations but provides little analysis of cause or solution. The effects are most clearly noted in the contrast and occasional conflict between generations—in the shifting of values that accompanies change in society. The standards of one generation are found inadequate for the next generation. The simple values of the emigrant whose single motive was the struggle to survive do not prepare his children for a more complex society. The placid, smug, sunny environment in which children grew up in the prewar years fails to condition them for the tumultuous problems of the postwar generation.

The youths of her fiction respond to doubt and insecurity with bewilderment more frequently than with rebellion and cynicism. Often the social scene suggests those segments of American society that adhered to Warren G. Harding's plea for a return to "normalcy." Her characters often seem to share in the "American mass desire to avoid the consequences of its reluctant maturity, to flee into the simplicity of its colorful, hopeful past."[6] Likewise they wish "to live in a plain house on a quiet street."[7] The images are patriarchal—Papa and Mama and the children, sitting on a green lawn in the twilight, with pigeons cooing in the rafters, the big brown cat asleep among the catnip, the church bells tolling, and the good smell of bread baking in a kitchen that is certain to look like a Currier & Ives print. The older generation cherishes such a dream and the younger generation never quite relinquishes it—as an ideal if not as a possibility. At least when disillusioned, they have nothing with which to replace the ideal of their elders. They question old values and find new ones wanting. They reject the comfortable platitudes and respond at times with cynicism and rebellion but are soon eager to capture conventional happiness. They admit the failure of the past but are timid in establishing a new pattern.

Ruth Suckow invariably examines the social scene and emphasizes two characteristics of American society: the social transitions and the assimilation of contrasting cultures, plus the intermingling of the old east and the new west in the most mobile society in history. Social transition depicted in its human aspects is central to all of her novels; indeed it is dominant in her fiction. This concept, more than change or development in character, directs her narratives. Changes in the social scene are more significant than changes in individual characters.

There is a repetition of certain aspects of the American scene presented with varying emphasis in each of the first five novels. Then in *The Folks,* a broad and expansive novel, her chronicle is brought to a close in the late twenties. She does not examine any later years. Following her studies of the contemporary era with its transitory values, she returned in *New Hope* to the earlier period of 1900 and affirmed the values which in the twenties were undergoing a test.

Country People is the shortest of the novels but, like her longest novel, it touches upon four generations. It is the sparse chronicle of the years 1859-1922, the life span of August Kaetterhenry. Brief as it is, this novel presents the chief topics and themes of a social significance: assimilation of the foreign element and social transition involving family and social patterns, the older generation's resistance to change, and their conflict with the younger generation. The emphasis is on the Americanization process.

The family and community pattern that becomes so familiar to the reader is introduced in her first novel. The Kaetterhenrys, like most of her families, trace their American beginnings to German immigrant ancestors who were attached to their native language, method of worship, and social codes. Three generations comprise the families: the German immigrant grandparents, one at least a dependent in the home of a son or daughter, suggesting the ideas of contrast as well as family continuity; their sons and daughters, the hardworking and industrious first generation in the new country, who despite the inbred values inherited from the old people, establish themselves in the new country and look upon material change with growing favor, if also a bit of awe; and their children who come to maturity in the period of the First World War, completely free of old country traditions and accepting without marvel or question the wonders of the twentieth century. In *Country People* material prosperity increased with each generation of the Kaetterhenrys and was accompanied by a consequent relaxing of thrift, industry, and social restriction.

All of the social elements that appear in her later fiction are present here and relate to the absorption of the German element into Iowa rural society and into the national character. The temper of the locale and the era is reflected by the way in which the Kaetterhenry family become identified with it.

The first generation born in this country of immigrant parents receives special attention. She reveals how German immigrants are assimilated through social institutions rather than through intermarriage as in later books. In his struggle to own and cultivate his land August Kaetterhenry quickly acquires the pattern of the rural Midwest in farming methods and social attitudes. The Americanization of his family moves rapidly as they prosper from agricultural developments and material progress, increase their ownership of land, and acquire from church and school the attitudes of rural society.

In response to his own need and the ideals of his society, August becomes representative of his generation in his pursuit of wealth and security. The desire for material prosperity born of a need to struggle for survival becomes the single motive in his life—so consuming a motive for him and his generation that it drains away all spiritual resources and with its fulfillment brings only a futile and meaningless existence. Opportunity in the new land instills in August a drive for relentless work and stringent thrift.

The land in this novel is something that pays the man who takes hold of it. August, like other Turkey Creek and Richland Germans—slow, hard-headed, hard-working savers of money who had come to make homes for themselves instead of profits for a Pomeranian landowner—was willing to toil from four in the morning to nine at night to get ahead. Everything else had to wait until "they got the farm paid for." He hated to do anything to the house until he had a better barn. Thrifty accumulation implied in August's case a "job well done." To him the farm stood as a way of life, a symbol of security, stability, and continuity of family effort.

The pursuit of this personal and social goal August comes to identify with the church. The materialistic impulse that brought the pioneer to the middlewestern soil persists even in his association with religion. His membership and attendance in the German Methodist church were closely bound with ideals of prosperity, security, and civic obligation. For the family, church membership meant respectability. Working hard, paying bills, bringing up the children right, and attending services were all part of the same thing. To the new American beset with insecurity the church became a deep-rooted bulwark against worrisome changes. It was a center of social life, the institution through which the immigrant family acquired the pattern of the rural community.

Changes inevitably affect the Kaetterhenry family. Departure from the family pattern is observed in the breakdown of German speech in the home and at church where services are in English, in better education for the older children, and in improved farming methods and greater prosperity.

August achieved his retirement after years of successful farming and moved into the nearby town until sickness necessitated a visit to the Mayo Clinic followed by an inactive life of meaningless routine until the final illness. Like many a successful Iowa farmer, August left his wife, Emma, "well fixed" and at least one heir to continue the family traditions and give permanence and continuity to the family pattern. Walter L. Meyers in writing about plain people observes that "folks are most folks" when they have settled down and taken on family responsibilities in which the old patterns are repeated. A man marries, grows weary of moving, becomes a part of a community in which neighborliness and uniformity are the deep-rooted values. He reverts more to his father's views, even to his forms of speech, and in turn becomes part of a conservative older generation.[3] Miss Suckow frequently makes use of such a cycle to emphasize the continuity of cultural patterns. She does not, however, ignore the elements of change.

Changes made sharp contrasts between generations. Freedom from need for hard labor meant greater ease amid the growing prosperity. The abundance the children enjoy is in contrast to the meager conditions known to their parents. But the simple principles by which the parents lived and prospered are unsatisfactory to their children. There is nothing in the narrow values of August's generation to inspire or vitalize the next generation which is not under the necessity to practice the same thrift and hard work. While August's children enjoy the ease allowed by their increased prosperity, his widow, Emma, seems as unable as he to relax her effort and thrift. As the story ends she commiserates with another widow and agrees that they should be thankful they have good homes and "don't have to be sent to the poorhouse."[9]

The novel suggests another pattern that appears in later books—the variation of response to the social scene represented in the lives of the children. The son Carl is a symbol of continuity. He lives on the land inherited from his father and becomes a fine farmer; the younger son Johnnie departs from the family pattern. He refuses to attend church, rejects the farm, makes an undesirable marriage and becomes a garage mechanic. A daughter, Marguerite, was said to be a "real Kaetterhenry, . . . she did her work well and disdained the slipshod ways of other stenographers. She was cool, hard, scrupulous, level-headed, a good worker."[10] In the character of Marguerite, Miss Suckow touches briefly upon a phase of society that is extended in the novel *Cora* in which there is the same type of young woman with German ancestry who follows a business career.

As social history, *Country People* reveals the manner in which the poor sons of emigrants with no resource but their willingness to work achieved ownership of land and prospered in its cultivation. This success was not accomplished through heroic virtues but through dogged work and thrifty accumulation of wealth for the next generation—an entirely material heritage. The novel makes real the virtue and the weakness of the immigrant's determination for a success which leaves the next generation spiritually impoverished and without even the motive for hard work.

The theme of assimilation of the German element recurs in the next novel, *The Odyssey of a Nice Girl*. In the marriage of Ed Schoessel and Etta Blossom the melting-pot process is presented with the intermingling of English and German immigrants who continued to live on a farm near Germantown and to keep their country ways, spoke broken English, kept German religious books and papers in their home, and attended the German Methodist Church where they prayed and sang in German. Ed had broken with this pattern when he left the farm to keep a store, married a town girl and attended her church. Etta's parents were native Americans from "York State" and leading members of the Congregational Church. Etta and her sister had had a year in a denominational college and had taught school. She was eligible for D. A. R. membership.

In Buena Vista as in so many Iowa towns the strength of the New England influence was apparent in the prestige of the Congregationalists; among them were the "very nicest people." From childhood Marjorie felt her English ancestry more congenial than her German background. She had a distaste for everything associated with the German grandparents and identified herself more intimately with her mother's family in her effort to eliminate the emigrant influence. This influence is very nearly eliminated in the course of the narrative which focuses on the third generation. The respect for the superiority of eastern culture leads her to Boston in her search of aesthetic development.

The mobility of American society that made possible the marriage of an Iowa farm boy and a teacher from "York State" is a characteristic which engages Miss Suckow's attention. In this novel Marjorie herself seeks culture in Boston, freedom and excitement in a secretarial job in Chicago, and the happiness of marriage in Denver, with no final indication that she will find any more satisfaction in the achievement of the last quest than in earlier experiences.

This disposition to migrate makes a radical change in the makeup of any community within one generation's time. At the close of the novel Marjorie's friends have moved elsewhere as she has done. Of her own family only the younger brother Bud is left in Buena Vista after her widowed mother joins Marjorie in Denver. Bud, in contrast to Marjorie, is like Carl in *Country People;* both are symbols of continuity and stability of pattern. At his father's retirement he took over the furniture store and suddenly was a "hardworking, responsible young man, suggested for the town council, a sponsor of the Chautauqua, soon to be married, and become a solid citizen of the town."[11]

This novel is the first of several which focus on the younger generation's response to its changing society in which the search for freedom and escape becomes the central problem of the era.

In the life of Buena Vista, Morning Sun, Valley Junction, Belmond, Fairview, and New Hope Miss Suckow has held up to view the values of the folks, and in almost every novel she seems conscious of a threat to those values in American society since the 1920s. Towns and family groups as well as individuals have changed. In general it is the transition from the fixed pattern to the unsettled, from confidence to doubt, from the optimism and idealism of parents to the disillusionment of hope for the future in their children. The theme of bewilderment and uncertainty of the age appears to some extent in every novel before 1934. In *Country People* it is largely expressed in the character Johnnie. In *The Odyssey of a Nice Girl* both Marjorie and Rich are groping for meaning in their lives. In *The Bonney Family* Sarah is the one most aware of the insecurity resulting from change. But it is in *The Folks* where Miss Suckow gives this feeling its most extensive analysis.

The most important historical event and the most influential force in bringing about social change and unrest during her own youth and that of her characters was World War I. It is with the generation and the social scene affected by the war that she is largely concerned. War never becomes a major interest in any of her novels, but it is one of the forces of change reflected in the social scene of her first three novels, *Country People, The Odyssey of a Nice Girl* and *The Bonney Family*. Its influences as exerted on the characters in *The Folks* are the delayed but more lasting social effects.

Her personal response to war as a young woman was perhaps her most significant experience in clarifying both social and religious ideas. Her opposition to the enthusiasm for war is closely bound up with her departure from the religion of her childhood.

In her memoir she spoke of the war as an "earthquake

shock" which "seemed to jar me loose finally from any form of 'organized religion.' " In her statement of the importance of the event to her she wrote:

The First World War, and the entrance into it of the United States, was a blow first of all to my love of country. A third-generation American with no emotional attachment to any older country, and no colonial heritage, I had grown up putting my national faith in the new country to which my grandparents had come with wholehearted commitment. I had taken the Melting Pot seriously; had believed that all who came and contributed to its upbuilding were equally welcome, as in the new town in which I was born; had conceived of a new and greater role for the young United States, not as participant in "the old quarrels of Europe" but as an impartial mediator and a center of aid and reconstruction—influential by example, rather than by direct partisanship. This aspiration was battered down—it seemed to me, was distorted and deteriorated—into the political doctrine of "isolationism"; its international aspect smothered out in the turn of national life.

. . . But the shock went far deeper than national feeling and hope—strong as these had been since early childhood—because I had grown up in the church, in the light of the Judeo-Christian religion, under New Testament precepts. In the atmosphere of war, it seemed that, after all, my upbringing counted, although I still lacked full and clear comprehension of its meaning to me. I could not at that time be called a "pacifist." I knew very little of pacifism as a movement. I did not belong to any movement—I was tending to steer clear of them and to find my way all by myself. I was not much influenced, therefore, by any stated theory or philosophy. In fact, I met that first shock of war fresh and green! My response to it was unstudied, spontaneous and actual, as I saw war from the home country, and felt its effect there.[12]

In the war-time sermons and the willingness of ministers to

support the war she saw the churches becoming merely the "religious arm of the state," and regretted that "those who had preached the gospel of love now preached the gospel of hatred." For the first time in religious matters she felt at variance with her father and she described the difference in their attitudes.

Now for the first time in my whole knowledge of him, my father threw aside his eminently sane viewpoint, his quality of disinterested judgment, and his independence of thought, and stood for what seemed completely opposed to the intent of his life and preaching. He became one of those preachers who ardently presented arms. Many things led up to such a position: perhaps his adoption of the war as a holy crusade represented partly the reaction of a second-generation American to his German ancestry, this war being with Germany; perhaps it was also affected by that sense of a slump in the creative church life of the time—in an atmosphere of spiritual dryness, he seemed to find a new cause that would absorb all his energies.[13]

Such responses to the war by the churches and churchmen she believed marked a powerlessness of religion in organized form.

But the permission to hate—to count hatred as a positive good, even a religious duty, as was freely done in churches as well as in the secular civic body during that First World War—had been like a brief opening of a great Pandora's box; the openers were appalled, but not all the evil things let out could be squeezed back in again. The emotions and decisions of that time seemed to mark (since I failed to take in all the elements of the situation—saw only in part) the meaninglessness of the churches and powerlessness of the Judeo-Christian religion itself as it had expressed itself through the centuries in organized form.[14]

If no characters of Miss Suckow's novels make such an analysis of feelings and response, two of them, Marjorie Shoessel and

Sarah Bonney, do reflect her attitudes toward the war and the organization of religion. Occasionally the treatment appears as part of the social background. In *Country People* war had been viewed largely from the attitude of the rural midwest and the immigrant.

In the first novel the effect of war on the immigrants and their families is obvious. Those from the old country "regarded with a hurt, sorrowing, bewildered wonder that it [the country] should be fighting Germany."[15] Those of German ancestry felt definite racial resentment and lost some of their own sense of security. August was made conscious of his German roots, but he also shared the attitude of other midwestern farmers who felt the war was not a vital concern of theirs or of their country and opposed the draft as unjust interference. August's two sons, representative of the generation who fought, did not respond identically. One came home ready to settle down for good, "saying that this old Iowa farm looked better to him than any place he had ever seen or hoped to see,"[16] and the other was restless, dissatisfied with farm life, and interested in mechanics.

In the *Odyssey of a Nice Girl* she presents the view of war largely through Marjorie's observations of its effects on the small midwestern town. Response to the war in Buena Vista reveals the narrow outlook and insular attitudes of a small middlewestern town: the ostentatious patriotism of the citizens, the desire among some for self-fulfillment rather than for heroism, the disapproval by others on moral principle, and general regret for its unsettling effects on the social pattern.

Like the farmers of *Country People* the townsmen of Buena Vista did not feel any immediacy or urgency in the cause of war.

To most of the people it had seemed far away, something that could never come close. Some resented it, others seized upon it now to help break up the long monotony of everyday living—more terribly thrilling than a fire in the business district, a drowning in the river, or the discovery that the cashier of the Farmer's Bank had been embezzling.

75

... Something had come, it seemed, to shake up that placid, solid, comfortable life of home, changing things around, shifting values that had seemed to be fixed.[17]

In Buena Vista different activities were substituted for card parties—Red Cross meetings in the Armory, formation of a league for conservation, dances for the boys who were going away. Marriages flourished and formerly obscure people came into prominence in military service or war-time occupations. When Marjorie's brother volunteered for service the family talked of his patriotism. From her knowledge of Rich's unhappy married life Marjorie knew he "was going because it gave him a chance at last to break routine, to indulge that old adventurous youth that had been early thwarted, turned aside; conscious like herself of qualities that he had never used, and seizing this chance to bring them to some kind of fruition." War brides and families who received letters from soldiers could see nothing but glory in the feverish excitement of war. The closest reflection of her personal response is to be seen in Marjorie's attitude.

In spite of her uneasy envy of Jessie and Rich, and all the others, she hated the war; and that old desire for integrity would not let her be quite illusioned, or use this thing for her own small purpose.[18]

She was in sympathy with old Mrs. Davison who had told the minister that "she could no longer be a member of a church where war sermons were preached and the Prince of Peace "denied. . . ."[19]

Marjorie observed that, with the war, astounding and upsetting things happened. Some of them were absurd, but the most absurd had in them an element of ironic cruelty. Her brother Rich died in camp during the influenza epidemic without having any of the adventure he sought; a hometown friend early in the war realized a brief flash of heroism but later became a deserter, driven and hunted. To some the war had shown sudden and shining promise which later "it had ruthlessly and savagely denied. . . ."[20]

While the effect of war on the community life appears particularly in *The Odyssey of a Nice Girl,* in *The Bonney Family* it is treated again in relation to the weakness of the church and to the disruption of a household. As in Buena Vista the strange business of war time settled "thicker and thicker" upon the campus, at first with pain and rupture and then with radiant excitement.

> The busy, happily provincial, mildly aspiring, secure life of the little college on the outskirts of the growing town was suddenly bitterly invaded from without and jerked out of its pattern. No one knew what to look forward to.[21]

Boys drilling on campus, Red Cross activities, groups meeting to pack kits, the recklessness of the unexpected and haphazard marriages all created a sense of patriotism and gave a false security. But when boys went overseas and reports of casualties came back, the brightness of beginning "changed, tightened, darkened into the strain of midway in action." Feelings of bitterness and hatred began to smoulder. There followed an enmity to German neighbors and a ban on German music; women in Red Cross work became "ardent, righteous and patriotic." Farmers did not understand how war had come in a strange and alien way to their quiet farms but did not think of struggling against it. They were vaguely but strictly patriotic.

Again a resemblance to Miss Suckow is seen in Sarah Bonney's disapproval of the churches' identifying with war purposes and her resentment of their zeal.

> On her way to the campus, she passed the brick corner church where the people in Vincent Park had been placidly "worshiping" all these years. Oh, of course there were a few good old ladies, one or two fanatical old men!—but the others had gone to keep up respectability and to sit down, with the pleasant feeling of duty performed, to big Sunday dinners and eat more than was good for them. But even that old mild, unvarying, Sunday service, with its "nice" hymns and "such a good" sermon and the singing of the big choir of college students who wanted to wear

surplices, was better than this zeal that marked it now.[22]

The business methods are equally offensive to her. The flaring signboard on the church lawn was an idea of a young up-to-date minister who wanted the church to advertise and who was busy

> hounding people to work in the Sunday-school, putting on drives, drumming up money and tickling the business men into giving by thinking up smart tricks, heading Liberty Loan campaigns, preaching war sermons, giving evening lectures on the atrocities he had never witnessed. . . .[23]

The war is seen as a blunder and failure of the older generation and as reason for questioning the validity of ideals taught in home and school. Sarah Bonney's own father, "the kindest man on earth," had plunged into the excitement of war. Sarah's resentment is toward all the generation who had taught the boys and girls ideals of "service" and "brotherhood" and then betrayed them, and she doubts that boys and girls can put faith in parents and teachers any more. In her own family and the small outside community the good firm fabric of her household was rent and torn and nowhere were there kindness and justice.

Miss Suckow stated in her memoir that she did not hold a church membership after she was eighteen years old. As her own aesthetic and intellectual interests developed she deplored the "pall of mediocrity" that hung over church services and activities and she resented the emphasis on what she called the "Martha aspects" in the church activities of the women. With her reaction to the shock of war came her complete break with formal religion until her affiliation in later years with the American Friends.

Most of her novels were written in the period when she observed the church to be one of the weakened institutions in society. All of her families have a strongly fundamentalist religious background which apparently offers them no positive values. Her young generation are indifferent or hostile. The waning influence of religious institutions as a theme in fiction is not confined to novels of the rural midwest. The Irish Catholic youths of James T. Farrell's South Side Chicago of about the same era derive little social or spiritual benefits from the religious teachings of home, school, and church. Despite his outward conformity to religion Studs Lonigan developed no spiritual resources to help him combat the brutality, injustice and cynicism of his environment.

While the church in most of her fiction is a prominent part of the scene it appears almost entirely as a social institution. It does not give a principle of conduct or exert any deep moral or spiritual influence. It is seen to be synonymous with "getting on" in *Country People* as well as instrumental in establishing a communal folk life. It has almost no influence on Marjorie Schoessel, who enjoyed the adulation of the younger girls whom she taught in Sunday School, but would not let herself consider whether she "believed" because she "must have something."

The Bonney Family is the story of a minister's family, and even they viewed the church in a practical manner. Mrs. Bonney's father "had been a minister, and she accepted the workings of a church in as matter-of-fact a way as if it had been a farm or a hardware store."[24] The hymns meant "exactly nothing" to her and while her husband preached she did some of her "hardest thinking" about household problems. Sarah's resentment of the church in war time was a development of the feeling she had held since an incident, very much like one in Miss Suckow's girlhood, when she had refused to join the Christian Endeavor Society. The church in this novel is portrayed as part of the changing pattern in the period of its history to which Miss Suckow has referred in actuality as its business period, when it glorified business and used its methods to attract crowds. Mr. Bonney had moved away from the simplicity of a small town church and had taken on more of a business assignment.

He had been knocking about from town to town, getting money out of people, getting in spite of himself into the devious byways of financial dealings, learning the ways of an institution from the inside office; and he had discovered things he would have liked never to suspect. He had lost his youth. What, then, was left but to grow in material comfort?[25]

The Bonney Family is principally a study of the interrelationships of family members, but these relationships are infused with the sense of change and the passing of values that promised stability and security. The family members are dispersed by the close of the novel, and as Sarah ends her visit in Morning Sun before going to New York for professional training she knows her love for Morning Sun is for what it used to be, not for what it is at the time. In this novel of a family are intimations concerning the nature of social forces and institutions.

One phase of the changing American scene which becomes part of the background of several novels and the main theme of one story is that of women's entrance into the world of business and careers, briefly suggested in *Country People* in Marguerite's secretarial job in Rapids City, and with a little more detail in Marjorie Schoessel and Sarah Bonney. But in the novels *Cora* and *The Kramer Girls* Miss Suckow deals more directly with the subject of business careers for women. Generally, there is no more happiness or meaningful existence in the search for fulfillment through business occupations than in small town life.

In the interlude between her dramatics course at Boston and her marriage in Denver, Marjorie held a job in a hosiery factory in Chicago. To the girl it proved no escape from dullness, monotony, routine or loneliness. Her secretarial job was a bleak and emotionless grind that meant long hours of work, burning eyes, and an aching back. Too tired at night to go out she spent evenings in her solitary rooms, and thought that "the 'interesting' contacts, the glamorous new intimacies were as far away as in Buena Vista."

Sarah Bonney's career is hardly launched at the end of the novel, *The Bonney Family,* but her strength and self-reliance shown throughout the story suggest that hers will perhaps be the most successful independent life of any of her feminine characters.

Cora has similarities to Sinclair Lewis's novel *The Job* (1917), in which a young woman, Una Golden, goes from a small town in Pennsylvania to New York and finally becomes successful in the large-scale development of real estate. Cora Schwietert resembles Una in her drive for success, her marriage to escape the job which proves to be an unhappy one, a return to the job and possible suitors, and finally the hope for combining marriage and a career.

Cora is a novel about a successful business woman. Very little of the business world itself enters the scene since Miss Suckow as usual concentrates on the human elements of the situation. Cora's rise to a business success through her secretarial positions is not detailed in the novel. But she becomes a reliable office assistant, gives talks on secretarial work for women at meetings of clubs and business schools, joins a club of business women and associates with the "best women in the city."

Cora Schwietert brings to her business career the temperament and personal traits of her German ancestry—not the sentiment and tender feeling for old country ways and traditions cherished by her father, Chris Schwietert, but the hard and scrupulous sense of duty and work which characterized the farming immigrant of a generation before her.

She is as unsentimental and undeviating in her drive for success as August Kaetterhenry had been in his stubborn thrift and dogged pursuit of work. Her ambition is motivated by the same kind of desire for a neat house, economic security, and well ordered lives for her family. With her love of order and efficiency, her contempt for loafing, her sturdiness and innate strength, Cora becomes a sharp-witted, sophisticated, and successful business woman, and ironically finds her achievement barren and meaningless. Devoid of humanity, she finds little satisfaction in her secure position.

After an unhappy marriage for which at the time she set aside her business future, her strength and hard efficiency enable her to take up the old pattern—the one more congenial and consistent with her own personality. At the end of the story she is a partner and business director of a specialty shop for children. Again she is living an efficient and orderly life and is thoroughly frustrated. She is bitterly amused at her fate and the irony of life in which people really did get what they were after—"only in such queer unrealized ways, changed and unrecognizable, and perhaps at the price of everything else."[26] The very business success that has stifled the woman illustrates another abortive effort of her generation to find happiness in material values that inhibit human values, and is a variation in the pattern of the search for security

When *The Kramer Girls* appeared serially it carried the descriptive sub-title, probably supplied by the editor, "Marriage or a Career?" Rose Kramer, the main character, is an "ordinary, neat, capable woman"—a type to be found in every locality. She is more human than Cora, more resolute than Marjorie Schoessel, and less self-reliant than Sarah Bonney. Her sisters had ambitions for her to become more than commonplace, and her scholastic honors gave promise that she might fulfill their expectations. She shared the contemporary desire for freedom and escape from the small town. Her opportunity to take a job in a Chicago office seemed to offer the possibility she desired. But as in Marjorie Schoessel's experience her dreams were not fulfilled in her life in the city. After a short period she welcomed the letter calling her home.

> Something had to happen to get her away from her job—from all jobs, from being lost in the hard, stony world of business and crowded streets and mechanical devices and cramped impersonal quarters, that she knew now was alien.[27]

At home in Valley Junction she seizes quickly the opportunity for conventional happiness in marriage—a marriage she regarded as a refuge that would settle everything. After a series of unsuccessful building ventures in a number of towns Rose must admit that her husband, "a rural Englishman in growing America," cannot be successful. His conscientiousness and love of work are not practical virtues in American society. With his need to do his work with "leisurely and careful perfection" he cannot become a successful contractor on a large scale.

Rose would have preferred to remain in the shelter of her domestic life, but she returns to business recognizing that "somebody had to change when everything was changing." Rose is commonplace, ordinarily competent and limited in ambition. Confident of her ability, she nevertheless derives her real satisfaction from the security of her family and her orderly home.

This novel ends on a more complacent note than that of earlier books. Rose has restored the pattern of the girlhood in her own home and has provided a continuation of all she had loved in the simple life of Valley Junction. She enjoys the comfortable security that eludes most of her generation in Miss Suckow's novels.

There seems to be little else of social significance in this book except in its presentation of life in the comfortable ways of homely folks. There is also the element of the intermingling of German and English. The contrast of the old country with the new is illustrated in Archie Carpenter's incompatibility with the rapidly progressing American materialism.

Perhaps Rose Kramer and Cora are not so different in their basic desires. Both have the wish for an ordered and secure life—more compelling than their yearning for freedom and experience—and they use the means available to them to obtain it.

In her fiction before 1934 she presented in faithful records the simplicities of old community life in the various small towns and recorded the social transitions which touched four generations. In *The Folks* (1934) she traces with the greatest detail the gradual breakdown of old ideals with her focus primarily on the years 1920-1930. The failure of familiar values to assure a course of certainty is explored in the lives of the four Ferguson children, each presented in a separate division. The era covered in the book is one beginning in pretense and ending in rebellion, years that were unsettled and uncertain but in general prosperous.

The familiar intermingling of nationalities in this family is seen in the marriage of Annie Luers, daughter of a German emigrant living in Ohio, and Fred Ferguson, whose family were Scotch and loyal Presbyterians. In the usual pattern they had kept pace with progress and become more prosperous than their parents. Annie's parents "had had so little all their lives" and spent their last days in three rooms provided for them in a son's home. Fred's parents owned a farm near Belmond but were nevertheless penurious.

As a banker in Belmond Fred achieved a position in the community and in the church, enjoyed a moderate prosperity, and from the fulness and abundance of his own security derived a sense of protection to family and church. For him loyalties were clear and simple—to the Republican party, the Presbyterian church, the old folks on the farm and the Ferguson clan, and the bank. The dependence of church and family members was both a burden and a pleasure. Fred and Annie never doubted the brightness of the future for their children. They are representative of their generation in their optimism, complacency, and desire for respectability—assured that their children had come into the "free inheritance of all the years that had gone before them"[28] and that leisure and prosperity were the "certain rewards of their time of life."[29] In the comfortable room surrounded by her pleasant things Annie held to her cherished belief in a simple and beautiful family happiness, and Fred was equally assured in his role of banker and father. All of the stabilities to which Fred and Annie cling are undermined in that era which hurled their children from the complacency of absolute security into perilous upheaval—economic, moral, and political. In the experience of each child security and peace give way to confusion and instability.

It is in the effects of this transitional era on the lives of her people that she reflects the social temper. In *The Folks,* as in other novels, she is not concerned to any extent with political or economic events.

The son Carl is a victim of his own compulsion to deny desires and impulses that threaten the stabilities of his life and to cling to the easy familiar certainties. He felt bound to marry Lillian White—meagre, narrow, provincial—or everything would be thrown into confusion. The tragedy of Carl's life comes from his efforts to avoid confusion and complexities in any departure from the pattern of his youth. His inability to restore these certainties results in his disillusionment and defeat.

In the lives of the other children Fred and Annie witness a rupture in the conventional pattern of prosperity and security. The younger daughter's marriage that began so favorably is threatened by economic distress. The intrusion of radical political ideas is intimated when the youngest of the family marries a student with liberal views.

In the rebellion against the optimism of the older generation there is little in Suckow's novels of the experiment in sensation, sex, drugs, alcohol, or perversions as escape. Margaret Ferguson is the one character who rebels against the sanely prosaic life of the middlewestern small town. The decadence of Greenwich Village attracts her, and she becomes the conventional devotee of the unconventional Bohemian life. She rejects her fundamentalist teaching and abandons all societal conformity.

By the time Fred Ferguson is ready to retire he has been sad witness to the alteration of everything he cherished. The beautiful family life Annie had tried to keep was cracking and straining. Through some strange force with which his children seemed allied everything of value was slipping away. The old folks were no longer on the farm; the Presbyterian membership had disbanded to unite with the Congregational Church; bank failures were threatening his financial security, and there was no Ferguson child to continue in his home or his business.

The faith of his fathers was gone, which they had come to found in a new land, carry with them, make greater and stronger than ever before. . . . His faith had been the church, which his father had left to him. It was the church that he had helped to build, the institution that he had tried to carry on. First the faith, then the institution to make it secure, then the faith diminishing and leaving the structure that was to hold it empty. It was the institution that had been left to him. That had been *his* place in this long sequence. Now that it was gone, what did he believe? Anything more than his own children?

. . . Now at the end of his life founded on trust, he was coming into uncertainty.[30]

Not only he and Annie, but the town also was getting elderly with little to look for in the future.

He had always thought of it as a young town, with all its future before it. But now it seemed that that "future" had become the present, was even here and there beginning to be the past. So long as Fred Ferguson could remember, trust in the future of the town had been as much a part of his life as his daily bread.[31]

The temperaments and fortunes of his children vary, but the story of each concludes on a note of uncertainty. Neither the conformity of the favorite son Carl and the normality of Dorothy nor the rebellion of Margaret and the youngest son Bunny provides an answer to the age. Each becomes aware of the failure of traditional values and the instability resulting from this loss.

Carl, "the good son" whose childish clinging to the old ways ironically brings him "close to the edge of the abyss of cynicism," feels in middle life a complete and devastating nothingness.

His whole career had been so feeble and minor that the thought of it choked him with satiric disgust. And part of this was because he had really, truly, ingenuously tried and desired to be good.[32]

For Dorothy on her wedding day—"fragrant with roses and bright with tears"—everything was "prosperous and fresh and sunlit" and held the promise of conventional prosperity and happiness. But the pattern did not continue, and in a few years she was threatened with financial distress.

The rebel daughter, Margaret, indulged her passionate need of exile which led her nowhere. The hedonistic pleasure of her trip to New Mexico with the married Bruce Williams was terminated when Bruce could not finally set aside his loyalty to his family. Later in New York he returns to Margaret insisting on his love for her but at the same time convinced that "I can't give up all of my responsibility." In bringing Margaret's story to a close Suckow again notes the instability and uncertainty in her future. On being reunited with Bruce, she accepts the transitory nature of their relationship.

They were ashamed, joyous, defeated, proud—all within the compass of that mortal bond, which for the time being at least, was stronger than anything. They had recovered life—on what terms it seemed they could—although it was jumbled and precarious, touched with derision, and they no longer knew where to find their footing.[33]

The youngest son, Bunny, who married the young girl with radical ideas, likewise is caught in a confusion of values as he tries to foresee his future.

His beloved would lead him along very strange ways; but he had to go, holding all the while to things of which she was unaware and which he had inherited, fusing the two in some difficult reconciliation . . . perhaps impossible . . . He and his bride were the inheritors of a stormy future, even here in the pleasant fastness of this middle-aged frame house on the familiar local street with the tall trees all up and down the asphalt.[34]

The older Fergusons too are forced to yield the confidence in ideals previously held invincible. As they view with disappointment and disapproval the changes in institutions and the lives of their children, Annie must admit that the illusion of the "ideal household" she had always dreamed her own would become some day had vanished. Fred Ferguson must relinquish his life-long principle of trust in the future.

And he wondered sometimes if the great day he had been building for his children—that they had been building, the folks—had turned out to be their own day, after all.[35]
. . . He had always trusted implicitly that his children were destined to do better; but now he was hoping they would do as well. Simplicities were shifting into complexities, and in the darkening twilight that he and Annie faced, along with the others that were left, he couldn't see what was beyond.[36]

With *The Folks* Miss Suckow concluded a series of six novels that present the social scene from 1900 to 1929. In them she described a solid and stable pattern of living which in each novel she saw as vanishing. In *The Folks* she admitted it was disintegrating and dealt with the new and restless era. All of the novels end on a note of defeat, uncertainty, frustration, and doubt resulting from the weakening of old values and the failure to establish satisfactory new ones in a changing society.

For the next novel *New Hope* she shifted the scene from the end of the era and returned to the opening of the century. With the collapse of traditional values among the Fergusons of *The Folks* she seemed to see an era completed that must be followed by a fresh beginning for which reliance on an old pattern was insufficient. A time in which both the older generation and the young regard the future with such uncertainty requires a renewal of faith in the principles and values of American society.

In *New Hope* Miss Suckow professed her belief in change, progress and a forward-looking quality as essential characteristics of American life.[37] In this novel what she considers the central experience of American life, the fresh beginning, is symbolized in the origin and life of this community. The same elements presented in other novels appear in *New Hope* but with original strength and vitality. Here she gave fictional embodiment to her concept of the folks idea in America; she presented a community where the values of the folks are still the realities.

The novel portrays a community in its golden period of youthful exuberance and hope. New Hope was made up of people who came from everywhere—unlike the nearby settlements that were homogeneously English. It had emerged from an earlier community that had been restrained by Puritanic strictness and aristocratic tendencies imported by its settlers of New England and southern origin. The two-year period in the history of New Hope comes at a stage when it has attained freedom and independence from most of the traces of the old community, and its faith in its own future is as yet unshaken. It is a cooperative, democratic community where freedom and equality and natural comradeship characterize all of its home-like institutions.

Everywhere is felt the natural comradeship of being all together at the beginning and working together for the future. The feelings of enterprise and growth submerged differences and gave all a desire to work together. In the Congregational Church to which the new minister comes there can be felt the characteristic temper of the town.

This church, with its plain furnishings, its uncolored windows, was bare. But the bareness was redeemed by the exciting atmosphere of youth, of communal fellowship, and of faith in achievement.[38]

Mr. Greenwood sounded the new note in preaching the doctrine of the New Testament:

its brightness of hope, its promise of new life, its creative spirit, turning away from the dark historic involutions of the old books. . . . It was the New Testament that Mr. Greenwood preached and believed in—the doctrine, not of power and might and darkness, but of goodwill, of love, of communal not tribal effort, and of light, more light. The words sounded with a peculiar relevancy that came home to people, here in the bare frame building in the new town just beginning its growth in the great opening country.[39]

Innocence, simplicity, genuineness, and basic goodness dominate all relations in the neighborly community.

Within the small town and rural scene occur the characteristic mixing of foreign and native and the mingling of east and west affecting institutions as well as families and resulting in a drift away from the puritanism of the east. The Millers were not Yankee but came of mixed strains even more common in the western region, "the father, 'Oh, just American, I guess,' as Dave had once said vaguely, and the mother of Pennsylvania Dutch origin."[40] The wife of one brother is of German descent. The families of the other two make more social pretensions and possess more of the native culture.

In this novel there is the characteristic emphasis on change, although its time span is too short for the sweeping alterations recorded in *The Odyssey of a Nice Girl* or *The Folks.* New Hope does not emerge from the social and economic conditions of the horse and buggy era, but change is emphasized in the contrast with the old community from which it springs and in the changes that transpire in the years of its history.

Canaan, an older rural community, had been destroyed by a cyclone some years before the beginning of the story. It had also been by-passed by the railroads and, after the destruction by the cyclone, was practically abandoned for the new town around the railroad station called New Hope. Old Roger Harper, who alone remained at the old town, is a sort of symbol of an eastern element in this far west and also of stubborn but futile resistance to change. The Harpers, along with the early settlers John Budd and old man Broadwater, suggest the inevitable elimination in the Iowa rural and small town social development of some remnants of eastern aristocratic influence.

The child romance between Clarence Miller and Delight, the minister's daughter, also serves the author's purpose of emphasizing the instability of the society depicted and of the inexorable change, since after two years these two children are separated never to see each other again when Reverend Greenwood accepts the call to a greater opportunity in Oregon.

Old man Broadwater's son had deserted the small Iowa town to become a lumber baron in Oregon. When he comes back to his father's funeral he is so much impressed by the Reverend Greenwood that soon after, the New Hope minister receives a call to a large "Union Church" in some unnamed Oregon city, thus removing Delight from her association with Clarence. Aubrey Broadwater obviously becomes a symbol of the movement to the west, and the Reverend Greenwood is a confirmation of this movement. "And the great western coastland to which he was going had suddenly become the horizon of the inland prairie town."[41] He was also a symbol of a change in ideas. Brought up in another sect he had turned to the Congregational Church because of its independence and lack of organized control. In the opinion of some he was moving a little too far to liberal views. He welcomed the opportunity in Oregon not merely because it was a larger church and a better salary but because it was a "Union" church. He left the town in the brightness of the morning when only a few first shadows had fallen; the promise of the name was still a promise—so it seemed to him.

With the departure of the Greenwood family and the close of the book Miss Suckow recognizes that the early innocence of New Hope is fleeting—its first morning glow is gone forever, but its promise and heritage remain. During the two years the Greenwoods were in New Hope the sensitive child Clarence had awakened to his world. He had only vague memories of any earlier life.

> It seemed to Clarence now as if that were before he was awake—almost before he was born. He had begun to live on the summer morning when he had gone down with his father to meet the train, when the little girl had come—had been awakened to that bright early hour of time, with the freshness of beginnings upon it.
>
> It could not last. It was not here any more. Those who could see only by that unstained morning light must push beyond and look for it elsewhere; keep on looking for it elsewhere, always elsewhere. The glow was transitory.
>
> Yet it had been; it existed; and here, in his town of New Hope—exuberantly named, yet not without meaning—were the elements that could support fulfillment. That particular brief fulfillment belonged to the morning. But the elements had not vanished—they continued into the day. The individual who had experienced the combining of those elements, though in childhood and briefly, in the seeming magic of completeness, could not be satisfied merely to recapture that early time as in a dream—not unless, in later time, he were to count himself a failure. He had come to feel the force of that experience, the need born of a fortunate start: to renew the sequence and finish out the early promises in fuller light and mature form. He faced the austere, enlarged demand to place completion far ahead, if necessary, beyond his own time; beyond any time he could see or realize; but to find his individual fulfillment in acting in accordance with its realization.[42]

This closing passage of the novel recalls her appraisal of her childhood experience in Hawarden recorded in her memoir. This seems to have been for her not only a significant social experience but one that became a wellspring for all of her novels. The personal idealism explicit in *New Hope* is the system of values to which her characters cling in every novel and in which she herself seems to have faith and confidence. Indeed her eight novels mirror not only the Iowa life of the period but seem partially valid for other parts of the country. The era in which they were written has been described in words strikingly similar to those in which Miss Suckow defined her own purposes in writing fiction. In the words of Henry Seidel Canby,

It was a classic moment, the end and summation of an era, a moment also when criticism and creation were equal in power. It was a brief pause to define and distill American values before new and sharper changes in our mores and our philosophy began.[43]

Chapter IV

INTERPRETER OF CHARACTER IN THE NOVEL

Significant for the study of any aspect of Ruth Suckow's fiction and particularly for her interest in character is her philosophy of fiction. In the article "Friends and Fiction," she points out deep underlying similarities between certain Quaker principles and those of fiction. These principles she had been observing and practicing in her own writing from her earliest stories.

The material of a story carries convincing reality only when it comes from a relish for life in the concrete and the acute observation which goes with it—in Albert Schweitzer's term, a "reverence for life." This involves sympathetic understanding of actual life, particularly human life; what we get otherwise is without life's bloom and breath.[1]

A part of this reverence for life, she explains, is a care for individual lives that has regard for the "individual human being as he is, as well as might be."[2] Her purpose in fiction is to see people and concrete events as belonging to a larger whole that is consistent with abstract principle and truth. In notes prepared for publication in the volume *Some Others and Myself,* Miss Suckow quotes from a statement she had made in a letter to a friend.

My desire is to see some aspect of greater truth through a particular situation in a particular place with particular people, concretely presented, because I enjoy concreteness,[3]

Because of this preference for the specific, she has been thought to make extensive use of actual experience and acquaintances in her fiction. Yet concerning the source of her characters, she has said that neither individuals nor families are drawn from actual personalities.

> ... I don't draw my characters direct from life. ... Of course all of them derive from life. Traits of people you meet, people you remember, merge themselves more or less unconsciously with the portrait on which you're engaged.[4]

In answer to a question about the origin of her family groups, in an interview with Marion L. Starkey, she said:

> People always accuse me of being a member of every family I ever wrote about. ... And I admit I do stand in some relationship or other to families of practically every type I've described.[5]

Her selection and development of character are determined by her philosophical concept which perceives the embodiment of the abstract in the concrete; by her humanistic concern for the individual; by her literary criteria of objectivity and impartiality; and by her social concept of the folks idea. The folk life in which she finds her sources of character she defined as the common existence in the most basic terms of a group of people knit firmly together by family ties. Her special concern in fiction is for a character studied within the social structure of folk life; her theme and meaning usually lie in character and personal relationships.

In contrast to Sherwood Anderson, who found the significance of life in an awareness of critical moments when submerged ideas and emotions were expressed, Miss Suckow sees meaning in the totality and continuity of a life pattern as a character reacts to his external world as well as to his inner tensions. The psychic existence of her characters is never as isolated from the external and social environment as that of Anderson's characters. The frustrated and the defeated are subjects for both authors, but Suckow is not preoccupied with the distorted and deviate personality.

Her chief interest, she has said, is in understanding the individual, his link with other people, and his relation to a larger truth. Her capacities for perceiving emotional overtones and recording deep and enduring impressions that recreate the texture of experience are best realized in her short stories. But to convey interest in the common existence of a group of people through the detailed rendering of their life pattern, the novel is her best vehicle.

The effects of social patterns are gradual. The individual, to her mind, is best viewed over a long period if development of a character is to be realized. In her longer fiction Miss Suckow centers on the study of character as it interacts upon group life. Although the incidents are commonplace, her method subtly illumines the idiosyncracies that lie behind individuality.

The family group as the most important social unit is her best medium for studying humanity. In her novels the individual's experiences in societal relations are largely within family life. Within this matrix he finds either development or frustration. Analysis of the experience that leads to fulfillment or inhibition is the basis of her art. Of her humanism, Professor B. E. Boothe remarked in an essay,

In 1924 she wrote as one who believes in life, and for whom the purpose of writing is to reveal the truth about life, to make discriminations between the factors which draw out and build up human capacities, and those whose effect is to confine and kill.[6]

For her the interpretation of childhood is basic to her characterization. In the child's world she finds an inexhaustible well of material. She presents vividly the emotions and experiences of childhood and through them she witnesses the forces that shape the adult.

The main characters in a number of books are followed from childhood to adolescence and on to maturity. In tracing the psychological effect on the child she finds happiness as well as implications of tragedy in parental relations. The experience of childhood holds a special charm for her, and she turns to it time and again. As Professor Boothe pointed out she frequently turns to the childhood of a main character to point up some trait or disposition that will be permanent. In many instances the childhood experiences remain the most vivid to the reader. This importance of childhood against the backdrop of life is a recurrent theme, and more than one character voices the feeling expressed by Sarah Bonney.

How queer it was that childhood should seem all the time only a preparation—a prologue—and then, afterwards, the only part of life that was wholly real![7]

While the struggle against the dependency of childhood and the security of conventionality is partially a social *phenomenon,* an expression of the turbulence in the period and the milieu, it becomes for the characters in Miss Suckow's novels an individual emotional experience. She knowingly presents the psychological factors in her studies of family interrelations. Time and again a well-meaning parent prepares the way for personal disaster by encouraging or ignoring weaknesses in a child. With meticulous care she traces the cumulative effect from the repetition of a pattern of behavior.

While she insists that setting is secondary, time and place are important because they give flavor to lives. In the quiet and uneventful lives she portrays, she seeks to realize the meaning of inner responses. Edith Wharton's statement about the characters of Jane Austen seems applicable to the Folks. They also are " 'speaking' portraits" who "evolve as real people do, but so softly, noiselessly, that to follow the development of their history is as quiet a business as watching the passage of the seasons."[8]

In accordance with her belief that impartiality "while infused with tenderness and fellow feeling, puts truth above any form of partisanship,"[9] she keeps outside her stories as a detached observer. She writes of simple people who are not capable of articulate expression and who grope their way through irrevocable changes. She records their faults with an understanding and compassion that stand beyond any judgment. She sees with clarity their conscious and unconscious motives, their pitiable desolations, their small satisfactions. Some struggle with aspirations and ambitions but often accept usefulness to others as a substitute for achievement. She deals reticently with emotions. Among her characters warmth of feeling lies in the hold which the association of family and custom has upon them. Their affections and loyalties lie deeper than their desires. They seldom figure in dramatic situations, espouse causes or issues, or make choices involving moral values. Miss Suckow is concerned primarily with people conditioned by psychological limitations and external circumstances.

Beginning with group portraits Suckow, as she matured as a writer, accomplished deeper characterization by delineating more detailed and more complex periods of development. The family group recurs in every novel, but in later books she increases the number of individualized portraits. Thus she moves from the study of a typical family or individual to a more detailed study of inner emotions and conflicts and enlarges the area of their interrelationships.

There is not much characterization in the first novel, *Country People,* beyond the presentation of the typical. In its bare presentation, analysis of motives, emotions, and feelings is slight. In *The Odyssey of a Nice Girl* Miss Suckow focuses on one character. Other characters are adequately developed for their relationship to Marjorie, but she remains the dominant one. In *The Bonney Family* she widened her range to include four: Sarah and Warren Bonney and their parents, Fred and Myra, all developed with detail.

In the next novel, *Cora,* one character again holds the center of interest. Only in Cora's father, Chris Schwietert, does a minor character emerge strikingly. *The Kramer Girls* is the story of three sisters. There is a great disparity in age between the youngest, Rose, and her two sisters who are responsible for her care. Rose seems the central figure, yet Georgia Kramer has a greater appeal. In *The Folks* Suckow returns to a full family group, and enlarges and intensifies her characterizations and extends the relationships. She analyzes minutely the characters of Fred and Annie Ferguson and two of the children, Margaret and Carl. It is in their relationships beyond the family that the children are revealed most fully.

The novel *New Hope* portrays an entire community. The most carefully drawn characters are two children through whose eyes many of the incidents are experienced. The period is limited in this novel. The characters are not taken beyond childhood.

The John Wood Case presents an incident and the analysis of a young boy's bewildered emotions in the light of an aroused community feeling.

Her biographical treatments develop from bare outlines to lengthy analyses of individuals sharply set in time and place, stressing inner tensions of thought and feeling. Her portraits of women and children are the most convincing. Except in childhood and adolescence, male characters are less impressive. The evidence for these judgments follows.

Characters studied from childhood through adolescence, youth and maturity are the usual subjects of Miss Suckow's novels. In recording their disappointments and defeats, she has become identified almost entirely as a portrayer of the misfit, the inhibited, and the unhappy. But in one novel she demonstrated her skill in creating the brightness and happiness of childhood as sympathetically as she had penetrated its hurts and pains. In *New Hope,* her novel of a youthful community in a "morning world," it seems fitting that she chose two children as her main characters. The youthful exuberance that pervades the story of New Hope is due in a great part to the selection of the young children as the central figures. This account of two years in the busy and happy life of the town cannot be said to have a plot or to be chiefly concerned with the development of character. The town itself is the protagonist, and the theme of the novel extends beyond a single character for its significance.

Its purpose is to present a way of life, and it is through the eyes of the two children that the reader becomes acquainted with the local characters and the pattern of life. Miss Suckow's skill in this novel lies in her successful portrayal of a community and at the same time the creation of character—the blending of the adult world and the child world through the experiences of the two children.

The six-year-old son of Dave Miller, banker and leading citizen, and the daughter of the minister, Mr. Greenwood, became inseparable companions. Clarence, serious, sensitive and a little shy, with an insatiable interest in the conversation of older people, finds a perfect playmate in Delight. Clarence had believed with utter trustfulness his father's praise of the town, but with the arrival of the Greenwoods he felt a new brightness over everything.

The story is built around a series of holidays and special days important in the lives of children: they are caught up in the excitement of the minister's arrival and his first Sunday sermon; a day on the farm at Uncle Andy's place; the harvest dinner in November; the Christmas Eve party; the Washington's Birthday Bazaar; a day in the country to gather flowers for the May baskets and the May Day ritual of leaving the baskets with friends. The children are a part of all of the community life. They participate in church socials and pageants, are on hand for refreshments when the ladies meet, and watch furtively the courting of the older crowd at fudge parties and choir rehearsals. They also glean the more serious and darker aspects of life—the janitor's theft from the church collection and the deaths of prominent citizens.

From association with adults they sense attitudes and feelings not fully comprehended. Clarence listens to the enthusiastic and confident talk of his father and shares the feeling for the town. He munches cake under the kitchen table while Mama's cronies gather in the afternoon to gossip and drink coffee. "The gabble went on over Clarence's head: the hints, scraps of information, speculation, the rich mournful relishing of the worst. . . . The singsong repetitions sounded a dark refrain through the homely kitchen comfort."[10] The ladies were so accustomed to his presence, he went unnoticed. Clarence "both despised these meetings and felt a zestful enjoyment," but he became acquainted with the relish, the jollity or fear with which the women discussed rumored engagements, marriages and family troubles, sickness and death.

Too young to comprehend, Clarence and Delight were still exhilarated by Mr. Greenwood's first sermon telling them what the church would be, what the town could be, in the great continent "where all were to share equally in the boundlessness of light and hope."[11] They were thrilled by the grand-sounding titles when the minister and Dave spoke of the "endowments" of the people, of the Declaration of Independence and the Constitution and their implications for New Hope.

Seated with Delight at the Christmas service, Clarence for the first time comprehends the joyous message of the scripture; "in the scent of the evergreens and the unsteady candle light . . . he was happy, he hated nobody."[12]

The funeral of an older citizen of the community took on for the children the color of a "great, somber, community drama"[13] as they watched from the parsonage window and shared the grief of the community. They heard the music swell from the open church windows. With respectful gaze they watched people move slowly from the church and were awed by the "black, dense draperies that hid the widow's face and weighed down her head."[14] They looked with "a queer feeling of recognition" at the G. A. R. members "in a body" wearing their faded soldier coats, old settlers with beards, and women in small black bonnets and stuffy black clothes. They watched "group after group enter the waiting carriages, and the slow procession . . . led by the splendid hearse with its black festoons—something like the kingly procession in a fairy tale; but sad."[15]

The companionship of Delight made all of the community affairs more interesting to Clarence, but her coming to New Hope was more important in making him alive to a bright new child's existence. The greatest charm of the book is in the portrayal of this idyllic existence. In a review of this novel, Richard A. Cordell describes the two "as real and living as any pre-adolescents who ever played, dreamed, quarreled, wheedled, and strutted between the covers of a book."[16]

Miss Suckow presents with understanding the child's responses, intentions, and insights. In anticipation of the little girl's arrival Clarence was in a state of "restless ecstasy," alert and expectant. In the days of waiting, his favorite haunts—the haymow and the storerooms—had "seemed to be lighted with a mystical shimmer." At first too shy to play with the new little girl, he listened to the talk about the newcomers sensing that "something new had come into the life of the place—a brighter element."[17] His uncontrollable excitement is too great at first for his childish timidity.

He ran out into the yard, and kicked at the brown-painted

tile in which petunias were planted. . . .

He took refuge in the barn, pressing his face against the rough board wall, listening to old Mollie crunching oats in her stall.[18]

By dinner time his shyness gives way sufficiently for him to whisper a request to sit next to Delight. From that time they are companions in everything. They share what a reviewer called "a close, secret enchanted relationship which, though so innocent, is very nearly love and from which all others are jealously excluded."[19] They are eager companions in their own world and spectators of the adult life.

The older people smiled and watched as the two set out together for that first Sunday service—Clarence, with ears scrubbed red, was wearing his biggest ruffled collar and awful Sunday shoes, and Delight with her long blond braids wore a starched embroidered skirt.

They looked small and brave, comical and touching, setting off together down the long boardwalk in the hot July sunshine. . . . There was a childish innocence in the devotion of the little couple, a pristine quality, that strangely affected the older people watching them.[20]

They were in and out of the house together from morning until bed time. Even at night they didn't want to be separated and were allowed to say their prayers together. On drives into the country the two children sat on the hard buggy floor so as not to be separated. Whether riding in the buggy, singing, visiting older folks, or playing their own games, "There was always excitement in being with Delight—a naturalness that was touched with magic. Whatever they did together was fun." Delight was more poised, alert and imaginative than Clarence, but he was proud to be the protector of the new little girl. At the farm a queer wind came up suddenly one day frightening Delight, who thought it was a cyclone.

The windmill had started going loud and fast. Grit blew into their eyes until they couldn't see. Delight caught hold of Clarence's hand, and he stood protecting her, braced stoutly. Strands of her hair blew against his face and even got into his mouth when he shouted to her that this was just the wind. Clarence wasn't afraid of any cyclone out on his Uncle Andy's place.[21]

On the floor of the buggy, in the shocks or the haymow, or in a room closed off from the meeting of the church trustees, Clarence and Delight had a world that excluded others. They were Hiawatha and Minnehaha living in a wigwam, John Alden and Priscilla in a log cabin, the President and First Lady in the White House, a prince and princess in turreted castles in the midst of foreign scenes, or just Clarence's older sister Bess and her beau. It was the most natural thing to imagine the two of them living together some place.

Clarence had no doubt at all of their future together some-where grand and faraway; and at the same time no doubt that they would always live together here in New Hope.[22]

This idyllic life that began for Clarence in Delight's coming to New Hope and that he wanted to continue and never to change is shattered when Mr. Greenwood accepts a call to Oregon.
A defiant refusal to believe the report is Clarence's first response to the news, followed by a silent hurt which creates a barrier between himself and Delight in the last days together. Outwardly he assumed the community's attitude—pleased for the good fortune of Mr. Greenwood. The children pretended to make plans for future visits together, but at the same time they sensed the finality of their separation. At their parting, which is perhaps more emotionally charged than seems probable for their age, Clarence knows they will not see each other again.

The early love was gone and could never be brought back, even if they were to meet again some day—but they would not. Even then, he had come to believe, the little boy had somehow sensed that this marked the end of a time. The morning world where the two children had lived together, encircled by communal closeness, seemed already to have retreated; had become a vision that lived long ago.[23]

Although Miss Suckow chose to emphasize the serious thesis of the novel—the inexorability of time and change—through the experiences of the children, she creates for them an existence idyllic and at the same time convincingly real. Clarence and Delight live as real children in the ecstatic excitements, the confidence of their friendship, their frankness and innocence, and even in their intuitive grasp of the adult world she wishes to portray.

Young women who have lived in the small town environment from childhood are most frequently the central characters in the novels. They yearn to escape domestic limitations and at the same time cling to their homes. They aspire to aesthetic achievement, humanitarian service, independence and security, marriage, or freedom, excitement and unconventionality. All except Margaret Ferguson cling to the simplicities and intimacies of their childhood. Rose Kramer accepts most complacently the continuation of the pattern; Cora Schwietert is most persistent in her drive for security. Only Margaret Ferguson is defiantly rebellious. Through the accretion of numerous details from their daily lives, Suckow gives a sense of completeness to her portrayals of Marjorie Schoessel, Sarah Bonney, Rose Kramer, Cora Schwietert, Margaret Ferguson, and Lillian White, Carl Ferguson's wife.

For her first full portrait in a novel Ruth Suckow draws on autobiographical details for much of her material. Marjorie Schoessel in *The Odyssey of a Nice Girl* has German grandparents; grows up in a small Iowa town; delights in music, reading, dramatics, and visiting homes of the villagers from New England; attends a Boston school of dramatics; returns home to help her family when they are stricken with sickness; accompanies a family member to Rochester and to Denver in search of better health; feels attachment to the beauties of the Iowa countryside and at the same time experiences the thwarting effect of the small town. In all of these details Ruth Suckow undoubtedly makes use of personal memories and observations.

But in Marjorie Schoessel she sees sympathetically the young girl in an environment like her own, who was unable to achieve the desired fulfillment, who could not, as she had done, secure creative satisfaction in an art, and who found her attachment to

103

the homely beauty of the Iowa town restrictive rather than enriching.

Marjorie belongs to a thoroughly conventional pattern from which she never escapes. Intimations of her sensibilities and aesthetic cravings are vague and undefined. Her own emotional and intellectual limitations and her passivity, as much as the mediocrity of the town, are devastating to development. An unsatisfied yearning to seize "something" is her strongest motivation. Yet the very bonds of family ties and her contentment with the familiar from which she seeks to free herself are deterrents to her freedom.

When irrevocable changes disrupt the old life, Marjorie yields her emotional hold upon it and enters into a new world with at last a consciousness of her inability to attain the best—a long existent and deeply buried drive within her—or to reclaim the old life which she sees dwindling. As the story closes, however, Marjorie, amidst all her submissions, bewilderments, and failures, revived something of the childish expectancy expressed in the last revelation of her thoughts as she rides in the swaying train toward Denver to take a job in her cousin's garage.

> But under all the twistings and halting of her career, the selfishness, the ironic absurdities, she knew that there had been one thing after all—the need to satisfy the craving for something that was deep and beautiful and beyond what people called "everyday things."
>
> She didn't care how ridiculous she seemed, or whether anyone could understand or not. She simply had to plunge on now . . . and then slowly, after a long, long time, perhaps things cleared away.[24]

The novel is the story of her life and longings from childhood to marriage. Except for a final chapter Marjorie's point of view is maintained throughout the narrative; there is no scene, except the last, of which she is not a part, and in that one her mother returns to Buena Vista to tell the ladies about the marriage.

Through a steady accumulation of details, the succession of little happenings, and the interaction of simple people, Marjorie emerges as a plausible, if unaccomplished, person whose life is apprehended with a sense of wholeness. Robert Morse Lovett commented thus on the method. "Neither in her own person nor in that of any character does she thrust comment or synthesis upon the reader."[25]

With her confidence in letting facts speak for themselves, she recounts every phase of Marjorie's girlhood and youth. In the narrative of four parts she relates incidents and experiences from Marjorie's childhood, her high school life, her two years in Boston, and finally her groping for meaning in her adult life.

From the opening chapter where Marjorie shows her distaste for the strangeness of her alien farmer grandparents and the crudities of country ways, her daintiness, fastidiousness, and desire to feel superior are characteristic traits. The account of her vacation days at the country sets forth her tastes, her reticences, her pleasures and inhibitions which gradually mold the maturing personality.

Her aloof withdrawal from the country cousins and neighbor children, the daydreaming in which she imagines herself becoming important, and the intensely personal nature of her little aesthetic pleasures are all experienced in her lonely days on the farm. She is imaginative in her dramatic play with friends. Her pleasure from playing the organ in the parlor is lost when mother and aunt come into the room to listen. In later instances she is childishly ecstatic when complimented for a well-performed reading or music lesson, but she is unable to talk about her pleasure at home.

There is nothing unusual in most of the happenings with her friends or at school—there were the cliques and petty rivalries among young girls, their shy interest in boys, a desire for prominence in school elections and activities. Illustrative of her little satisfactions and triumphs is her experience in a declamation contest in the town of Forest Bluff. She was not the winner, but her achievement was sufficiently admired by her family and school friends to satisfy her pride. More important to her was the meeting with a boy contestant and the excitement of the ride at night with him to the auditorium when he had kissed her. Such were the events in her life until graduation from high school. In these years she experienced some awakening of aesthetic aspirations and adult longings, and was alternately satisfied and disappointed. In her reading, music, and dramatics, she had sought an inner pleasure.

Always , beneath her tense preoccupation with the harsh, wounding, absorbing present, were the old dreams—dim, and yet stirring—of going away to Europe, studying music in that great room with the polished floor, finding something that she must have; and she held herself a little apart.[26]

Only after her graduation did her real dissatisfaction begin. The life that had been so crammed with meaning in every tiniest detail had lost that meaning, and even her books made her impatient with Buena Vista.

She wanted to "learn things"—to go where people wore evening dress, and where there were butlers and grate fires and afternoon tea . . . people hailing a passing taxicab, and casually going on board an ocean liner . . . where you could see real authors, and artists. . . .[27]

Her first rebellious feelings came from her parents' efforts to keep her close to home after graduation. A gift of new bedroom furniture she felt made it necessary to compromise with her desire to go East and to attend a college near home for the first year.

In the large section of the book where Marjorie spends two years in Boston studying dramatics, Miss Suckow, with knowledge and understanding, portrays the young girl with the strange name and midwestern speech who meets the culture of the East. Marjorie attends concerts and art exhibits, visits the historic shrines, the shops, the tearooms. A Baptist minister's daughter who professes to be an atheist becomes her best friend. With Emily she tastes, somewhat timidly, her first freedom to experiment. They attend readings by poets and subscribe to *Poetry*, go to the Drama League, and attend anarchists' meetings in a big barren hall, stand in line to get tickets for plays, and sell clothing when necessary to buy concert tickets.

They learn to smoke, buy pamphlets on sex and atheism, and dream of going to Europe by steerage. Marjorie, however, reveals little intellectual reaction to these exposures. Her real moment of glory came with her successful performance as Titania in *A Midsummer Night's Dream* in the final recital at the dramatics school. Except for acquiring a contempt for Chautauqua and the kind of readings presented at local club meetings, she returned to Buena Vista visibly unaffected. Of her venture Frederick J. Hoffman said,

> Ruth Suckow honestly posed the Midwest against the East, found Buena Vista, Iowa, sane and sound after Boston, and thought that it provided a quiet cricket-laden context for the eternal verities, Midwestern style.[28]

Encouraged by Emily, Marjorie also wanted something "different" and "interesting" but could never ignore the strain of breaking away from Mama and Papa. Although she talked of the steerage, "she saw the fresh white curtains in her room, the sweet cleanliness . . . the smell of warm cake in the kitchen. . . ."[29]

More analysis of her gropings and conflicts appears in the last part of Marjorie's story. After having passed a second milestone, the completion of her study in Boston, she again struggles against inactivity and loneliness and feels that something ought to happen right away, her real life begin. Neither the private lessons she gave nor her work in her father's store seemed purposeful. At home she was struggling against her desire to satisfy her clamoring needs and her attachment for daintiness, sweetness, and security of home. In another effort to escape home bonds she went to Chicago and took a secretarial job which meant only fatigue and loneliness. It was no sacrifice to return when she was called home because of her mother's illness. With her purpose determined by circumstances, Marjorie accepts the return to familiar things with a mixture of unconscious courage and a secret happiness.

> Now, when she went into her own little room at night, she loved passionately the pink-and-green rug getting softly

faded, her white bookcase and old books. She felt an intimacy with these four narrow walls, with their silvery pattern and border of little roses, that hurt unbearably at times, and at times was more beautiful and satisfying than anything in the world. Lying in her bed and reading, stretching luxuriously between her smooth white sheets, slowly turning the pages and reaching over to get the apple that she had put on her chair, hearing those sounds of home that she remembered—coal dropping in the furnace, the faint tiny bang of an attic window, the movement of branches outside—she knew that she was happier at home than anywhere else, when she was needed, when there was actually a reason for her being there.[30]

In the days and events that follow she sees the town in both its idyllic leisure and its dreariness. The war, the deaths of her brother and her friends, and the disappointments in the lives of others bring Marjorie to a sad realization.

Their childhood seemed real, but their grown-up selves queerly distorted. She herself, and all her companions, seemed to have passed, without her knowing when, out of that bright certainty of childhood into some limbo of middle youth.[31]

Bewilderment, weariness, and lassitude possess her for a time. But after a trip to Rochester for an operation she returns with a new sense of expectancy and excitement, rid of her old shocks—"of the war, Rich's [her brother] death, her old submissions and bewilderments and failures."[32] Her new eagerness and quickened interest in friends and the beauties of the countryside are interrupted by the threat of an illness to her father and the dreary familiarity of illness, grief and pain again—another trip to Rochester, her father's retirement from business, a visit to relatives in Denver cut short because of his failing health, a return home, and his death.

Subsequently she finds it useless to think of staying in Buena Vista and rebels against the role of becoming companion to Mama. "The old life, now rich and beautiful in retrospect, had closed in, was dwindling."[33] A letter and invitation from Uncle Albert in Denver provided the necessary escape. On her earlier visit to Denver Marjorie had known briefly the old satisfaction of exciting beauty—reckless and gay—when her cousins had taken her into the mountains for a picnic supper. That experience becomes one in her thought with all the moments in her life that had brought her happiness and some intensity of feeling, in contrast to the everyday, commonplace contentment.

> Somehow she must get that satisfaction that was a warmth in the blood, that gave all life a glowing centre. The two ways made each a different pattern; but the patterns were intertwined.[34]

This last surge of ambition leads her to the stenographic job in her cousin's garage and to marriage with a man who had refused to continue a law course to become an automobile tire salesman and had bought a 200-acre fruit farm—hardly a promising situation for achieving the satisfaction for which Marjorie had longed.

In this story of a village-bound girl are the themes for which Miss Suckow has a predilection: the inability to escape one's beginnings; the conflict between the attachment to the comfort and contentment of home and the desire to avoid its restrictions; the futile search for a meaningful existence; irreconcilable change and loss of the confidence of childhood. Marjorie, like the characters to follow her in Suckow's novels, has a kind of latent courage and capacity for self-denial when circumstances determine her course.

Among Miss Suckow's women characters is a recurrent type whose ambitions are never as self-centered as those of Marjorie Schoessel. Sturdy and reliable, self-sacrificing and lonely, they never possess the affection of their family or the companionship of friends. Yet they are required to set aside personal pursuits for the interests of others. Jenny Robinson, Hester Harris, Sarah Bonney and Georgie Kramer are characters whose loneliness is more pathetic because of the unappreciated sacrifices demanded of them.

In two complete short novels, published in *Smart Set* but

never reprinted, Miss Suckow established the pattern. From the time she was nine years old, Jenny Robinson in "The Best of the Lot" was burdened with family responsibility—first the case of the younger children and later of aging parents. Emergencies at home interrupted every effort she made for an education. Her only compensation was the satisfaction she derived from feeling needed. In time the children left home and the parents died. Jennie was left worn and lonely, with only one interest in life—the care of the cemetery lot.

Hester Harris in "A Part of the Institution" had a better social and economic status than Jennie Robinson, but she also had a lonely, unrewarding life. She sacrificed her life for the principles of Adams College, pioneer college of the prairies, dedicated to the interests of Christianity and higher learning in the West. First a student and later a faculty member, Hester was zealous in her loyalties to all the ideals of Adams College. She became, in the minds of students, a part of the institution as fixed as Recitation Hall, and her enthusiasm amused former friends who returned for a twentieth class reunion.

After years of being the dependable family member, Sarah Bonney set out for the second time, alone and in search of a career. Georgie Kramer died without having had appreciation or understanding from friends or family.

Lonely characters of all ages appear in Suckow's stories, but she depicts with especial sympathy and insight the poignancy of loneliness and isolation among her adolescents. As a minister's daughter she experienced in her own girlhood the meaning of a barrier that prevents complete acceptance by others. She gives expression to this solitary suffering in many forms and characters.

Sarah Bonney is one of her big and strong, capable and dependable characters, whose fate it is to be of service to others—to care for children and make old people comfortable— and to receive in return little appreciation or sympathetic understanding. In her own family as well as among others her plainness and bluntness remove her from the intimate companionship she craves. Required to sacrifice personal desires, she carries a dark, inarticulate pain in the knowledge that she is the least loved, least cherished of the children. This realization does not shrivel or embitter Sarah; on the contrary, her loneliness and strength drive her out of narrowing bonds and finally set her free.

Into the character of Sarah as into Marjorie Schoessel Miss Suckow put some of her own external circumstances and emotional experiences. But they are different facets of her life from those utilized in the earlier book. Sarah is a minister's daughter and knows parsonage life; she loves the rural town; she enjoys reading and writes poetry which she throws into the wastebasket. She attends a small denominational college for which her father solicits funds as Ruth Suckow's father had done; she views the college, the church, and the war activities from the same vantage point and with misgivings similar to Miss Suckow's.

While Marjorie Schoessel's longing was to possess beauty and inner satisfactions, Sarah is impelled by the need to use her strength to achieve something, to benefit people.

Sarah is first presented as in the family group but not of it. She silently reads her novel by Dickens and snickers to herself although no one laughs with her. A big girl, she is regarded as clumsy and queer by her brother, Warren. Her mother depends upon her and seldom worries about her, but gives indifferent attention to her confidences and her questionings about religion. Matronly for twelve years old, among girls of her own age, she is already conscious of an aching forlorn feeling. She is out of tune with them and doesn't belong to the crowd which is beginning to go with boys. Her social uneasiness is emphasized by the family's visit to Morning Sun when she feels a widening of the gulf between old friends—an alien, cold, lost feeling. Everything she starts to say sounds clumsy, and her sentences remain unfinished as listeners turn their attention elsewhere.

While she is one of the strongest characters and stands next to her mother in importance in the family, the story does not focus on her until her college days, and more fully in later years when she takes on the role of her mother in the household. Her development is most significanct in those years, and through her perspective both the passing events and the memories of family life are reflected.

Sarah is as unobtrusive in the narrative as she is in her family,

111

but it is largely through her reflections that the personalities of her father and mother are best revealed. Pleasant memories of Morning Sun are stronger in her than in other members of the family. Her independence is emphasized by her brother's conventionality, and her stability by the dependence of the twins, Wilma and Wilfrid.

Sarah entered eagerly into college life, made one good friend with whom she shared her love of nature and reading, and became enthusiastic over literature courses, but she continued to be recognized as staunch and dependable and remained a little outside. Unlike her brother Warren, Sarah did not feel a completeness in college life. She was conscious of a strength that required use in the life ahead of her. After two years of teaching she went to Chicago to live in a settlement where she seemed at last to have found a place for her energy, services, and desire to achieve.

Self-sacrifice more than opportunity for accomplishment appeals to Miss Suckow as a testing ground for character. Like Marjorie Schoessel and Rose Kramer, Sarah receives the summons home. In her case it is a sacrifice, not a refuge. This necessity for feeling needed is a persistent theme in these novels. Sarah "had wanted 'real life,' a hot push of struggle and ferment that would test her purpose and her power and put a sharp edge upon all her abilities."[35] When needed at home she threw away the thought of the eager life she had left and was happy to be acknowledged as the stand-by. She had through her own energy, resources, and forward look gone from Frampton College to a larger world of activity, but her return home destroyed her prospect for a life ahead and threw her into a nostalgia for the past.

After her mother's death she is buoyed up by a "tireless magic" as she takes charge of the household and the care of her father. Sitting alone in the kitchen she feels at the heart of the old household life. In the knowledge of defeats, war, and disappointments, she finds the memory of the old life the only good thing left in the world.

In the interim at home she witnesses in her family the death of Wilfrid, Wilma's marriage, and Warren's growing conventionality as a professor in Montana. In the upheaval of family life, the turmoil of war, and the changes in church and community, it is Sarah in this novel who perceives that things work out in the wrong way and who laments the shifting of old relationships once solid and profound. When her father's remarriage brings dissension in the family, Sarah alone is tolerant and sympathetic. Following this event there is no further need for her at home and in an anticlimax she sets out again to make an independent life in a career. She still wanted to use her strength, accumulating and almost untouched, to benefit people. Her independence, born of loneliness, and her latent strength enable her to become more self-reliant than any of her family.

> Now it seemed to her that she had got that strength free at last, with pain and blind struggle and outward necessity, from the something narrow and concentrated that most women had— . . . Her own loneliness—the least loved of all the children—had both driven her out and set her free.[36]

While Rose Kramer is the central character in *The Kramer Girls,* her actions are directed largely by her sister Georgia's propulsive influence. Georgie Kramer does not belong with the young women of the novels nor with the matrons. She is another of the strong, reliable, and unappreciated. She knows none of the satisfactions of personal achievement or the warmth of human affections and lives to see her sacrifices resented more than appreciated. Her efforts to provide the younger sister with opportunity denied her were accepted reluctantly. In her generosity she could withhold nothing from Rose or Annie, a sister near her own age but less aggressive.

Sometimes hurtfully mindful that she was allowed to be "nothing but an old hack horse," she found consolation and support in giving strength to weakness.

> She wanted someone to override her, to care enough. But there was never anyone strong enough to do it. It was her own strength, partly, that had always got in the way of happiness.[37]

In the household with an invalid mother and a younger sister she liked to be the "prop of the household." She stayed home from church socials, visits to friends, and out-of-town trips to give Annie relief from home cares, and always planned that Rose, the youngest, would have a different life from theirs. Proud of Rose's grades she had ambitious plans for her future.

"I don't want you to be dependent upon anybody. I want you to do things for yourself. I tell you, that's what all girls ought to do."[38]

Rose's marriage to the kindly but ineffectual Archie Carpenter was a defiance of Georgie's aspirations for her. Disappointed and defeated, Georgie was, nevertheless, free after her mother's death to use her energies for herself. She moved to a larger town, studied to become a chiropractor, and opened an office for practice. At last absorbed in her own affairs, she had a profession and money of her own and took an interest in clothes. Her brief period of freedom ended when it was discovered she had cancer. In the depression of her illness, she confided to Annie her sense of failure—her regret for not having accomplished anything worthwhile.

"It was all unnecessary. As I look back on it, it seems as if we didn't really have to do a thing that we did. Papa would have hired somebody to take care of mamma—he'd have had to.

". . . I thought I was doing so much! I really meant to. As it turns out, it's nothing but meddling.

" . . . It'll be better for the kid to have me gone. She won't have me, and then she'll have to stand on her own feet. You'll be better off, too. As long as I'm around, you do what I say. If you don't have me, you'll do what you want to do. Folks can't do much for other folks."[39]

Through all of her rebellion against her sister's domination Rose had a vague and humble realization of Georgie's superiority on which she relied.

"Georgie gave everything to me," she said. "I wish she

hadn't. She cared for me too much. . . . I feel that if I hadn't always had Georgie back of me, if she hadn't done so much for me, I could have done more for myself."[40]

After Georgie's death when Rose did achieve a self-reliance, unknown to her before, she was at times remorseful "that she could be working, and living happily, depending upon herself, with Georgie gone."[41]

The futility of Georgie's life was sadly noted by one of her hometown friends who observed that people in Valley Junction had given her flowers and a big funeral, but they hadn't given her a chance. The pathos of her misspent, misunderstood, and unrewarding existence is characterized by the photograph that Rose had in her house.

But it hung in a poor light—and it was such a poor photograph, anyway, doing no justice to Georgie, and taken by a provincial photographer who didn't really know his business.[42]

The pathos of lonely and misunderstood people whom life ironically denies the satisfactions they seek is a repeated theme in the novels portraying this group of characters. Defeat and disappointment are experiences common to all of them.

While Sarah Bonney from childhood suffers the loneliness of feeling a misfit, she escapes a serious neurosis through her deep affection for family, her kindliness, her physical strength, and her eagerness to be helpful to others. Margaret Ferguson, on the other hand, cherishes her resentment and her sense of inferiority and determines to find compensation in defiance of family mores. With Margaret Ferguson, as with other major figures in *The Folks* Miss Suckow widened her range of interest in characterization, probed more deeply into the thoughts and feelings of her characters, and pursued further the effect of childhood conditioning on adult lives. The introspective, sullen, misunderstood child becomes the iconoclastic rebel who accepts social exile first in a promiscuous existence in Greenwich Village and later in a liaison with a married man. In many ways Margaret Ferguson is unique among Miss Suckow's characters.

She has none of the loyalties and affections for home and the small town. She is the only one who separates herself emotionally from her Iowa beginnings and defiantly assumes what she believes to be the manners of sophistication. She is the only character in any of the novels to become involved in an unconventional sexual relation. At the end of her story it is assumed that Margaret will continue as mistress of Bruce Williams.

At home Margaret was "always so different, always at odds, and incalculable."[43] She sensed the family's disapproval of her and felt that she could never please with anything she did. Sullen, distant, and remote, she was unlike the loving Carl. She was jealous of Dorothy's curly blond hair, yet took pride in her own long dark braids and the dark eyes she always hoped someone would notice. At school she chose the peculiar rather than the popular children for friends. But through her misery she always felt "that somewhere there would be a wonderful, shining, special fate for her."[44]

She attended a normal school because it offered a means of escape from home, but she continued to be bitter and lonely and chose the wrong friends. Suspended for helping a girl to elope, she returned to Belmond. The family's embarrassment at her disgrace made her frustrations and failures more keen. In her loneliness reading was her only solace. The Brontes were among her favorite authors "because in the seclusion and stormy emotions of the Yorkshire sisters she felt some of her own loneliness and rebellion."[45] In her solitary walks her reveries were always of some exciting future for herself.

> Margaret's final dream, no matter how she started out, was of herself in marvelous clothes and long earrings coming back to Belmond—not to stay, of course!—but interesting and a little weary, after a life of passionate, tragic and glorious experience, such as no one could have here at home.[46]

After her younger sister's wedding, life in Belmond became more intolerable as she saw herself "getting older and older, a spinster daughter and a fixture in the house." She felt humiliated by the superiority of the married women whom she held in contempt.

> To marry anybody in this town would be to forfeit the real story of her life. What she wanted was to look *down* upon this town—to know something wild, rapturous, free. . . .[47]

Margaret craved something that would "break the narrow, intense, self-bound world in which she was imprisoned, and to make her complete. Not marriage, though. . . ."[48] Her dreams for herself had never contemplated marriage.

> Regular marriage meant being like the folks, presenting a united front to the world, neither one doing as he or she wanted to do. . . . Marriage, Margaret had always thought of as just the end.[49]

With the assistance of the librarian in Belmond Margaret made plans to take a library course at Columbia University. At twenty-seven she escaped to New York. At first she lived with friends from Belmond and carried on her work. But as she became more restless her friends became doubtful and suspicious. She was attracted to Greenwich Village, and in a tearoom she met a girl from home—from the wrong part of town. Soon after, she began to be included in the "aristocracy of exile," bobbed her hair, and moved into a cellar apartment.

Joseph E. Baker saw in this portrayal of Margaret's life in Greenwich Village a concrete illustration of the analysis in Spengler's *The Hour of Decision.* "In Spengler's language . . . Margaret 'sinks to the bottom' and becomes a part of the aesthetic underworld of New York, hating 'ethical, religious, national ideas, marriage for the sake of children, the family, state authority.' "[50] She is attracted by anything that sounds shocking.

The description of the party at which she is christened Margot with a few drops of gin Baker cites as a picture of New York "satirized from the point of view of the 'hinterland'; in contrast to the literature of the 1920's which preferred to satirize the 'hinterland' from the point of view of New York."[51]

The wonderful Dr. Finkbein had got up from his cushion on the floor and sat down very close to her on the couch. Margaret was afraid that she would give away her innocence and inexperience. She was impressed but not attracted by his dark Jewish looks. Still, she wasn't going to be judged any more by Harry and Carl. They would be out of place among people who lived in New York, and talked about music, and sex, and perversion. The wonderful Dr. Finkbein was interested—she could see it in the alertness of his eyes, and feel it in his body as he pressed close to her, breathing too near her face. Now it seemed that all the old values were overturned. The things that had been held against her were her assets. When she told them that she had been fired from the Normal, she achieved her greatest success.

. . . But she never, never could go back to the Bellows' apartment. Now the gin was gone and they were all eating hot dogs and drinking coffee out of chipped Italian pottery cups. Jane embraced Margaret, and hid her head, wailing. There was Lossie's apartment! Daggie had the key. Lossie had left it with him when she had got a chance to go abroad as secretary to that woman with the sandals and fillets who was going to revive the ancient arts of Greece.[52]

After a few casual affairs with men Margaret meets Bruce Williams and feels herself ready for the fate she has always dreamed.

Yes, at this very moment, she was on the thrilling, exquisite edge of becoming the very sort of person she had always meant to be—and she liked her name, her hair was exactly right at last, she had experience instead of ignorance behind her, and there was a man—a married man!—in her life. It had taken her all these years to

118

struggle up fiercely from diffidence and innocence and provincialism. Now—when she was over thirty—she was coming into her blooming.[53]

To Bruce's fears concerning their future Margaret's reassurance is, "I don't *want* to be married. I want to be perfectly happy."[54] Bruce takes her on a trip to the Southwest where for a time she thinks herself perfectly happy. But Bruce regains a sense of duty to return to his family. When he returns to the East Margaret goes back to Belmond. Bitter and uneasy under the suspicion of her family, she finds Belmond more unbearable than ever and returns to New York. After a short time Bruce locates her in New York and they reestablish their relationship on terms far from satisfactory for her present or future—a future as dark for her as that of her brother, Carl, in his submission to the unhappiness of conventionality in his marriage.

Margaret Ferguson is one of the characters selected for comment by Dorothy Yost Deegan in *The Stereotype of the Single Woman in American Novels.* In her analysis Miss Deegan points to comparisons with Jennie Gerhardt, Mattie Silver, and Meta Beggs, who precede her.

Like them, she becomes involved in an emotional relationship of an unconventional pattern. Like them, she is faced with the necessity of earning her own living, though not quite such grim necessity as the others experienced. . . . Like Jennie, . . . she has a strongly fundamentalist religious background which apparently offers her no positive values.

. . . Margaret Ferguson's story parallels that of Meta Beggs particularly in the force and nature of her rebellion, . . . Both rebel against the small town, against middle-class morality, against their respectable professions, against the limitations of every sort which their communities place upon them. Both have a deep yearning for an indefinable something they call "life," both flee to the large city to seek for it, but being women conspicuously lacking in talent and stamina, find neither success nor satisfaction there.[55]

In the more worldly Margaret Ferguson, Miss Suckow treated a facet of society and human experience untouched in other novels. Her inclusion in the Ferguson family emphasizes the changes in social and ethical mores. Unlike characters whom deception or necessity brings to a similar fate, Margaret sought the unconventional in an effort to disprove her inferiority. Her victory is a bitter one and there is little satisfaction or hope indicated in her future. Here Suckow demonstrates her skill in portraying a scene beyond the Iowa locale and in capturing its atmosphere as truly as she had presented the small town.

Lillian White, the wife of Carl Ferguson, illustrates Ruth Suckow's most pointed treatment of a Freudian theme with an analysis that is almost clinical. Conditioned from childhood to the habit of reserve under suffering, Lillian even as a wife and mother is unable to free herself from her inhibiting reticences. In her fears, her sense of inferiority, her powerlessness to communicate, and her sexual unresponsiveness, she suggests the distorted and tormented grotesques of Sherwood Anderson's stories. Her love of Carl is sincere, but she is sensitive to her own inadequacy and is instinctively aware of his unacknowledged attraction to more sensual and more worldly girls and women. In hurt silences she buries the knowledge that he married her without loving her. Sensitive to misinterpretation and neglect, in any crisis she is seized by a powerlessness and inactivity. In moments of tension her helplessness and distress are manifest in her breathless struggle for words to release all that is bound and aching within her and in the spasmodic jerkings and almost convulsive movements of her body.

The dissension concerning Carl's change of positions is only the spark that ignites her long smouldering tensions and drives her to an admission of her failure and to the drastic, but unsuccessful, effort to commit suicide. The accumulation of deeply buried hurts and the knowledge of her helplessness overwhelm her. Even her violent act is not a sufficient catharsis to enable her to speak everything to Carl.

He was the only boy, the only man she had ever loved or could imagine herself loving. And yet she had never been

120

able to come up to him! She should never have tried. Now she felt herself slipping into some deep abyss, where she could lie gratefully, beatenly helpless. She could keep it up no longer, she had to let it fall from her hands. Marriage with Carl was the sum of all the happiness she had ever dreamed of. When she was a girl, she had never dared let herself be certain. Carl must always make the first moves. She had felt that it would be a happiness almost beyond her. But when she had it, she could not rise to it after all. She was a closed flower, that had grown in too chill a shelter. Shadow was her habitat, and she could never open out under such sunlight. She had only wilted beneath it without opening. Now she could never say any of these things to him! They were too deeply buried. She had too long held the habit of secret familiarity with them only in herself.[56]

Only the completeness of her wretchedness evokes the disclosure of the most deeply hidden of all her secrets. She speaks the truth that she has known and wouldn't speak, and that Carl would never allow himself to acknowledge even in his own consciousness. In her agonized utterances, "I should never, never have married you. . . . I married you when I knew you didn't really love me," the weak and suffering Lillian becomes stronger than Carl who, in his need to justify himself, had always skirted the truth.

The pathetic failure of Lillian's life illustrates another disastrous effect of a lonely and thwarted childhood. Meekness and passivity, forced upon her as a child, determine her attitudes as an adult as inevitably as the pattern of acceptance and approval influences Carl. She was brought up in her grandfather's home in an atmosphere of strictness and severity where even her parents were suppressed by tyranny. In the necessity to remain silent about their own concerns the three maintained a tacit reserve among themselves in which there was no need of speech. After the long conditioning to silence it became impossible for Lillian to break the habit of reserve.

While he [her grandfather] was alive, it seemed, no matter

121

how far away she was, he had forced her to keep on being what she had always seemed to be. She dared not come out into the open. The sense of his eye upon her had gradually grown into some great, undefined, stern watchfulness, so that she was guilty whenever she stepped from the strict path, or showed any desire beyond what he had permitted—when she bought a new hat, spent a few cents of money foolishly, caught herself talking or laughing too freely. But after he was gone, when her mother had died, and her father was no longer hers—the two who had known, with whom her secret being could live—then she saw herself being carried farther away from Carl than ever, alone in the great blind cold.[57]

Marital conflict is treated at length in only this one instance of Carl and Lillian Ferguson; one character, Cora Schwietert, is abandoned by her husband Gerald Matthews, who is scarcely characterized in the novel except through the romantic eyes of Cora. His desertion is motivated by the desire to escape responsibility when Cora becomes pregnant. Elsewhere Miss Suckow portrays moderately happy marriages, but she does not idealize them. Among the older generation she emphasizes the suppression of individuality and the necessity for pretenses. The younger generation experiences even more disillusionment. In *The Odyssey of a Nice Girl* difficulty is presented only briefly in the marriage of Rich, Marjorie's Schoessel's brother, but it is sufficiently serious to cause him to volunteer for military service in an effort to escape it. Marjorie's own marriage can be regarded as an escape from the monotonous small town. Rose Kramer, who seeks marriage as a refuge from her distasteful business job, finds contentment but is forced to return to the business world to support her family. In *The Bonney Family* marriages are not disastrous but neither are they promising. In the case of the younger daughter, "The marriage seemed to be turning out neither as badly as Sarah had feared nor as radiantly as Wilma had believed."[58] Warren's marriage to the hometown girl climaxed his effort to make himself accepted in the college crowd. Little attention is given to it in the novel except through Sarah's observations.

Since their marriage he and Ethel had, in many ways, gone through hard times. Their second child, . . . had lived only an hour. The other two children, and Ethel herself, had had illness after illness, draining Warren's salary as a new professor in a small school. Ethel was faded and over-wrought. The effort to care for delicate babies, and still be Warren's "pal" in all his undertakings had worn her out. Warren, in spite of their difficulties, had matured and grown stronger; but Ethel—as Sarah had seen when the two had come home at the time of Mrs. Bonney's death—still combed her faded hair as she had done in college, still wore her heavy rimless eye-glasses, which put fiery marks on each side of her little nose, and talked about Warren's work with nervous enthusiasm.[59]

The Ferguson children are confronted in marriage with psychological, social, and financial problems. Only Carl's marriage is analyzed at length in the novel, but threats to happiness are intimated in Bud's marriage to the alien girl. Close observation reveals Dorothy's marriage to be far from the idyllic, fairy tale existence Belmond believed to be hers.

The failures in marriage do not result from infidelity but from restrictions and inhibitions imposed by conventional mores and the limitations in the emotional depth and sensitivity of these passive characters.

In the numerous family groups delineated in Suckow's novels the mothers are all of somewhat the same type. In some novels they occupy a more significant role than in others, both in the family structure and in the narrative. But always they are quiet, self-effacing, and uncomplaining. If they possess any pretentions they are for the niceties of respectability.

Margaret Lawrence in her book, *The School of Femininity,* views Ruth Suckow as a modern matriarch who is interested in the avenue to the adult through the child. She describes *The Folks* as the work of a matriarchal mind who has taken enthusiastically to the study of interrelated human psychology and sees that life eludes the fixing hands of the matriarch who has to realize that nothing can be done about it—that psychological scars are inevitable in any kind of group life and that some form of frustration is the general human lot.[60]

Miss Lawrence's comment expresses not only Ruth Suckow's attitude but specifically that of all the matriarchal characters in her novels. The families of the novels vary in social and economic status, but there are likenesses in all of the women who head their households—Emma Stille, Etta Schoessel, Myra Bonney and Annie Ferguson.

A combination of quietness and strength makes all of these characters more impelling than their husbands, with whom they are reticent and docile. All are reserved in expressing opinions and decisions; all appear to have lost their own personalities in the interests of husbands and families, but at the same time to possess unvoiced, and almost unconscious inner conflicts—submerged but uneasily alive. Annie Ferguson is most sensitive to her husband's failure to comprehend and is most aware of unresolved tensions.

They crave, first of all, their children's security, comforts, and acceptance in a conventional society. They have a firm trust in respectability, find their chief social outlet in the Aid Society and the Ladies Clubs, and have a certainty in a brighter future growing out of greater material prosperity. All experience disappointments in their hopes which they accept with stoic resignation, yet they are reluctant to abandon their optimistic view.

The positive quality they all possess lies in a placid strength to endure reverses and their unwavering confidence that a better existence is attainable through a conscientious conformity to standards of duty, goodness, family loyalty, and self-improvement. "To build a firm household" is the way Miss Suckow so frequently expresses their idea. In the context of the books that implies a comfort and stability without upheaval or shock of change, which can eliminate or ignore the inner rebellions, struggles, and agonies existing beneath the surface of the external.

Emma Kaetterhenry, August's wife, reveals the sobering effect of marriage on the pretty, giggling, farm girl whose personality is submerged by a life of hard work and docility until, as a widow, she experiences a timid blossoming and finds outlets for her small interests.

August courted Emma because she looked like a good worker. She was pretty and sensible, she had taught school, but she also knew how to wait on the threshers. As August's wife she had added to the hard work of the farm the care of Grandma and Grandpa Stille. It all came on Emma, more washing, more cooking, more cleaning. These were the hardest years of all. Her feelings toward Grandma were all related to fear, defense, rebellion, care and worry. After Grandma's death "relief slowly seeped into everything." August's prosperity made an easier time for all of them and Emma became "dumpy, shapeless, and middle aged." Only once in her married life is her role important in the eyes of others. She achieved a strange and unaccustomed importance in her trip to Rochester to the Mayo Clinic. The trip, the acquaintances from other places, the personal attentions to Emma in the hospital, and the telegram that had to be sent home all made her seem important. But at home after the operation she threw off her invalid ways. When August retired, Emma liked living in town better than he did. She joined a Social Circle Club that met every Tuesday to eat and talk and the Aid Society at the church. She took pains with her housekeeping, but still knew nothing of business affairs. After August's death Emma felt timid and out of place in a bank and was cautious about spending. She was afraid to draw out a cent and still liked to keep silver and odd change in an old teapot in the cupboard. Like other widows in the town she had an independent income from rent on two farms, stock in the bank, and a piece of land in Montana. She gradually became accustomed to doing what she pleased; she had friends outside her home, worked in the kitchen at church suppers, kept the grandchildren, was sent for when there was sickness in the country, and took pleasure in her flowers and garden.

Her personality, smothered and silent for many years, was blossoming out, very faintly and timidly, but a little, enough to shed a kind of light of content and freedom over this quiet end of life.[61]

In her last years she found a congenial friend in another widow. The two sat in the twilight together sympathizing, condoling, and narrating the troubles and hardships of their lives and their gratitude for the blessings they had in the end of their days.

Not all of Miss Suckow's women characters have as limited and uncomplicated a life as Emma, but in her are the essential qualities of all of them: docility and self-denial, submergence of personal hopes and fears, a stoic acceptance of hardship and suffering, resignation to disappointment, and inability to express dissatisfaction.

In *The Odyssey of a Nice Girl* Mrs. Schoessel's anonymity is almost as great as Emma's. In some respects it is greater because the novel centers on the daughter, Marjorie. Mrs. Schoessel's role throughout this novel is trying to please and understand her daughter. She like Mrs. Ferguson brings refinement to the coarse country ways of her husband's family. She has a comfortable home, respect for appearances, and the optimism of her generation. Only once does she utter a mild protest against life's dispensations. After her son's marriage, his enlistment in the army, her husband's death and Marjorie's persistent dissatisfaction, she complains "I don't see why it all had to be when we tried so hard. . . ." But her concern that things be right before the public will not allow any prolonged dissatisfaction. In her great desire for the appearances of respectability she made a trip from Denver to Buena Vista just to assure the ladies that Marjorie's marriage was desirable and she concludes on a platitudinous note reminiscent of Emma Kaetterhenry.

"I might have chosen to stay here—but it didn't come out that way, and we have to take it as it is. And I can see that there are going to be some good things about it."[62]

The only distinctive trait with which Etta emerges is the simple quality of unseeking goodness and affection which she possesses and regards as essential in her friends.

Mrs. Bonney balances the warm effusiveness, youthful idealism, and sentiment of Fred Bonney. Matronly in appearance and outlook, impersonal and dispassionate in her pity and kindness, she approaches all crises with a practical calm outlook. D. B. Woolsey described her as "practical and serene—her once separate self so long ago set aside for the family she sustains as to be forgotten by her and unimaginable by them."[63]

Among the parishioners she was not as well-liked as her husband. Coolly independent she was without any of the nervous affability and humility that seeks approval from important church members. She more than her husband was sensitive to the family's needs and the ways to obtain them. Aware of a falling off in Mr. Bonney's sermons and the presence of different elements in the congregation, she foresaw the necessity of the move from Morning Sun. She saw clearly the problems, merits, strengths and weaknesses of each member of her family, and Grandpa Bonney found her strength firm and placid, equal to his needs and ready to give itself. Her quiet restraint is best demonstrated in her understanding of Warren's problems. He more than any of the family depended upon her guidance, and she is best portrayed in her relation to him.

In all of his self-consciousness and queerness she understood his suffering but was careful not to betray her pity or to allow his indulgence in self-pity. Always respecting his reticence, she tried to let him feel her comprehension without forcing upon him a solution. She was convinced that Warren "must not be permitted to make an outsider of himself."[64] and assumed calmly and steadfastly through all the turbulent vicissitudes of his boyhood that her son would be a splendid man. Her lasting monument is in having brought Warren from his agonizing isolation into the safety of the group. In the eyes of Sarah, his sister, this accomplishment was a dubious triumph.

In the ironic workings of life not even the assured, reasonable, and dispassionate direction of Myra Bonney could stabilize her family as she would have desired. In Sarah's appraisal of the family's achievement is recognition of the futility of Mrs. Bonney's strivings for her family that is similar to Georgie Kramer's lament that "Folks can't do much for other folks."

"But nothing she did lasted. That's the awful part. . . . Things work out just the wrong way. It's so crazy. I mean, the things that are started right. . . . I don't see how

127

mother could have done any better than she did, but just *because* of that, it seems to me, everything's worked out so kind of queer."[65]

Of all the mature women, Annie Ferguson is presented most fully as an individual, as well as in her relations with her family. So insistent is her desire for an ideally happy family that she maintains the role of the fortunate wife satisfied with everything. The submergence of her own personality results in a life of pretense before her husband, her children, her friends—and an accumulation of secret resentments and almost unconscious conflicts with the divergent personality of her husband. It is not until all the children have left home, and the youngest has caused the deepest hurt, that Annie consciously rebels against the denial of self. She yearns for someone with a sympathetic comprehension of her feelings and for a release from the troubling anxieties. A brief vacation with a wealthy sister in California affords a taste of the detachment she craves but fails to provide the intimate confidante she seeks. She perceives in her sister's life of luxury and lack of responsibility an arid marriage, a pretense of happiness, and a hardening to the cares of others. She returns home after her holiday "just for herself" glad to be home again—satisfied in the comfort and security of her life in Belmond, more complacent and appreciative.

When Annie Luers, the pretty teacher at Buck Township school, married Fred Ferguson she tried to conform to the pattern of his rural, Scotch Presbyterian family. She forced her girlhood self into what Fred seemed to want without regard for her own desires.

> She pretended to side in with the Ferguson thrift, like a good wife, but in her heart that was not the way she wanted to do things. She wanted to be lavish, fine, abundant, like her sister Louie.[66]

She had something of her sister's rich, lavish, socially ambitious streak but she was afraid to let it out for what Fred's folks would say. She was removed from her own people so his family became the folks. She silently resented the plainness and meagre ways of the country Fergusons and the necessity to get eggs and vegetables from the farm to save money. She chafed under the necessity of being apologetic for any assistance with her work or any fineness of possessions, but always she felt "Grandma Ferguson's sharp eyes were upon her housekeeping, even from out there in the country."[67] Fred's sister, Ella, had to be invited when she entertained, and "mute and defiantly humble" she was always out of place. Reluctantly Annie supported Fred's loyalty to the Presbyterian Church.

> Certainly nobody could have guessed from Mrs. Ferguson's face what she was thinking. Since she was Fred's wife, she was of course a leading member. . . . But she had never quite felt as if she belonged here, even in this nest of Fergusons and their relations, or felt as if her real place was among this congregation. . . . If she could have chosen, she knew secretly that she would have gone to the Congregational church, which was of brick on a pleasant shady corner, and where all the ladies she liked best belonged.[68]

Despite the adjustments of her tastes and inclinations Annie knew "that no woman had a better husband,"[69] and she was generally content in the "warmth of Fred's indulgence and dependability"[70] all around her. In the comfort, security and abundance of Fred's prosperity nothing should interfere with the beautiful family life Annie envisioned. To that end she ignored uncomfortable little disharmonies and strove to create even before Fred a placid, smooth surface.

No matter what the discord among the children, "It seemed as if they all ought to eat as a happy family in harmony with the beautiful sunshine."[71] Dorothy from childhood had seemed to be "in a secret feminine league with her mother" to keep the peace.[72] Margaret's sensitive and defiant manner disturbed her, but she feared to seek out its causes.

> She had the knowledge that more was involved in Margaret's actions, like this morning, than had ever been unravelled—but she thrust it off, it made her afraid, upset her cherished belief in a simple, beautiful family happiness,

129

with something that seemed alien.[73]

Annie likewise refused to see Carl's overeagerness as a failing. His fearfully sensitive need of approval "always seemed to stir his mother's love for him to an aching tenderness."[74] Not until after his irrevocable failure will she admit him capable of error. It is only on rare occasions when mutual understanding exists between Annie and Fred. She can feel what he thinks, but he is rarely aware of her real thoughts—yet he relies entirely upon her for his happiness and mutely appreciates the richness and fineness she has added to the old plain bareness of his life.

For a long time Annie maintained the image of her family life. Dorothy's marriage appeared to be perfect. In the crisis of Carl's marriage the family maintained their discreet silence and presented a united front to the community, never admitting to each other the real nature of Lillian's act. Margaret's absence from home and family made it possible to avoid disturbing reflections on her self-exile. Feelings of guilt, frustration and pain concerning Margaret could be dismissed with the knowledge that she had chosen her own way.

Toward Bunny she felt a special kind of affection.

> Now it seemed to her, if she could *have* a choice (and of course she couldn't, it would be treachery to her mother's heart), she would say that the last was the best of all.[75]

After Bunny's marriage Annie felt the strain of keeping up appearances to be unbearable. His marriage to the alien girl, older and rough, was a "cross-blow that had struck at the roots." With all of her children taken from her Annie felt for the first time painfully conscious of the impoverishment of self that marriage and family had imposed upon her.

> She could never say that her marriage had not been happy, in spite of all of its secret failings. Nevertheless, her own separate life had gone down beneath it; and now that she needed that life again, she could no longer find it.
> . . . She had pretended to accept all kinds of things she had never actually accepted. Now when she tried to look

ahead, there wasn't anything that she could see. The children hadn't known her as herself. Fred, either—or if he did once, he had forgotten. Maybe there *was* no self any more. It was all dissolved and lost. She had gladly given it away—but now she felt defeated.[76]

In other family crises Annie was able to maintain an appearance as if nothing had happened—with Bunny's marriage the strain became too great. She felt the neighbors could penetrate the "falseness of her smile."

Before people in town, she could never let down for a moment from being Mrs. Ferguson, a fortunate woman, satisfied with everything just as it was.[77]

In her rebellion at the pretense she longed for somebody with whom to be honest. "Fred was no use. All he did was try to soothe and console her—just as false with her as she with him!"[78] The smooth surface was cracking and straining, and even to Fred she could not voice the depths of her feelings. Years of "womanly silences and bright pretenses" had made her unaccustomed to honest confidences with him, and in her misery she struggled "to preserve her old attitude toward him, to withhold her secret from him."[79]

A vacation to California presented Annie with the possibility of having something for herself, of being free of her role of maintaining appearances for the family—freedom from responsibility, need of pretense, anxiety—and an opportunity to be herself. Visits with Dorothy—her child whose fairy tale existence Belmond delighted to talk about and with her weatlhy sister Louie promised the deserved release and indulgence. This vacation was to be "all sunshine."

The first stop in San Diego was a disappointment. Dorothy had rented her home and furnishings and moved into a small furnished house not adequate to accommodate visitors. While Dorothy maintained a cheerful attitude, Annie detected in it merely her own code and that of all women which refused to permit even a suggestion that her married life wasn't perfection. Annie was torn between her desire for a vacation of undisturbed pleasure and sympathy for her child. While she recognized the vanishing dream of the "fortunate child," she never solicited a discussion of their financial troubles.

Pampered and indulged at her sister's in Pasadena, Annie felt far removed from the concerns for her children and the plainness of life in Belmond. Amidst the luxury and the numerous servants in her sister's home, she felt "the past drop away from her."[80]

On occasion she was "frightened by the dreamy unreality that had come over old attachments that seemed to be slipping away from her." Henry and Louie saw that Fred and Annie had nothing to do but to enjoy themselves. They went to the movies, attended the Tournament of Roses, took long drives, made frequent shopping expeditions, but Annie never found occasion for that long awaited talk with her sister to unburden herself of all her accumulated anxieties, and there was something still unsatisfied in her heart, beneath all the pleasure. She had worked too hard; she could not accept Louie's way of life.

When Annie finally went to Louie to confide all of her pains and fears, she was unable to talk freely; she could do it only haltingly and not in the luxurious detail that she had imagined. She wanted to admit the "bitter truths and painful intuitions" and speak out her bewildered perceptions of Carl's defeat under his apparent success, their trouble with Margaret, her uncertainty about Dorothy's financial state. But she found all the space of the large, uncrowded room between her and Louie, isolated in her ease and luxury. Blandly unresponsive, Louie wanted to smooth the surface so that she not open her heart to trouble. Annie perceived that Louie also kept up the "pretense of perfect happiness according to the ancient feminine code" and was unwilling to risk any impulse of confidence or intimacy—"Her shining peach-tinted robe was a symbol of the immaculate good fortune by which her beauty was surrounded and it must not suffer a touch."[81] The aloofness of Louie, disappointment with the Iowa picnic, and bad news from home were factors in the Fergusons' return to Belmond.

Back home and again the center of her own small admiring group, Annie answered their questions happily; she could never admit the disappointments of the trip. At home familiar objects made their mute appeal. "Now she couldn't believe in her own secret turning away. . . . Her small rebellion—smothered, only partly acknowledged even to herself—was over. Again she would have to make the best of everything."[82]

She assumed again the role of the wholly fortunate Mrs. Ferguson. Her children were gone, matured, and set in their ways. She and Dad had come to the place where they must accept what was with realization that there was nothing any longer they could do about it.

While the life of Annie Ferguson is revealed in much more detail than any of the other matrons' of the novels, she relfects in the conclusion of the book their same resignation to the inevitable.

Among the male characters of the novels the adolescents are the most successfully realized. In Warren Bonney, Carl Ferguson, and John Wood, Miss Suckow portrays perceptively the bewilderments and adjustments of the adolescent boy. The story of Warren Bonney is carried in detail through his college career. By that time his resolution of conflicts points to the man to come. In his agonizing trials in high school and college years he is portrayed largely through the sympathetic eyes of his mother, and his later years, presented in much less detail, are viewed from the not so sympathetic attitude of Sarah. Carl Ferguson, the good son, is presented in his fortunate and youthful days in high school and college, and his early maturity. His most disturbing problems that occur after college days in his profession and his marriage grow out of the conditioning of his environment in childhood and adolescence. John Wood, a high school graduate and valedictorian of his class, is studied during a few crucial weeks of his life. His future years are indicated less specifically than those of Warren Bonney or Carl Ferguson.

Warren Bonney, the adolescent rebel, through the unpropitious efforts of parents and school to socialize him, grows into a conventionally bound stereotype. He is more comfortable as a conformist than as an individualist. As an overgrown boy of fourteen, with wild red hair and flaring ears, and a sprawling bony figure, he knew all the agonies and hurts that can be inflicted upon an awkward, self-conscious, and queer-looking boy. By the time the family left Morning Sun he was thought defiant and unsocial and was suspected of having genius. At that time he was sorely torn between two possibilities—freedom to be entirely different or opportunity to make himself the same. In his secret existence he had known terrible hurts, disappointments, and humiliations and had retreated to books, music, science, and painting. In his first years at the academy and at Frampton College he continued to be hurt by jokes at his appearance and pranks that emphasized his unpopularity. He held to his lonely, twisted, embittered satisfaction of being a grind. He attracted a coterie of the talented, "outside" queer group, and took a sullen enjoyment in being unkempt, lonely, and scornful.

To escape his hurt from a particularly painful prank he took a summer job in a camp at Yellowstone Park. At first he tried to maintain his romantic solitude.

> The world here was in two parts, sharply divided: the world of the timber, of stillness, grandeur, and solitude; and the small, gay, rough, noisy human world of the camp. They were opposed; and yet, because he felt himself inadequate to possess the one, he could not freely possess the other.[83]

In the rude world of the camp he was attracted to a cheerful girl from Montana who had worked in a drug store. She spooned with all the drivers, but her warm responsiveness to his first youthful excitement enabled him to break the old straining bonds. On his return to Frampton he found himself beginning to dislike queerness. His new attitude brought him an invitation from the college glee club. His acceptance required stepping down from his chilly, but lofty, isolation and getting into the midst of the despised, terrifying life of the school. Even in accepting the new position he was uncertain whether it was triumph or ignominy. But having taken the step, he determined his course from that time. After graduation he accepted a fellowship to study Latin and Greek, married a girl from the right crowd, and became a classics professor in a small Montana college—regular in his standards and in his dress. Mrs. Bonney's sympathetic efforts to lead him to security were successful.

Sarah explains his reactionary attitude to an old friend in Morning Sun.

> "Mother worked so hard to help Warren—but it seems as if just because he was so different before, he settled down all the harder. He's just a regular college professor, . . . He's the *most* regular kind."[84]

Defensive against Sarah's antagonism to his craving for safety Warren justifies this role to himself and explains his central emotional struggle:

> —no people who did not feel too painfully, too passionately, could ever know—what safety meant to him. Mother had known, he thought. She had led him into this security. Now he was—or could successfully pretend that he was—like other people.[85]

Carl Ferguson, as much as Warren Bonney, is the victim of a mistaken parental love that unwittingly prepares the way for tragedy. Carl's strongest motivation as a boy and later as a man is to be well-liked and to have approval of friends and associates, but particularly of his parents. The approval and popularity that were so rewarding to him as a boy become thwarting and frustrating to his development. While Warren Bonney was led into the security of the conventional, Carl Ferguson was bred in the standards of conformity and could not break their bonds for any self-assertion or gratification. From childhood he suppressed any impulses that might incur disfavor. The story narrates something of Carl's life as an adult. As a middle-aged school superintendent Carl still acts from the same need for appearing right in the eyes of the world. In portraying Carl's marriage Miss Suckow presents the most complex and most intimate marital conflicts to be found in any of her novels.

As a child Carl's need of approval drew his mother closer to him than to any of the other children. In high school he was a football hero; at church he was the most reliable member of the young people's society; in the small denominational college he attended he won academic honors. Throughout these years he could never do anything that would make the folks disappointed in him. Nothing meant as much to him as their pride and faith in him. Any inclination to step beyond their world filled him with guilt and the need to reestablish himself by some act he thought expected of him. He felt ashamed if attracted to any but the "real nice girls" and never thought of going with any girl outside the church. He was not impervious to attractions of girls more sensual than the pale and timid Lillian White, the hometown girl whom his family expected him to marry. But after any recognition of his own response, however slight it might be, he was driven back in desperate need to an understanding with Lillian, who belonged to the ways of simplicity he craved. Anything that threatened the expected marriage threw everything into confusion. Whenever Carl felt briefly the urge to break loose from the pattern, circumstances made it seem a necessity. In his first summer days after college graduation he felt the pull of his idealism against his old pressures.

He was back again under the stress of his old necessity to excel, to do what (he thought) everyone expected of Carl Ferguson. At the same time, he had a blind new desire to strike out for himself, go away somewhere, start out new, work out his great glowing ideas without the cautious limitations that he felt somehow the folks imposed upon him, even while they demanded great things of him. And at times he caught himself looking again into the dazzling newness of that different possibility.[86]

An offer of a principalship and his father's money gift to enable him to get settled left him little alternative but to make the expected proposal to Lillian. On the evening he proposed

he was aware of something in himself crying out after that barely glimpsed new perilous delight, for striking out into what was unmapped and unknown, something that would have forced his life out of the clear daylight course he had set out on in his childhood.[87]

These feelings were temporary and did not deter him from asking Lillian to marry him.

Carl's yearnings for more adventurous and vital experience continue after his marriage as his dissatisfaction increases with the narrow, meagre, and provincial Lillian. In his accustomed attitude of needing to think himself right he attributes the mediocrity of his career and his marriage to his wife's deficiencies. The crisis in his marriage and Lillian's attempted suicide bring him to the recognition that he, not she, was responsible, and that beneath her mute fear and docility, Lillian had the strength and integrity he did not possess to see and speak the truth. He could no longer hold up her deficiencies when he felt so deeply his own defects and inconsistencies, and he could not bear to contemplate separation from her.

> Part of him was buried in his marriage, as part of him was buried in the atmosphere of his childhood. Now he felt as if he could never do anything else, or be anything else, with conviction. The break was too great after all. He never could leave Lillian. He suffered helplessly with her. It was himself who had barely escaped this death—and yet himself who had driven her to it. He must protect her from that. They seemed to be small and together. He loved Lillian with humble, wounded respect, and with protectiveness.[88]

At the close of the section of the novel devoted to Carl and Lillian, their outward lives belie the anguished crisis through which they suffered. The finality of Lillian's act had "put them down on a low hard level, where it was better to be."[89] Carl was both disappointed and rehabilitated by his acceptance of a position in Geneva, his old college town. His decision had the approbation of his parents and home friends and his world could go on without much change, but inwardly he knew defeat and resignation.

> A certain hope, expectancy, feeling of boundlessness was gone from his work. He felt sure—he thought—of his com-

petence, but he expected only to do what he could. The old innocent "ideals" of his college days were like a tale that had been told. And yet he felt a kind of firmness—not wholly cynical—underlying the future.[90]

In her last novel a young boy, Philip Wood, is the main character. Her approach to characterization here is different from any of the preceding novels. *The John Wood Case* is a narrative of a single incident compressed into a period of a few weeks. The response of a community to a fraudulent use of money by a highly respected citizen, John Wood, and the effect of the incident on the lives of others provide the basis of the novel. Into the account are woven numerous interrelationships of major and minor characters.

The town of Fairview found it difficult to comprehend an offense so incongruous with their image of John Wood and his family. The drama is not in the presentation of the act or in the analysis of John Wood. He and his wife are revealed largely through the impressions of others from external evidences. Their inner lives—thoughts, feelings, and motives—are not explored. In this novel, the only one in which characters really come to grips with a moral question, Suckow's consistent interest in the bewildered adolescent is reflected in her selection of the youthful mind and emotions for a resolution of the issue. The impact of the offense is felt most keenly by John Wood's seventeen-year-old son, Philip.

The discovery shatters the image of his parents and shakes his "bright-eyed confidence," his faith in humanity, and his trust in religious beliefs. Out of his confusion from shock and dismay Philip emerges with a new kind of strength. The novel is chiefly concerned with Philip's conflict and with those characters who help him through his suffering.

In the opening scene, Philip, alone in the brightness of his room on a May morning, thinks pleasantly of his good fortune in his family and in his prospects for a bright future after graduation. In the last scene, only a few weeks later, again in his room, alone and in darkness, Philip has matured and saddened. He somewhat fearfully looks ahead to the family's start in another town in which he must take the responsible leadership.

Before the incident Philip had in the school and town the standing of a "youthful king." Admired by girls and envied by boys of greater wealth, he was bright in his studies, and he excelled in games. He shared in the love and care for his invalid mother. He was "confident in his family life, which was closely knit and yet allowed him freedom." He felt his happiness made sharper, more poignant by his mother's frail health. "This put an edge of precariousness upon what was otherwise unalloyed security."[91] He had moved through his life with "unconscious princely ease" and satisfaction. On the threshold of graduation he could see his path leading only to a golden future.

At a Sunday service in the familiar Congregational Church he became conscious of the few remaining Sundays he would spend in this church he had known from childhood. In a reverie of memories and hopes,

> He became lost in a vision of himself, grown up, noble, and in fact perfect in every respect, coming back to Fairview from—somewhere, Washington, D. C., all the capitals of the world; he felt the joy of the welcome, the pride, the love of old friends. . . .[92]

Philip's golden future seems even more likely when the Merriam family so long associated with his family take an interest in him. Colonel George Merriam, "a benevolent local autocrat well past eighty," offers to finance his college education. The colonel, his wife, and their son Bradford, all for different reasons, have hopes that Philip's childhood friendship with the granddaughter Elaine will lead to marriage. The hope of this bright future is shattered by the knowledge of his father's moral defection. Even though his father had first told him of the situation, Philip is unable to accept the sudden reversal of his family's status and keeps hoping that the thing cannot be true. The attitude of his parents kept him from asking the questions he wanted answered. Confused by his mother's defensiveness, he could make little of his parents' behavior and felt excluded from the tight union they had formed with each other. He held to the hope that at the meeting of the churchmen the whole thing would be "fixed up" and he could step back into the bright springtime, the opening world, and regain the place that was his by rights. He had not yet lost that place among his largely unknowing schoolmates and teachers. . . . Surely that other clear world was the reality, not this one of fogs and bewilderment.[93] But in the presence of the men gathered in his house his hopefulness sank.

> The atmosphere which prevailed in this room taught him all over again that, although these men might come as friends, the disaster was real. At the same time, he looked to friends to change it. They could not let disaster go on being real for John and Minnie Wood—and it could not possibly be real for himself, for Philip Sidney Wood. It was totally incongruous.[94]

While he knew that his own life's foundations were shaken, he at the same time felt "welling up in him a sense of passionate protectiveness toward his father."[95] In his father's admission he saw the manly fortitude and loving care shown his invalid mother. But he could not give a firm answer when his mother asked: "You wouldn't go with those men and allow your father to stand trial, would you, Philip?" To this he could give only a bewildered answer, "Mama, I don't know."[96]

Humbled by his disillusionment and shattered faith he receives his first hurts from some of the townspeople and is supported by the loyalty of others. Mrs. Lydia Merriam more than anyone else helps him to regain self-confidence.

In the following days the uncertainty of his own moral attitude is not eased by the unapproachable attitude of his parents. "I don't feel as if I know my mother and father any more," he told Jerry Storm. "They almost hold away from me."[97] He is unable to reconcile the goodness of his father with any moral weakness. At the same time he cannot be certain that the church and friends should protect him and "pass over the thing as if it were not there." He feels rebellious against any faith: "if my father . . . didn't act out what he said he believed all these years, I don't know what difference the whole thing makes."[98]

Jerry Storm, the young minister, who had himself known

little love and respect for his own father, can only say, "You have to stand on your own feet, Philip. You have to find your own faith and make your own decisions."[99] Cut by some former friends and supported by the loyalties of others, Philip is torn between his sense of right and his urge to join his parents in a tight little triumvirate against the world.

There are things to be resolved in his own affairs. He must call on Colonel Merriam and decline the offer of money for his college education; he must withdraw his invitation to Elaine for the senior picnic. He is opposed in his decision to forfeit his honor of valedictorian by the principal who reminds him that "If you drop out, it will be harder for you to go ahead all your life."[100] A fellow student, Gladys Cornwall, refuses to be salutatorian if he is not on the program.

On the night of his graduation a mingling of devotion and estrangement in his parents causes Philip to regard their solitude as more tragic than his own.

> His parents seemed to Philip to be living in a world of their own, a dream world, while he had stepped out of the dream into actuality. His father had showed suffering but had not openly accepted responsibility.[101]

Philip's call on Colonel Merriam had been brief and humiliating. But while he was in the house Mrs. Merriam had sought him out for a longer talk. Shut out of any intimacy with John and Minnie, she had centered her sympathy on Philip. Because of her pleadings for John Wood, her husband did not prosecute. In a strange exchange of confidence Lydia Bradford Merriam pours out her life's suffering and guilt to the boy of seventeen. She assures him that error is not irreparable, that he is of worth in himself, aside from his father and mother, and urges him to rely upon spiritual assistance. At this time she gives him a graduation gift and two envelopes. The gifts, she explains, represent an old woman's choice who had committed many grave errors.

The full meaning of her words and her gifts was not clear to Philip until the night of his graduation. His gift was Mrs. Merriam's own treasured family Bible. He recognized that in giving him the family heirloom Lydia Merriam no longer rested hopes on son or granddaughter to carry on things she valued but seemed to be saying that she trusted him to understand and cherish the things she cherished. The envelopes contained the most astonishing gifts—two hundred dollars for his family's expenses while they were getting settled in a new town and a check for two thousand five hundred dollars to finance his college education. Philip now is the one to take the lead for his family. He feels a new strength in himself of a different kind from his old exuberance as he knows he must step out of his half-illusory world.

In the darkness of the night Philip loses himself in his thoughts. Although still confused, he is no longer fearful of the days ahead.

> Philip's last image was that of a long, dark tunnel, at the far end of which there seemed to be light; although he could not give a name to the light, and did not know what its meaning was, or why it should be there.[102]

A question might be raised concerning the likelihood of a communion of interest between a boy of seventeen and a woman of Mrs. Merriam's age. Miss Suckow has anticipated this doubt by her emphasis upon the long and cherished intimacy between the two families and by the mature responsibilities that Philip had shared. More incredible are the gifts of large sums of money to the young boy. But again the narrative states that George and Lydia Merriam had separate fortunes and were independent of each other in many areas of their lives; and that Lydia's actions were motivated by her own sense of guilt at having "failed as a mother to comprehend the nature and needs of her own children."[103] In the resolution urged upon Philip by Lydia Merriam, she seems to be stating a gospel of love and faith which comprises an acknowledgment of error and the recognition of evil out of which come a compassion for human weakness and a growth through suffering.

In her gallery there are few fully developed characterizations of men. They are uncomplicated people with simple loyalties and affections. Viewed entirely within the domestic scene they exert less force than the mothers in the families. Where they have interest and appeal, their portrayal is achieved usually through the attitudes and response of their wives and daughters.

In *Country People* August does not emerge from the typical first generation farmer stereotype. The simplicity of his thoughts and emotions requires little analysis. The quietness and lack of assertion attributed to Ed Schoessel's life also apply to his role in the novel. He remains someone Marjorie thinks and talks about, but he seldom enters the story directly. His role of provider for the family is clearly felt as well as something of the pathos of his estrangement from his German parents and sister and of his sickness and retirement. But Ed Schoessel is never dramatically presented. His family background is presented, his kindly generosity is inferred from the attitudes of his wife and daughter; his provision is apparent in their comforts. He is respected as a tradesman in the town. When he is aware of the onset of sickness, he retires as quietly as he had lived.

> Papa did not talk about the store. On the day when he had come home at noon and not gone back, he had tacitly given up the store and left it to Bud.[104]

The store had become one of the landmarks in Buena Vista. Gifts and kindly attentions of friends during his illness gave assurance that

> Papa had had, after all, his need of appreciation—his quietness, his lack of assertion, had not concealed what he was. People knew.[105]

With Fred Bonney as with other characters in *The Bonney Family* Miss Suckow gave a more individualized portrait of human weaknesses and virtues. In her first portrayal of a minister, she undoubtedly put some of the affection and respect she felt for her own father and his calling. In his loyalty to the friends of his youth, in his deep-rooted affection for a place, and in his business assignment with a college Fred shows a similarity to Mr. Suckow. But he is no more a full portrait of her father than Sarah Bonney or Marjorie Schoessel is a self-portrait. Fred Bonney has none of the intellectual vigor or effectiveness of preaching she attributes to her father. These qualities are more characteristic of a later character, Mr. Greenwood, in *New Hope.*

Fred Bonney is most strikingly portrayed in his role as pastor in Morning Sun, in his simple goodness and warm affection as he ministers to his parishioners' needs; his reluctance to leave this pastorate; the clinging desire to return; and the sad disappointment in discovering the town, the church, and himself too greatly changed to make a return possible.

He had entered the ministry because he knew no other way to use the fund of human affection that made him want to deal only with people—as the helper, father, elder brother of his people, the comforter to a household in trouble. The solitary uncomprehended human beings in whom he took a personal interest had a pitiful gratitude. He was not an excellent preacher, was not at home in the pulpit. Even his own family recognized in his sermons a letdown and a tendency to use old material. Their chief value was in the earnestness of delivery. "But there was something likable about his sermons, because they were like his own mind: unpretentious, honest, with glimpses of a warm, yearning human sympathy."[106] For fifteen years in Morning Sun in the confidences and the affectionate friendships he found response to his own warm feelings. The people, the church, the very building, "the streets and roads over which he had walked and driven so often, were deeply rooted in his affections."[107] The idyllic pastoral quality of Morning Sun is best depicted as it is held in the memories of Fred Bonney and Sarah. Early in the novel he takes an institutional job because of the larger salary and better educational opportunity for the children. A few years later his aching desire to return inspires a visit to investigate the vacancy in the pastorate. His most deeply experienced emotions are portrayed in the disillusionment of this return. He finds it impossible to retrace steps or to take up beloved ties where he had left them. First greetings were warm but old friends took it for granted that he no longer belonged, and only a few times was he able to recapture the old feeling. The disappointment grew slowly into a flatness underlying all that he did. Recognition of so great a change shocks him into the realization of a lost youth and a meaningless future. This feeling is the central emotional experience with which all of Miss Suckow's novels are concerned. Usually it is felt most keenly by her younger characters. The simplicity and naïveté of Fred Bonney are revealed in the severity of this shock to him in maturity.

After the disappointment of this experience he becomes a less important figure in the novel, and his personality is lost in his colorless role at the college. In the years after his wife's death he seems to Sarah no longer wise and mature, but an innocent, lovable, grown-up boy. His second marriage to a woman twenty-one years younger is narrated principally through the children's response. All except Sarah are indignant; she sees it as a satisfaction to his need for warm human response which he had missed since his life in Morning Sun.

Fred Ferguson is the character in *The Folks* through whom she portrays the social order and the older generation's response to change. Fred is uncomprehending of the complexities of personalities and of human emotions—his own are bound up in his loyalties to family and community and his role of protector. He has the devotion to family, industry, thrift, and piety recognized by his generation as requisite for a stable family and a solid social order.

He derives a deep silent satisfaction from his growing responsibilities—"the sense of protection grew deep and warm within him."[108] A good son, husband, and father, a successful small town banker, and the mainstay of the Presbyterian Church, he has nevertheless an obtuseness and lack of comprehension. Earnest in his efforts to make the future secure for his wife and children, he is a failure in his capacity to share their feelings. Any display of feeling made him awkward and he was inarticulate in his affection for Annie, but appreciated the finer and more ample life he had with her. She always meant more to him than their children and he was both hurt and bewildered at her occasional outbursts of accumulated resentments. He was always taking for granted that Annie felt as he did when all at once he discovered he didn't know what she was thinking at all. He is more emotionally involved in his world of order and stability than in any individual relationship—yet he has no knowledge or interest beyond his family, church and bank.

He responds to the changing social order with painful bewilderment and sadness. One by one he relinquishes the responsibilities that had been both burden and satisfaction to him and feels both sadness and relief when he steps out of his place.

At the bank he was fearful of expansion and the new order of business—was never at home in the new building. The dark interior of the old building, "narrow and homely," was the reality to him. He should have regarded the town's growth with a natural pride but things were getting out of hand too rapidly. Confusion and resentment destroyed any feeling of pride. The shabbiness of the street where the church and manse were located "seemed to proclaim the dwindling meagerness and poverty of the congregation, and to be a slur upon himself."[109]

He was hurt when the children chose their own ways. After the youngest son's marriage he retired from the bank partly to enable him to take the trip with Annie but more specifically because he felt outmoded in the new ways of business.

The vacation in California was not satisfying. Fred was unsympathetic to the idle life of Annie's wealthy relatives; leisure was not enough. He was disappointed in the lack of loyalty among Iowans he met in California. The return to Belmond impressed upon him "a sense of diminution" and a "narrowing of range" in his life. But in the presence of physical comfort, security, and familiarity of home he comes to think that much error and weakness can be minimized. Somewhat humbled by the failure of his old values to be sustained by his own family, church and business, he can feel sympathy for those for whom he formerly had contempt, and can admit the possibility that Bunny and his wife are right in their social theory. But he is not really shaken from the complacent view that, as things went in this world, he and Annie had no cause to complain. "It had been a pretty good day for them."[110]

Suckow's gift for sympathetically portraying old people is demonstrated in her characterization of immigrants in the novels.

In *Country People* she treats the German newcomers more fully than in any other novel. Two kinds of German immigrants

146

are represented by the Kaetterhenrys and the Stille family. Casper Kaetterhenry had been a farm laborer in the old country; in America he could become a landowner. He worked hard and brought up his children to know little but work. He used Low Dutch expressions, was tyrannical, stubborn, silent, and "dumm." When his wife died of cancer without having received any medical aid, he offered ten dollars to anyone who would find him a new wife. When his son August rebelled against the domination of the old man, hired out, saved, and married Emma Stille, he married into a different type of German family. Emma's father, Wilhelm Stille, is described as much like Ruth Suckow's grandfather—"a gentle dreamy kind of man" having eyes "with mystic ardour." In his old age spent in August's home he could do little but sit in a wooden rocker with a calico cushion, smoking a black pipe, reading old German religious books and papers, and at times singing in a faint, high-pitched voice.

The picture of Grandpa Stille living a lonely life in his daughter's home recurs in other stories and novels just like the more difficult character typified in Grandma Stille—stingy and crafty, sullen and suspicious—whose tantrums and angry mutterings become familiar in the household.

Aging grandparents are a part of almost every family group in Suckow's stories. Ed Schoessel's parents still live at Germantown and appear crude to Ed's children in contrast to the mother's English family. The German old people in these families talk and sing in their native language, attend churches where sermons and prayers are in German, and read German papers and books. The Bonney family make provision in their home for parents who never leave their room. The Fergusons' grandparents, Scotch not German, continue to live on their farm. They are all akin in their bewilderment at the war—their attachment to the new country and their fear of innovations that separate the young people from them. In his advice to Carl Ferguson, the old man states the simple formula of his generation for success and happiness characteristic of all of them.

"Take to yourself a good wife, and don't drink nor smoke nor gamble your money at cards, and work hard at whatever your work is—then you'll get along, my boy," the old man repeated. "Those are the principles I've always stuck to. And uphold the Lord and His holy works."[111]

In the character of Chris Schwietert in *Cora*, she gives her only picture of the non-farming immigrant. Chris, a German tailor, had moved from city to city always with the eternal hopefulness that the next place would be best. But he never found the place where he could make enough to support his family. In him she portrays the tragedy of the foreign tradesman unable to adapt to factory production and the ways of the city. In one town he had his own little tailor shop. In the city he had gone to work in a factory. Unable to endure the harsh working conditions, he was forced to give up the job and accept the humiliation of becoming just a helper at home. He raised vegetables, kept the chickens, helped with the food and washed dishes for his wife's boarding house. When an attack of illness made him unfit for this work he set up a little tailor shop in the kitchen of his house. Throughout his pathetic defeats, he was gentle and kindly. His need never destroyed his high spirits, his love of music, pleasure, and hospitality. In his work he is one of the few who find a modicum of delight in living. His generosity and good spirits enlivened the gatherings of friends. He told stories, played any one of six instruments, and always had a little wine or beer to put on the table. His shop in town or at home was always a favorite of children who thought his jokes and stories funnier because of his quaint, broken speech. His backyard with its "neat German look" became a haunt for neighborhood children with the two chairs painted light blue, the little blue table under the tree, and the rococo bird house, blue, white, and yellow. His shop in the kitchen became a neighborhood institution, and he himself a "character." His humor, story-telling and dramatic ability recall Miss Suckow's description of her grandfather Suckow.

To his daughter, Cora, however, his good humor and gentleness did not compensate for his inability to provide for his family. It is not until his illness requires him to give up all work and she sees him patient, sweet-tempered, and gentle in suffering that Cora feels any sentiment for her father or really perceives his personality. In his illness he becomes like the other old German people—withering, pathetic, and lost, in an alien atmosphere.

When a novelist repeatedly portrays characters in the same physical and cultural milieu and in a limited number of circumstances there is likely to be similarity in types and repetition of themes. Her character types are repetitious and their psychic world is exceedingly circumscribed. Her characters evoke sympathy and pity but remain without imagination. Their extremely commonplace lives lack drama and intensity of emotion, and the characters themselves are restricted in their range of thought and feeling. Indeed much of the pathos they arouse is due to the impoverishment of their spirit and their irresolute ambition.

As a consequence of her emphasis upon the domestic scene and the unproductive years of life, there are absent from her Iowa many kinds of characters one would expect to find—the rural doctor, the county judge, the country newspaper editor, people in the other professions, the arts, business, and politics. Some of her characters become teachers, but the novels do not deal with their contact with ideas nor their roles in the academic world. Some of the young women have ambitions to escape routine lives but set them aside for commonplace marriages.

The rebellious youth, with whom so much midwestern fiction was concerned, appears in only one significant instance, in *The Folks*. And Margaret Ferguson's rebellion is motivated by a desire for excitement in the unconventional rather than by any artistic or intellectual ambition. The rebellion of Marjorie Schoessel and her brother is not of consequence in the narrative.

The preoccupation with children and old people also eliminates characters from the world of intellectual or artistic endeavor and from economic or political strife. With the exception of farming, only in the stories of ministers does vocation or profession bring significance to character or narrative. And even in farm stories there is a minimal concern with natural or economic forces.

In the portrayal of the family members, the hopeful years of childhood and adolescence and the vacuous years of retirement receive more attention than do the years of struggle and achievement. In the period of maturity before the onset of reminiscence and senility. Suckow's characters accept resignedly the frustrated dreams of youth and resist everything that disturbs the securities and stabilities which remain from that youth. Defeat may be the common lot, yet one prefers to see a more valiant struggle.

The extreme moderation in the lives of her characters, the absence of major conflict, and the almost complete failure to consider evil seem to limit the vision of life presented with such scrupulous realism of method.

Suckow's themes are few, the variations of them are multiple: the inescapable conditioning of childhood environment; the nostalgic yearning for simplicities and the inability to cope with complexities of adult life; the shock of disillusionment in adult awakening to inexorable change; the loneliness of inhibited, uncomprehended and meagre lives; resignation to the ironic reversals, defeats and disappointments; and the enslavement to places, people, or values that obstruct freedom. Her people almost seem to prefer bondage to freedom.

Her method varies little in any of the novels. It is that of the naturalistic school. The meticulous observations from the prosaic lives result in the accretion and enumeration of details rather than in analysis or story telling. She builds the structure of lives and narrative out of literal fact and precisely documented circumstances. This massing of detail makes for the illusion of life and what Philip Rahv refers to as the "endless bookkeeping of existence."[112] Her naturalistic technique, however, is tempered with a delicacy of sentiment, a poetic feeling for her scene and a tender compassion for pitiable lives.

Interest in the folks pattern overshadows her individual characters. The villagers become almost as numerous as the characters in a Dickens novel, but their relation to the narrative or character is never melodramatic or contrived. They are essential to the environment. The spirit of the environment and the group life is always faithfully narrated. The nature of this group life sometimes keeps the characters from being interesting.

Her skill in characterization is in her ability to perceive the emotional overtones in situations and events that are externally unimportant in everyday existence; to discern significant impacts of people and events upon an individual, and to comprehend sensitivities in the outwardly passive character. She excels in her ability to create successfully the world of childhood with its joys, ecstasies, and sufferings; the complexities of adolescence with its fears, desolation, and bewilderment; and the loneliness and isolation of age. Her adult characters are never sufficiently dynamic to capture the imagination, but they are real in the limited world in which they exist.

The method of narration is inextricably involved in her presentation of character. Design in her narratives and their thematic implications evolve from the life cycle of her characters more than from any arrangement of incident. Her purpose to catch a reflection, to hold, to keep the image of the life she depicts requires skill in description, summary, and analysis rather than deft manipulation of incident and plot. In her novels, the sequence of events is temporal, not causal, as her narrative follows a life pattern. The effect is to create a series of pictures caught in reflection not action. Yet so skillfully does she present her family histories and her community portraits that her novels do not appear static but have a quiet movement. The changing scene in which she frames her portraits provides that necessary progression. Her narrative follows a coherent and consecutive process in which as a detached spectator she creates an impression of a milieu.

One understands the identity of form and content that achieves the necessary congruity between subject and mode of treatment in the fiction of Ruth Suckow by examining the way in which she shapes and develops her material into a recognizable design.

Her subject interests—the pattern and social structure of the folks and the individual's experience within that pattern—require, in general, a technique involving pictorial rather than dramatic treatment, with more emphasis on character and setting than on incident. Her technique varies in relation to her emphasis on an individual, a family history, a community, or the interrelationships of group life. Primarily she relies on the chronicle or the biographical account. The presentation of an entire family, sometimes several generations, or of a community involves too comprehensive and loose a subject for scenic treatment.

The chronicle method with which she began in *Country People* provided the method of *The Bonney Family* and was extended in *The Folks.* In *The Odyssey of a Nice Girl, Cora,* and *The Kramer Girls* there is more concentration on a single character. *New Hope* and *The Folks* might also be said to approach the method of a period novel since they have the specific purpose of communicating the life of an era. *Country People* is sparse and tightly narrated with large periods of time treated briefly and only the broad changes indicated.

The Odyssey of a Nice Girl follows the life pattern of Marjorie Schoessel and maintains her point of view from childhood to her marriage. She is the only character in this novel whose thought processes receive analysis. *Cora* is a novel of one major character, but her relationships both within and outside the family are more complex than Marjorie's.

In *The Bonney Family* and *The Folks* there is a similarity of pattern—the family group presented first, with the focus then moving from one individual to another at their significant stages of development. The group relationship is maintained to a greater extent in *The Bonney Family* than in *The Folks,* which presents in separate sections the old folks, the good son, the fortunate daughter, the rebel daughter, and the youngest. At the end the story returns to the parents—the folks—for synthesis.

The method of *New Hope* is similar to that of the pageant. Outstanding days that reflect the life of the community pass before the reader as he follows with interest the activities of the two young children.

Only in *The John Wood Case* does she concentrate on a single event. There is some use of the dramatic method in the novel, but she is still more interested in the interrelationships revealed in the community's response than in the motivation or the causal sequence of events. At least two characters, Philip Wood and Lydia Merriam, are revealed in detail in their relation to the incident.

The characteristic opening of the novels is a domestic scene which gathers together the entire family, presenting them first as a group and then focusing upon the idiosyncracies of individuals and their relations to each other. From the home scene the characters move to town, to church, or school as the camera eye of the novelist takes in the community and the citizens, usually in some group scene. From that point, time is a more important factor than any other in the movement of the narrative in which the lives of her people are detailed.

The last scenes of the novels frequently return to the starting point of the story—to the same locale or mood of the opening. *The Bonney Family* begins and ends in the neighborhood of the old parsonage at Morning Sun. In *The Folks* the story opens and closes with Fred Ferguson's feelings for home. The action of *New Hope* takes place within a two-year period marked by the arrival and departure of a minister. *The John Wood Case* begins and ends with Philip contemplating his family's status and his own future—bright and confident at the opening, sad and uncertain at the close. The cumulative effect of selected details and emotional overtones of the intervening incidents enrich the connotations of these last scenes. Within the framework of the novels her portraiture and narrative evolve in the pattern of life itself.

Chapter V

SHORT STORY WRITER

Ruth Suckow expressed herself more often and more explicitly on the subject of the short story than on any other aspect of her writing. In two magazine articles, the preface to *Carry-Over,* and in an unpublished essay written from lecture notes presented to college and university groups, she has made a number of observations about her own concept of short story writing.

In 1927 in an article in *Saturday Review of Literature,* she protested efforts to define and formalize the method of writing short stories. As the one vigorous native expression of American life in fiction, the short story, she believed, must be unrestricted in form if it is to retain vitality and originality. She observed regretfully that Poe's definition, the evidence of his struggle for originality and perfection in the chaos of early American literature, boomeranged.

It was the chaos, the unevenness, the diversity of American life that made short stories such a natural artistic expression in the first place. . . . It [the short story] was the first eager, hasty way of snatching little treasures of art from the great abundance of unused, uncomprehended material. Short stories were a way of making America intelligible to itself.[1]

The imposition of standards presupposes that beauty is a rule and not an effect. In denying the efficacy of definition she insists, "If that effect is poignant, deep, and lasting, then the right means have been used."[2] Short stories may be whatever the author has power to make them—"A running commentary upon life; fireflies in the dark; questions and answers; fragments, or small and finished bits of beauty."[3]

In a later article, in *The Outlook,* she directed her comments to aspiring writers in "search for the master-key" for successful writing, and again denied the efficacy of a single approach:

> there is one important door which, through eager fumbling, may be opened. It is the door to consciousness. When that mysterious region is entered, we can do without our keys.[4]

She discusses the writer's response to the realm of consciousness in the essay, "Development of a Story." Citing as a valid explanation of the desire to record an impression in enduring form, she quotes a statement made by an eleventh century Japanese novelist, Lady Murasaki:

> We write because something, in our own life or in the lives of others, has so impressed us, for good or evil, that it must never be lost. There must never come a time, we feel, when people do not know about it.[5]

She selects for discussion in the essay a single hypothetical incident that might occur within a child's experience, and then suggests possible methods by which a writer, as experiencer and spectator, translates the experience into some creative experience. Among others she indicates two possible methods that describe the creative processes through which many of her own stories seem to have evolved. A writer may, she says, translate his knowledge of the world at large back into a small world and tell his story from the viewpoint of a child. He may show the quality and the implication of human experience through his evocation of a childhood drama, not necessarily the same, in which he himself has participated or which he has witnessed. "Yet it may be the same scene, or his memory of it, added to or substracted from to get what is essential."[6] He may, on the other hand, carry on into adult terms of emotion and experience what so impressed him in an experience of childhood. In either case the artist transforms the real and the actual that have impressed his consciousness, and fashions in an original design an experience that has the quality of the real, but is not the real.

155

It may be written quickly, while the impression is fresh. It may stay in the writer's mind for years, almost for a lifetime. Observations, reflections, experiences, insights, cluster around it—broadening, deepening, enlarging. Our author "finds the right form." This comes to him in a flash, or the form is slowly perfected. Instance is balanced against instance, with light thrown from one to the other, in order to illuminate the situation and to test out what holds true in general. Finally the writer is able to tell a story, perhaps very far from that which holds "the germ," regardless of the method used which is no longer autobiography slightly veiled (the silver cord unbroken) but has undergone a sea change of imagination.[7]

Her short stories were her first published fiction, and they remain the best expression of her narrative purpose and method. In them she portrays the underlying sadness of existence in those whom Florence Haxton Britton called the "sparrows of life."[8] Her characteristic concern for the minute detail of environment, which sometimes obstructs narrative and gives a sense of monotony in longer work, is her most effective technique in presenting a single situation with fullness and meaning. Her artistry lies chiefly in her capacity to select and marshal details that evoke the implication of a situation and to penetrate with sensitivity the incommunicable responses consciously suppressed or submerged in her inarticulate characters. In her deft treatment of a single episode she communicates the essense of a character, the texture of an experience or mood, the meaning in a situation, or the subtleties of human relations.

No pattern can be defined with exactness to describe the method in every story. The revelation of an emotional experience may require the narrative to illuminate a moment or a day in a character's life, or even an entire life span. She is adept in limiting her selection of material to what is necessary and in choosing the most effective method for her particular purpose in each story. Her talent in the short story from her first publications has been recognized for its vigor and originality.

She, like Sherwood Anderson, became a pioneering figure in the history of the American story, and if now her gifts seem less extraordinary than they did when H. L. Mencken first praised her work, it is because others have tried to follow the path she made. No short story writer in this country has done more to release the story from dulling "requirements of the trade." No writer has been more scrupulous in maintaining a high level of accomplishment.[9]

The stories collected in *Iowa Interiors* and *Children and Older People* are similar in subjects and themes—the rural scene with its impoverished and circumscribed lives. Underlying almost every theme are irony, pathos, and bitterness. In each episode her narrative method is adapted to the revelation of some inner response, a character trait, or a pattern of life. The situation is usually commonplace, uncomplicated and not dependent on dramatic incident or sharp conflict. Yet in each small tale plot is "complete with emotional culmination and decline clearly enunciated."[10] She has greater concern for capturing the essence of character than for plotting a story. In H. L. Mencken's words, "the salient thing is the anatomizing of character" which he believed her to achieve with "penetration and understanding."[11]

The stories in these volumes have such familiar homespun situations as the gathering of families in reunions and councils; an anniversary celebration; a Christmas entertainment; a family vacation; Iowans touring in California; the reopening of a home-place long closed, and the return to one's birthplace. Among the people are sensitive children, the failures, the disappointed and the unrequited, and the aged pathetic in their isolation. Small tragedies grow out of such relationships as those between a young girl and her first employers, a sacrificing daughter and a selfish mother, a reliable but unfortunate member of a family and the more prosperous brothers and sisters, old folks and the younger generation, renter and landowner, a minister and church members, a sensitive and sentimental woman and a grumbling pessimistic husband.

Characteristic of subject interest and skills are the stories that focus on a group of figures sharing in an act or moved by some common experience. The situation provides the means for exploring the interrelationships with which she is so frequently preoccupied. The revelation of emotions aroused by a situation that touches the lives of a family group becomes more important than what happens in the story. The situation is sometimes viewed through the perspective of one character. These stories are penetrating family portraits that reveal the characters' thoughts and emotions as well as their external appearances. Stories that illuminate motives and emotions of a group of characters responding to a single situation include: "Uprooted," "Four Generations," "Mame," "A Rural Community," and "The Resurrection."

"Uprooted," her first story, portrays family members assembled to make a difficult decision. In an atmosphere of suspicion and hostilities, brothers and sisters are gathered in the dank chill and close musty air of the Shafer's parlor. The children and the old people are excluded.

Dominant in the family council was Sam, the successful brother from Omaha, who took the lead and assumed a brisk cheerfulness. He sat large, amenable, prosperous. His wife, Lou, spoke with a "majestic sweetness that created an instant atmosphere of suspicion,"[12] and sat with smiling unconcern "with her large hard bosom plastered with silver and beading, and her maddening air of being only remotely, and by virtue of her own graciousness, connected with the affairs of the Shafer family."[13]

Art, the brother who was a preacher, spoke in his ministerial tone, "for which he hated himself," and searched for excuses on a moral basis. His wife, Jen, sat "ready to fly off the handle if anyone winked."[14]

Mattie, a "bulkily built woman who seemed to overflow the small cane-seated rocking-chair," wore a look of protesting stupidity. Her husband, little Henry, summoned from his feed store, "swung his foot and examined the cracks in his finger-tips. No one needed to consider him."[15]

From the beginning there is conflict in the selfish scheming and distrust among them. Their hypocrisy is obvious in every statement. More poignant is the mute resentment of the old mother unwilling to admit dependency and the slow comprehension of the old man who had the "unfathomable look of old peasantry." He had "grown sweeter, vaguer, and more useless with the years."[16]

The physical and emotional setting is presented in the opening scene.

> The sense of conspiracy that attends family conclaves lay heavy upon them. The air was thick with undercurrents of feeling, schemes, secret alliances and antipathies. They had all eaten too much and they sat with the discomfort of middle age in the stiff old-fashioned chairs. The three men were making a pretence that the whole affair amounted to nothing. They refused to meet the meaning glances, full of dire warning and portent, which their wives cast at them from time to time. Whenever, in a pause of the furious squeaking of Jen's rocking-chair, the clatter of dishes and shrill children's voices sounded loud from the kitchen, they were suddenly stricken, condemned with an obscure sense of guilt.[17]

When the conversation shifts from neutral topics the pretense of a pleasant gathering is shattered. The cleared throats, the solemn quiet, and the shifting of positions mark the tenseness. In their evasive statements, lacking any subtlety, all express concern but decline to assume responsibility. Silently they seem to settle on the one least articulate and also least able financially to shoulder the burden. There is no love, sympathy or gentle sentiment among these people who neither feel nor comprehend the old people's attachment to home. Together they resolve nothing. But alone with the old woman her favorite son Sam, the most affluent, wins her trust.

The old lady distrusts all the others, but puts a pathetically mistaken confidence in Sam which he betrays by directing the action against her will. He resolves the problem hastily by proposing the home of his defenseless sister. He knows Hat is incapable of opposing him.

Through their expressed statements and the analysis of unspoken reservations, Miss Suckow reveals the pretenses and jealousies of these characters. She communicates with feeling the mute and resentful submissiveness of the aged and the inarticulate. Characteristic of her subdued irony is the solicitous comment of Jen: "It's good they [the old folks] have their children to look after them."[18]

Often attitudes of characters are indicated by a consciousness of physical details as in Sam Shafer's observation of his sister-in-law. "He smiled sardonically as he saw Jen's tense listening back."[19] Henry, the poorest, who had the least to say, sat swinging his foot and sucking in his breath. When a suggestion was made that affected his home, "he sniffed slightly but made no answer."[20] All of the characters have something of obstinacy and selfishness and the only judgment implicit in the story is in Sam's reflection, "But it was too bad that the way of life was as it was."[21]

Another story which explores thoughts and feelings of family members studied in juxtaposition is "Four Generations." In this instance conflict does not evolve from the incident itself but from the long-cherished and innate feelings that are merely brought to a sharp focus by the situation. An old homeplace is the scene of a family reunion at which four generations are represented. The story has more the static quality of a picture; in it the characters are ranged as in the photograph for which they pose.

While a heavy stolid country group waits against the wall of the farmhouse, four members of the family stand before the snowbushes to be photographed. Each one is described largely in physical details observable by those waiting.

Grandpa sits in his chair, small, bent like a little old troll, his blue far-apart peasant eyes with their still gaze, his thin silvery beard, hands gnarled from years of work, wearing the checked shirt of an old farmer. Next to him is his son Charlie, a small town banker, dressed in the easy garments of good quality and yet a trifle careless. Charlie's daughter Katherine is slender, haggard, worn, with dark intelligent weak eyes behind her thick-rimmed glasses. The child Phyllis, dressed in a yellow frock vivid as a canary bird, has "liquid brown eyes" and shining gold-brown hair, her bare arms round and soft and tiny, white and moist in the heat.

Both the party, waiting the right light for the photographer, and the onlookers are conscious of every detail of the setting in the brightest, hottest time of day—the flowers and green foliage, the orchard and the "green spreading cornfields where little silvery clouds of gnats went shimmering over the moist richness of the leaves."[22] At the moment for the picture their breathless silence is emphasized by the contrast of the long whirr and rush of a car on the brown country road beyond the grove.

The rest of the day lags for the visiting relatives from town eager to get away. The inaction provides a quiet appropriate for exploration of the moods and feelings of the individuals who were photographed. Every analysis points to the persistent theme of the unfathomable disparities between generations—each is an enigma to the previous.

The great grandfather, like Grandpa Stille and Chris Schwietert in the novels, is uncertain and bewildered. Alienated from his children, he lives in the memory of the past. The old man had little to talk about with his son, a town man, banker, who smoked cigars and rode in a new car. The two sit silently in sight of the automobile, a coach with blue draperies on the windows. It is always a reminder of Charlie's wealth, his separation from the country family, and his readiness to leave the farm. Charlie is unsuccessful in drawing his father into a conversation about business or the crops. The only thing comprehensible in the old man's reverie is the muttering, "Dot was all so long ago."

In the long silence Charlie too reminisces with resentment at his own daughter's aloofness. Unlike her country cousins she had studied music and art, gone to college, married, and lived in the East. In her fastidiousness with Phyllis and her rigid attention to schedule she did not allow her father much freedom to enjoy his grandchild.

Katherine among the "womenfolks" is offended by the feminine grossness and vulgarities in the country women's talk which she has associated from her childhood with the family's visits to the country. She feels no ties to this ancestral home so unlike the quiet old frame house in New England that belonged to her husband's family. The fragile daintiness of the child Phyllis seems most incongruous with this rustic setting.

In the account of her few minutes alone with her grandfather the story takes on a touch of that tenderness which in Suckow's stories often relieves the drab and prosaic element that is so pervasive. As her grandfather rocked in the doorway of his room Phyllis stood outside and watched.

> The late afternoon sunlight shimmered in the fine texture of his thin silvery beard. It brought out little frostings and marks and netted lines on his old face in which the eyes were so blue. One hand lay upon his knee. She stared wonderingly at the knots that the knuckles made, the brownish spots, the thick veins, the queer look of the skin between the bones. She looked at his black pipe, his funny little cap, his slippers with the tufted flowers. . . .
> He stretched out his hand slowly and cautiously, as if it were a butterfly poised just outside his door. A sudden longing to get this small pretty thing nearer, an ingenuous delight, possessed him now that he was alone with her.[23]

Old songs had been murmuring in his mind and in a faint quavering voice he sang one to the child. For a moment she was quite near, they understood each other. Then suddenly, instinctively aware of the strangeness of the place, she flitted away to her mother.

The story successfully evokes a scene and notes effectively such ironic contrasts and incongruities in the situation as the pose for the photograph that suggests an intimacy, closeness and pride in continuity that denies the actual lack of understanding, and the reunion in the ancestral home that is bitterly alien to the younger generation. It also contains the delicate touch suggested in the momentary grasp of some fleeting awareness of gentleness in usually stolid lives.

It may be said that in its lack of narrative action and static quality "Four Generations" is hardly a story. But it produces effectively a poignant impression. It also has interest in its inclusion of so many subjects, themes, and motifs of later stories and novels: the immigrant ancestry, the remote German grandfather; the conflict between generations; the movement from country to town; the preference for the East among the young; and the contrasts between rural and town members of the family. In this story, written in 1924, the character types selected to represent each generation are ones that receive repeated and extended treatment in longer fiction.

"Mame" also is a story that involves the relationships of a family group. The willingness to shift responsibility and to rationalize guilt feelings characterizes this family exactly as it does the Shafers in "Uprooted." Mame's letter stating her need to raise money for taxes is the occasion for her brother Louie's visit to the farm. Little happens to change the status quo. Mame and the other family members emerge through the conversation and the thoughts of the brother Louie. Her generosity, sacrifice, affection, and hard work all become known through Louie's rationalization of his need to avoid too great a sympathy.

On his way to the country he stopped first at his brother George's house. In the prosperous and hearty household his foreboding about Mame was minimized. The brothers agreed "there would always be something" with Mame and her husband, that "they were bound to be unfortunate." Exasperation was the accepted family attitude to Mame.

When he comes upon Mame's blind and crippled husband, Alick, whose "eyes were filmed and uncertain, his face sunken in mournful, hopeless lines," Louie's "eyes slid away from the painful sight. He would not admit it to his sympathies—must not, could not."[24] His prudence would not let him pity. In Alick, Miss Suckow portrays the bitter and pathetic suspicion of the dependent and infirm. Mame's appearance tells the story of her life of toil. "She was a loosely built woman with straggling hair that had once been red, a corded neck and a kindly, sunken, helpless face."[25] In her presence Louie is conscious of guilt for her eleven years of sacrifice for the old folks before they died. He had a remorseful affection for her, but it was tempered with his fear of his wife, the need for caution, and an irritation at her helplessness. Everything on the place was in poor repair like the "old rocker" that was still loose on its standard and came forward with a jerk that rasped Louie's nerves.[26]

He is able to maintain a sympathetic attitude without obligation beyond a twenty-dollar payment on a sewing machine. This gift made him feel less guilty for what he did not plan to do. He also protects others in the family by discouraging Mame's plan to move in with them. In his resistance to any consciousness of affection or attachment to his home place, he is much like Sam in "Uprooted," who is eager to get away from the sight of the wretchedness. The relationship between Mame and Louie is like that of the mother and Sam in the first story. In her simplicity and trust Mame feels that Louie is more kindly than the others and puts more confidence in him than he deserves. Mame's troubles become more remote as he drives toward home; by the end of the trip he can almost dismiss any sense of guilt or responsibility. This story presents the poverty of the rural life, the pathos and ill temper of the afflicted, the impatience of the prosperous with the unfortunate, and the uncomplaining acceptance of hardship. Here as well as in "Uprooted" Suckow perceives the drab, the mean, and the selfish among the rural folks.

Another story in which the situation is a visit to the old homeplace is "A Rural Community." The main character, Ralph Chapin, has grown away from the rural life in his years of writing and travel. In the story he is more an observer and interpreter than a participant in any action. More sophisticated than the villagers, he possesses a self-awareness that they do not have. No longer a part of their life, he shares in it through his reminiscence and associations with the past. The country scene, the folk gatherings, the people, their conversation and rural ways are all seen through this perspective. He analyzes with some nostalgia his own responses to childhood scenes revisited and looks objectively at those who have stayed close to their own soil. In so doing he sees both the stability and the circumscribed pattern of their lives. This is one of the few stories in which a character becomes the interpreter of the rural life.

The story in which a family group is portrayed is sometimes merely a revelation of a momentary emotional response of one of the characters. In "The Resurrection" Suckow writes of an old woman's appearance in death—inexplicable and inscrutable. The familiarity of the beauty and strangeness which awes her children and grandchildren is preceptible only to her husband, an old man. He knows the look and half unconsciously struggles to know its meaning: it is the spirit of her girlhood—the spirit that had underlain the acquiescence, the seeming patience of everyday; her thoughtfulness that the children might not be frightened; her sense of propriety to look her best on important occasions; her religious spirit. A little hurt that the toil and familiar way of their life together had not erased her girlhood beauty, yet proud and tearful, he is unable to speak any of these thoughts. None of the emotion that stirred him is detected in his restrained comment, "Your Grandma looks—real nice—don't she, Nellie?"[27]

The revelation of a character is achieved in some stories through the narration of a single incident that illuminates an entire life by arousing reflections and observations, his own or others. A retrospective view gives meaning to the incident in relation to a pattern that extends over a period of time. The essential qualities of the character are brought into focus by some situation in which the story "picks up the thread of a life at some moment when the swell and ebb of an emotion are most decidedly marked."[28] The stories convey a sense of the totality of a life determined by some combination of circumstances or psychological factors. Largely concerned with her spinsters and her aged people, these portraits resemble the effect produced with brevity in the epitaphs of "Spoon River."

In "A Home-coming" the description of the town of Spring Valley, the almost forgotten Summer Street with its drabness and old houses, and the musty, gloomy interior of the Haviland house all prepare for the introduction of Laura Haviland. Her return to Spring Valley and her reopening of her house create interest in the townspeople. A visit from a friend of her youth is the main incident for stimulating Laura's sad feelings and her reflections on her past life.

Every detail emphasizes the consciousness of a spent life—of its loneliness, emptiness, and uselessness. The darkness of the room and the gloom of the unused house claim her attention more than that of the caller. Absorbed in bitter thoughts of her lost youth and empty future, she listens to her visitor's conversation with only polite attention. The demand for her help which had destroyed her opportunity for making a life no longer exists. Her hopes for marriage and her interest in music, like all other desires, had been relinquished to her mother's demands.

The poignancy of the story is achieved through the creation of atmosphere and the evocation of feeling. The return to the gloom of the unused house emphasizes for Laura more sharply the emptiness of her life without purpose, ambition, or meaning—all destroyed by family claims. Life here is a kind of entombment in the musty atmosphere of the neglected house and furnishings of outmoded splendor. In the realization of her loneliness Laura likens her life to Summer Street, which youthful drivers pass by, laughing and gay, because it "doesn't go anywhere."[29]

"The Daughter" is a story with a similar theme. It has more of bitterness than the sad melancholy of "A Home-coming." The pervasive atmosphere of this story is the morbid gloom of sickness and death created by the descriptions of the place and people, all unlovely. It tells the meagre life story of Mary Lane who had cared patiently for an invalid mother. To her even the recurring spring brought sadness with a sense of time passing, and unfilfillment. Since her high school years Mary had been engaged to Henry Acres, a clerk in a hardware store who had never lost the country look. The delayed marriage took place after her mother's death. Mary was frail and broken and never escaped the sense of her mother's presence. After one year she died in childbirth.

In a second marriage her husband recovered from his loneliness and overcame the shy and clumsy ways for which Mary had pitied him. The child grew up with queer ways—she was sensitive, unresponsive, and reticent, a mystery to her stepmother but not to the ladies of the town who said, "It was easy enough to see whose daughter she was."[30] The story, like *Country People,* reveals the lives with a conciseness and economy of analysis that communicate their meagreness.

"Susan and the Doctor" develops a similar subject and theme in which Susan's love affair with the doctor obscures all the rest of her life. The town maintained a consistent concern with the prolonged courtship. At first, Susan was a figure of interest and mystery, but later, one of pity.

While the doctor's obligation to an aging mother and aunt prevented their marriage, the lonely quiet surgeon found sustainment and release from his gloom in the reassuring devotion of Susan. Her own tastes, interests, and personality were submerged in her love for him which had to remain unsatisfied. But her dissatisfaction and apathy turned to fear when the doctor made no proposal after his mother's death. Forgetful of the love affair bound up with the old days of gloom, he turned to a girl younger and gayer than Susan had become. Emotionally depleted, Susan became resentful of the patronage of old beaux and the pitying tone of older women. Regardless of her own determination that her life was not finished, the women would never look at Susan as long as she lived in the town without thinking of the doctor.

"Mrs. Kemper" is a story of a woman's need for the security of affection. The women in the town observed her nervous manner and sunken figure and wondered why she need look like such a "bedraggled piece," a woman who had a nice home and a good husband, someone to look after her, and not a real trouble in the world. A timidity of manner and a halting approach spoiled all her attempts at sociability and dignity. Like Lillian White in *The Folks,* Mrs. Kemper required the assurance of her husband's love. She could never be sure he had forgotten the dead girl he had first loved. Because he had never said he loved her, a furtive uncertainty prevented her pleasure in her husband's success, their well-furnished country home, her social position, and even in her own sons. She dared not claim any of them.

> All her own treasures were sunk within herself, within this drooping pallor, and could never be loosened . . . she could not possess even herself without the key that had never been laid in her hand.[31]

Her own brightness, laughter, and tenderness were all thwarted by her timid uncertainty. A lifetime of repression and humiliating suffering is compressed into the sketch of her life.

Miss Suckow's stories of the aged depict the meagreness and futility of their entire existence. The characters and the situations are much alike. The details of a single day's routine in the life of Seth Patterson in the story "Retired" epitomize the vacuousness in the lives of her inactive old people. The feeling of uselessness experienced by all of these characters is expressed in Seth's thought, "When a man's work was over, what was there to live for, anyway?" The loneliness and yearning for home that the old feel in unfamiliar settings is the theme of "A Pilgrim and a Stranger." In "Just Him and Her" reliance on each other gives the only meaning to the lives of an isolated couple. They feel their age that was setting them apart from everything else, was pulling them together. So necessary are they to each other that their lives seem to stop almost simultaneously. The death of one follows that of the other after only a day's interval. In these three stories the sense of leftover, lingering life prevails, revealed in the characters' restricted activities, the limitations of their conversations, and even in the furnishings of their homes. In the nostalgia for the farm these old men show some of the most sensitive responses to the beauties of the rural scene that are to be found in the stories.

While characters always control the plot, some stories are more compact and are more sharply focused on a single incident to illuminate the character. One pattern in the stories is the narration of a single episode presented chronologically in the natural order of events, with dramatization of a conflict culminating in an emotional experience. The significance is in the single incident which has its beginning and end within the story and its action usually confined to a single day or some short period of time. These stories convey a greater sense of movement than those previously discussed.

"A Start in Life" is the story of Daisy Switzer's first day of hiring out. In the one day's happenings she realizes the difference between her status as the oldest child in her own home and that of a hired girl in the home of a young farm couple. Unaware of the anxious fatalism beneath her mother's warning, "this ain't like visiting,"[32] and unconscious of her homeliness, the skinny, unappealing child "stood at the little mirror preening herself,"[33] eager to wear her best ribbon. The child's pride at "starting to earn" and her anticipation of the venture are contrasted with the mother's sadness in her knowledge that

168

Daisy "had so many things to learn."[34] Every action and every word exchanged emphasize the contrast in moods. The day itself has a "cold rainy loneliness" and "chilly wind." The drive with Daisy seated in the back seat of Elmer's car which skidded over muddy roads soon puts her own weathered house out of sight.

Her arrival is temporarily ignored as the couple go in the house ahead of her and exchange conversation about their plans for the day. Her telescope with her clothes is almost forgotten and left in the car. A little saddened by the parting with home, Daisy still has the child's eagerness "to prick up her sharp little ears" at the mention of a ride later in the day and to watch hungrily where Edna put the sack of lemon drops. In her confidence that she is one of the household she leaves her unpacking for later in order to be "where the rest of them are." Throughout the afternoon Edna's efforts to clarify Daisy's status are persistent with the reminder "You know we got you to help."[35] From Edna's impatience with her clumsiness and forgetfulness, the indifference to the child's efforts at conversation and to her complaints of a toothache, Daisy begins to feel a queer ache. "She sensed something different in the atmosphere than she had ever known before."[36] The greatest rebuff is from the children. Her efforts to play with them send them crying to their mother. The lowered voices behind shut doors are only partially understood. But the consciousness of her new status, which she had been unable to comprehend in her mother's sadness and Edna's efforts to exclude her, becomes painfully real when the family drive away in the car and leave her at home.

> There wasn't anything, really, to be done at home. That was the worst of it. They just didn't want to take her. They all belonged together. . . . She was an outsider.[37]

The baby's rompers scattered on the rug and the Big Ben clock in the kitchen ticking loudly were reminders of her desolate loneliness.

Her ugly little mouth contorted into a grimace of weeping. But silent weeping, without any tears; because she already had the cold knowledge that no one would notice or comfort it.[38]

Every detail of the girl's appearance, her home, the drive, the chill and rain of the day, the trivial incidents, and the conversation in the household emphasize the pathos of the situation. Her final clear perception of her own desolateness is anticipated by every word and action of the story which gradually affect her own consciousness.

"The Man of the Family" is the story of a young boy's emotions. Very little action takes place in the story, but Gerald Rayburn, like Daisy Switzer, assumes mature responsibility. On the day of the school picnic he goes to work in Floyd Oberholzer's drug store to help support his mother widowed by his father's accidental death. On this holiday for other school children he sets about with dogged earnestness to learn the new job. With silent concentration he keeps busy at the little jobs made for him by the druggist and his wife.

His attitude toward his new role is expressed in numerous little actions which he identifies with his growing maturity. When his sister comes to the drug store, he rebukes her for wasting her time and money. At home he takes on his father's pattern; he washes his hands in the kitchen, drinks coffee for supper, accepts the extra servings because he had worked hard, and after supper sits on the porch.

He is at the same time stirred by boyish feelings—his disappointment at missing the picnic, the aching pain when he thinks about his father, and his burning embarrassment at a conversation overheard in the drugstore about his mother and a widower. But "above that ache of unmanly tears he felt a hard exultance in his new role."[39] The culmination of this new feeling is expressed in the protective attitude to his mother and his rough dismissal of Art Fox, the widower, who comes to the house with a box of strawberries for the family. Resentfully he declines the gift and tells Art his mother is not at home.

He was the man of the house now. Art Fox could stay at home where he belonged. This was *their* home. She was *his* mother. . . . They wouldn't laugh any more in the drugstore. They wouldn't talk about her.[40]

170

His mother's resentment at his hostility is softened when she sees how proud he is of his strength. "He was only a little boy, after all—her little boy, sitting small and pitiful and unapproachable in the twilight."[41]

The emotional impact is in its portrayal of Gerald's pride in responsibility along with his boyish sufferings. In this as in other stories of hardship and toil details are recorded with objectivity and restraint.

"Eminence" depicts the temporary joy of a child who has performed brilliantly turning almost imperceptibly into a bewildered loneliness. The parents of Florentine Watkins were vain in their desire for her superiority in everything—appearance, performance, and possessions. From the opening of the story with Mr. Watkins proudly carrying Florentine in his arms until the end where he carried her home through the snow, the parents were self-consciously proud of her superiority and tensely alert to hear every word of praise.

As the parents made their way through the church they were "thrillingly aware of the whispers all around them."[42] Sunday School teachers, parents, and older girls gathered around the child in eager delight to admire the prettiest child in the Sunday School with her pale-gold curls, who was wearing white slippers and a white silk dress and a crown of silver paper tipped at the center with a star. Florentine, aware that she was the star of the evening, stood on the register, a little princess, small, calm, and sure of herself.

Beneath her little smile, the glory of the occasion, of the moment, of the worship, was shining and singing through her.[32]

During the program Mr. and Mrs. Watkins smiled slightly and clapped perfunctorily. They could not give ready applause until after Florentine's performance. Waiting for her turn, Florentine sat whispering her piece over and over to herself, almost in terror as she realized she "was Florentine Watkins. The whole church expected her to do well. . . . She could not breathe or live until this was over. She moistened her lips and moved one cold little hand. She was the most miserable one on the program."[44]

While Florentine spoke, her mother's eyes were fixed in an agony of watchfulness on that small face, and afterwards "her heart steadied into a happy, elated beat as she drank in the applause."[45] She could be happy that her child was the best on the program. Florentine accepted the homage with sweet childish royalty, but in her mind under all the glory was a tremulous, shining wonder that craved to be reassured.

The entertainment was followed by a party and a distribution of gifts. Florentine received an enormous doll, expensive and beautifully dressed. "She was mute with a surfeit of bliss."[46] Other children crowded around her—their reactions of excitement, wonder, disappointment, and envy were noted by Mrs. Watkins. Soon satiated with the vision of the fairy princess and the big doll, the children drifted off to enjoy their own modest presents and to play games in which Florentine was not included. Other children received attention and praise. Florentine, who had been noticed by everyone, was no longer one of them. As she looked after the other girls with a strange loneliness, she felt timid and no longer cared what people said. At the end of the program, the proud father carried her home and the anxious mother, mindful "that tomorrow will be here," was eager to put her to bed.

The nervousness of the attentive parents, the child's strain to excel, the childish perfection of her performance, and the admiration of the church members came to a climax of glory for Florentine. After the gift of the doll, however, the atmosphere changed. Other parents revealed envy, jealousy, and disapproval. "The Watkinses, on the very peak of glory in showing it off, did not know,"[47] and they remained insensitive to the child's loneliness and to the emptiness of her life, as unreal as that of the expensive doll she "must never let any of the girls handle."[48]

The situation and occasion that provide setting for the little drama involve more personalities in the interplay of feelings—the parents and child, other parents and other children. The narrator moves from one to the other in recording actions, conversations, responses. A complete little drama is fully enacted between the arrival and departure of Mr. and Mrs. Watkins.

In "Good Pals" a couple's desire to fulfill a youthful

romantic dream to watch a sunrise from a mountain peak is frustrated by the demanding needs of their frightened child who is left behind at a halfway cabin. The story presents more conflict of characters in relation to a particular incident and a desired achievement than is customary in Miss Suckow's stories. Here she shows her ability to present with feeling and delicacy the beauties of a scene other than the Iowa countryside and to give reality to characters who have a capacity for a physical delight in the beauty of the natural world. In describing the mountain climb she communicates with vitality their sensory response to the primal freshness and savage hugeness of the scene as the party comes upon the splendor of great pines, the plunging waterfall, the abundant wild flowers, the chipmunks and birds, and the chill fresh snow. The weariness of the toiling climb is also real.

The story centers on Hazel Benson's mingled feelings—her own youthful eagerness and romantic sentiment, her maternal protectiveness of the children, her sympathy and her resentment toward her husband's impatience at being disappointed. The conflict in loyalties to husband and children is resolved in a compromise that makes each more comprehensible to the other and strengthens the bonds of understanding and affection.

The Bensons have only done things they could all do together, but on this vacation Roy and Hazel plan to fulfill the dream they have had since their college days, to climb Black's Peak. The children's first protest at being left is pacified when they agree to stop at the halfway point for the rest of the night. Roy and Hazel have just started their dangerous climb in the moonlight when a frantic cry takes them back to the cabin where one of the children is sobbing in terror, the caretaker certain he is in great agony. Hazel immediately recognizes the cry as one of fear and not pain. She recalls a former occasion when he wakened in a strange place. Sympathetic to the child's fear she is defensive against Roy's impatience and at the same time resentful that he agrees to make the climb alone. Her grievance, however, lessens when he returns in a short time, unwilling to go without her. They compromise on a less difficult climb they can all make and half remorseful Roy and Hazel comfort each other in their disappointment.

In the experience of Miss Suckow's characters moments of exaltation that lift commonplace lives from their every day existence are rare and transient. The closeness of the familiar and the ordinary presses upon them while the dingy happenings of every day tarnish their splendor. "Golden Wedding" is a story of the celebration of a couple's anniversary. It is another of the stories that portrays character through the narrative of a single incident.

The dramatic conflict is one of character revealed in the responses to the events of the day—a day of unusual importance in the ordinary uneventful lives of Mr. and Mrs. Willey. Mrs. Willey's hopefulness, sentiment, and sensitivity struggle against her husband's pessimistic grumblings, his insistence on the prosaic, and his uncommunicative disposition. In the developments of the day she experiences that exaltation her spirit longs for, but by evening the radiance of the day begins to elude her.

It is through little details that conflict is expressed. Angie Willey, in anticipation of the festive spirit of the day, puts on her grey silk dress, lace collar and brooch to look her best before the people who, she is confident, will join them at her granddaughter's house. Asa, reluctant to acknowledge any excitement of the occasion, grumbles about putting on his best tie, utters forebodings about the weather, and doubts that anyone else will get out in the snow. This characteristic insistence on their insignificance and meagreness seems to Angie to deny their one achievement of continuity.

Beginning with the bobsled ride to the granddaughter's house the excitement mounts. The strangeness of the falling snow in the new, pure whiteness makes all feel the exhilaration of a festival. The cheerful welcome, the air of preparation in the subdued bustle, the perfect order of the mission table, the chairs set so neatly suggest something beyond the ordinary. Mrs. Willey's expectations are gratified when friends arrive shouting and waving from a bobsled. The dinner is the big event—the abundance of a harvest dinner served on a table set with the best china, silver, and tumblers in a room festively decorated with yellow crepe paper, wedding bell and cake. The occasion is enlivened by the arrival of a telegram from an absent son, the minister's speech, the presentation of an engraved silver loving cup, and even a speech from Mr. Willey.

After the dinner comes a ride in a sleigh furbished and decked with sleigh bells. The merriment in the greetings of friends adds to the hilarity. The stop at the photographer's climaxes the day's happy intoxication. Even the old man is lifted above the gloom and forebodings as he raises his wife's hands clasped in his and shouts back at the people.

The happiness of the day gradually slips away. When the sleigh returns the best of the sunshine is over. At the grand-daughter's house, friends are gone, and the women are weary. But they revive their cheer for the night meal of remnants after the outsiders have left.

Back at her own home standing bleak and silent with no shine from the windows and no smoke from the chimney, Mrs. Willey enters "with the feeling of a traveller from splendid scenes who still carries a trace of their radiance with him to shed upon the familiar home."[49] In the house together there is nothing for the couple to do; alone they have so little to say. Their room is too familiar, their knowledge of each other too intimate for their speech to go outside its daily boundaries. Mrs. Willey wants to linger and talk about the details of the day; he is impatient to go to sleep. A thin bitterness "seeped through her proud exaltation, tincturing it with the familiar quality of every day."[50] She knows she has to keep to herself her incommunicable thoughts both of beauty and bitterness.

In the story is the characteristic treatment of country scenes, houses and furnishings, family gatherings, and characters whose incommunicable thoughts are smothered in commonplace utterances. The excitement that mounts to an exhilarating peak is but a brief interlude that cannot restrain for long the intrusion of the drabness in their daily existence. The order of the story that begins and ends in the plain home of the old couple emphasizes its theme. The narrative movement toward a culminating but transient happiness dramatizes briefly the life of Angie Willey with its fleeting moments of brightness.

In two stories she uses a moderately satirical approach to her treatment of characters and situations. In "Midwestern Primitive" the situation is slight—a tourist party from the East stops for dinner at a country inn near a small Iowa town. Two characters are portrayed with an almost satiric, but not unsympathetic touch.

In the story, Mrs. Hohenschus, a stubborn German peasant, refuses to dress or act according to the manner her daughter thinks proper. The daughter Bert manages The Hillside Inn. Bert has made every effort to make her dining room conform in decoration and service to the city tearooms photographed in her cooking magazines and has copied the napkins, decorations, and menus that appear in household publications. She is both bewildered and hurt when this special party from the city take delight in Mrs. Hohenschus's dandelion wine, her old-fashioned garden, her geraniums planted in old brown tile, and her plush album. They encourage her to make her naive revelations of family history in a "voice rich with chuckles and drolleries of German inflection,"[51] while they show their disappointment in the obvious standardization of decorations and menu where they expected to find rusticity.

The situation is one that might have been presented with Sinclair Lewis's biting sarcasm to ridicule the visitors as well as Bert for their standards of conformity. In the whole recital only Mrs. Hohenschus is free from pretense. Yet in the presentation there is a sympathetic understanding of Bert's defeat and disappointment.

The story "Auntie Bissel," appearing in the volume *Some Others and Myself,* was written and first published in 1935. Like the others in the book, it is the sketch of an unusual character who lived intimately and vividly in the memory of the narrator. Otherwise it is unlike any of the other stories in that collection or in the earlier volumes. It is beyond the shadow of gloom and suffering, of sickness, age, and death.

In Reverton, Iowa, in the early 1900s Auntie Bissel had lived in a regulation house which could have been preserved as a museum enshrining all the bad taste of the period. After her husband's death, she moved to California where some years later an Iowa friend visited her. There in the golden sunshine of southern California, the matron from Iowa blossomed in the atmosphere of youthful happiness. With a comic touch almost unique in her stories, she describes Auntie Bissel's fulfillment in the humanly conjured fairy land.

Her visitor found her living in a semi-Spanish house with a

gleaming up-to-date porcelain kitchen, her appearance and dress evidence of her new good fortune. The great coil of hair formerly worn in a topknot was bobbed and frizzled. With an effervescent delight she took her visitor to see all the marvelous sights in her newly found Paradise, climaxed by a trip to an elaborate memorial park with a mausoleum, the "most effulgent blossom of this civilization."[52] It best symbolizes the ideals to which Auntie Bissel responded.

In that resting place the ancient gloomy symbols have been replaced by a statue of a child, the symbol of "eternal youth and invulnerable happiness."[53] It represents a curious mixture of an exalted worship of the ancient and a modern up-to-date aspect. The ashes of the great reposed in urns more grandiose than those of ancient Greeks.

> those of other humbler ones . . . were stowed away in what resembled nothing so much as glorified white marble post-office boxes—and to make the resemblance complete, and to give the whole idea of burial the personal touch, these boxes were labeled with "exact reproductions" in everlasting bronze of the actual autographs of the owners.[54]

This extravaganza of a grandiose American dream is the only instance where Miss Suckow looks critically at the superficialities in American culture. But in the presentation of this farcical and melodramatic tribute to birth and death there is no barb in her portrayal of Auntie Bissel's delightful naïveté.

The stories collected in *Some Others and Myself* (1952) are a departure from her familiar objective portrayals of commonplace lives. They are less compact, intensely personal sketches of the unusual and the non-typical, differing from earlier stories in narrative method, tone, and attitude. In five of the seven stories the narrator is a first person observer with an intimate knowledge of the characters whose lives are sketched with a gentleness and tenderness. The narrator's tone sometimes approaches that of the personal essay more than of the short story and allows the author greater freedom of interpretation Mood, however, more than structure distinguishes these stories from earlier ones.

She continued in them to be the marvelous observ-

177

er, but in these stories her impressions are more than clear reflections. In three of the stories, "Mrs. Vogel and Ollie," "An Elegy for Alma's Aunt Amy," and "One of Three Others," the narrator reminisces from the point of view of one who returns to scenes where years before she had been charmed by the rare qualities of the women she depicts. In retrospective mood and with deft strokes she creates her vignettes, lavishing on each the art, care, and attention that produce the reality of a bygone time. In all the stories of the volume there is a sense of picturesque but decaying charm in which ghosts of a life gone by linger with an enchanting tenderness. There are touches of the macabre, the mysterious, the fanciful, and the childlike wonder. Interpreter as well as narrator, she searches for meaning in the lives of the "odd discards, half hidden . . . and yet spectacular." These fond tributes to characters she had known and loved are inspired by the same appealing quality she eulogizes in her sketch of Amy Root.

> Her life was an air that sounded muted and interwoven with others, with no one ever to play and to make audible its separate music.[55]

Some shadow of sorrow or mystery pervades the atmosphere of most of the stories and the lives of the characters. In "One of Three Others," Jennie Gruenwald's deafness and later her mental aberration enshroud her life in half darkness. In her late years only a few intimate friends can recall the charm of the woman who became an aged and withered child clutching a rag doll. There is charm in the slight madness and childlike wonder of Mrs. Vogel whose yard is like an "outdoor attic, full of horticultural relics,"[56] and her orchard "a witch's orchard"[57] with its fallen misshapen fruit nested in the matted grass. In "Merrittsville," a faded gentility and an air of mystery impress a visitor with the feeling that "the clocks were stopped and the whole household lived on in an unmeaning timelessness after time was over."[58] The spiritual grandeur of her husband's nobility lives in the memory of his widow. The sad and waning beauty of Amy Root reveals some sense of disappointment held and cherished. The faded flower of her girlhood lingers about the room with the little reed rocker, her satin sachet on the dresser, and the old-fashioned perfume bottles tied at the neck with blue ribbons. In her shadowy role in her sister's home she keeps her life closed in the box of faded photographs and keepsakes shown only to intimate friends in a kind of plea for recognition of the unanswered claims of her pretty girlhood. In the story "Eltha," an ethereal quality and a sad enchantment of a stricken child give her the appearance of "Snow White lying in trance in her crystal coffin."[59] Another story reveals memories of family sorrows and pent-up sufferings struggling for release as a woman visits family graves on Memorial Eve in an atmosphere of impending war.

In her last collection of stories and in her last novel, both of which came after the ten-year interval from 1942-52 without publication, Suckow's art shows a less stark realism and a less rigid objectivity. The retrospective view of the stories is not unlike that of the "Memoir" with which they were published. They could and probably do contain much actuality—memories stored up from childhood impressions of the old ladies to whom she was always attracted. A fondness for the nostalgic and an interest in the eccentric, flavor these reminiscences, most of them about women in the twilight of life. But in their somber and sad lives there is less sense of futility and bitterness, and more courage and dignity expressed simply and movingly.

A woman in "One of Three Others" accepts with resignation the burden of a helpless sister and lavishes upon her all her care and goodness of heart. The strength of the ordinary daughter, Ollie Vogel, remains firm and reliable in contrast to the whimsical fancies and aberrations of her childlike mother. Mrs. Merritt and her daughter are sustained in their poverty by the memory of her husband's integrity. Mabel Mosher in "Memorial Eve" releases her pent-up suffering by easing the bitter aloofness between two families. "Eltha" is the story of the confining and wearing care of an afflicted child which becomes a service of love transcending duty and ennobling a mother.

In one of the stories Miss Suckow's own regard for the significant in life and in fiction is ascribed to a character to whom the story of Judge Merritt is disclosed. The judge's experience had been a disaster resulting from the bank failures of the depres-

179

sion. When his wife recounted the details to George and Mary Sedgewick, who were paying guests in the Merritt home, George Sedgewick fitted the bit of local history into the "framework of social-economic reference." But Mary expressed a consistent attitude of Miss Suckow's when she contended

> that what happened in a particular way, under its own particular terms and circumstances, mattered too. A particular instance mattered.[60]

Setting forth the particular circumstances in the destinies of non-spectacular lives remains the purpose of all Suckow's fiction. The variation of her method in her later stories points to the extension of her earlier purpose but not to a contradiction. In 1951 she reiterated a previously stated concept but with some expansion of her original idea. Her last publications indicate that the statement described her intention for later writing.

> On my own part, I would liken a story (as I would like to tell a story) to a reflection in very clear water, which seems to give back the scene itself, but with a depth and a slight mystery, sense of atmosphere and meaning, there being a current in the stream as well. I also feel more and more that slight touch of elegance . . . may be given by the author and in this way add a certain personality.[61]

Chapter VI

CONCLUSION

The foregoing study of Ruth Suckow's novels and stories examines her fiction in the light of the total body of writing and in relation to her statements of purpose and intention. The analysis indicates some of the enduring qualities that give her fiction significance and suggests restrictions that are inherent in her choice of subject and method. The preceding analysis has considered separate elements. In conclusion, I turn to the fiction in its totality for a more comprehensive evaluation of strengths and limitations.

Her originality stems from her choice of the Iowa scene as subject matter, to which she brings knowledge, talent, and compassion. Genuine affection and intimate acquaintance are combined to create an authentic delineation of scene. Her eye for visual detail imparts to the scene a convincing reality, created by a faithfulness to minutiae. In her interiors, every object has the preciousness of the familiar and cherished, and the power of her landscape descriptions is the result of her aesthetic response to the scenic beauty of Iowa.

Her narrative technique is most successful when she concentrates upon the small incident which has deeper implications for thought. The incidents themselves are commonplace; they become significant through her capacity to suggest these overtones.

Her portraiture also reveals sympathy and perceptiveness. Comprehension of the child's emotions of pleasure and pain enables her to portray him with convincing sensitivity. The old people, experiencing a variety of ills, are treated compassionately to evoke pathos. And in all age groups, she makes poignant the sufferings of the inarticulate.

A great deal of her interest in the individual character concentrates upon his relationship to others in the family, church, and community. Because she is interested in him as one of a social group, her novels become social chronicles. The events therein record the spirit and atmosphere of country living. As such their value lies in their complete description of the domestic pattern of rural life in the early twentieth century.

Valuable as her novels are for social history, most of them suffer to some degree from the confinements of her subject matter and method. It is not unique, perhaps, that the very qualities that give distinction and individuality to her art also confine her expression.

Her concentration on the rural Iowa scene limits the range of character types and the scope of their experiences. Frequently the consequence of her complete absorption in them and their locale is—monotony.

Her concern for detail burdens the narrative with its thoroughness and repetition. Furthermore, it impedes the action. At her best she can be economical with detail. When she is, the subject matter is usually the meagre, barren aspect of rural life.

Her characteristic narrative action lacks dramatic conflict, crisis, and the resulting intensity of emotion. It is a failing probably due, in part, to her concern with group portraits and communal experience. Her individual characters have limited emotional capacities and a narrow field of experience. Consequently they lack color, excitement and imaginative appeal. Furthermore, the character development she attempts is rudimentary, impeded by the lack of complexity in her characters. Their loneliness, defeat, and nostalgia are strongly felt and skillfully communicated; but her over-use of a paucity of emotional themes lessens their individual and over-all effectiveness. These flaws in Miss Suckow's fiction are most evident in her novels.

The three volumes of short stories are her best work. In them her feeling for the concrete which overloads the longer fiction gives fullness to the limited scene of the short story. Also, the nature of the short story does not require the dramatic for interest. Illumination and recognition are sufficient. Since almost all of her short stories concentrate upon the single character instead of the group, her focus is sharper, her emotional impact greater. Furthermore, the very types of emotional experience she studies are best conveyed in the short narrative. In themselves, they are not dramatic enough to sustain a long narrative because most of her characters do not engage in action. They are primarily passive. Consequently a brief view of their dilemma is moving; whereas a lengthy one becomes drab. The confinements of the short narrative enable Ruth Suckow to concentrate her pictorial and narrative talents upon a single stituation, character and mood. And in these stories, her tenderness and compassion attain their consummate expression.

This study has not been primarily concerned with autobiographical elements in her fiction. However, conjecture is inevitable relating to her preoccupation with a limited time and era (that of her childhood), and repetition of theme and character types.

Certainly she was not unacquainted with the world beyond her beginnings. Education and travel broadened her horizons. Yet, except in rare instances, she continued to depict the region she had first known and loved. The deeply felt emotions which recur most frequently in her characters are loneliness and isolation, nostalgic yearnings and the sadness that comes with the realization of lost security. Although she does on occasions show the narrowing effect of the rural pattern and the inadequacy of her older characters' oversimplified solutions to emotional problems, Miss Suckow usually finds the era of confidence and stability most appealing. Beneath the surface one detects a clinging to the status quo, a set of values which gives her fiction, when viewed as a whole, a nostalgic tone. Her choice of recurrent themes seems to be indicative of a personal involvement. There is the possibility that the writer uses her realism to assert an affirmation of rural values based upon an intensely personal nostalgia. Perhaps she was reluctant to relinquish her hold on the world she had known as a child.

Certainly some of the painful situations within the family life she depicts often concern problems similar to those in her own experience. Her mother's illness began before she was five. Years of sickness, the deaths of her mother, nephew and sister within a short time seem likely to have suggested some of her themes.

Attachment to some particular locale is frequently a theme in her novels. Undoubtedly in the frequent moves necessary in a minister's family, there could have been unhappy breaks with pleasant home associations similar to those sufferings of her fictional characters.

Another indication of her nostalgia for childhood is her use of her birthplace for the setting of a late novel, *New Hope,* 1942, to portray a quasi-utopian society with enduring values of communal fellowship which she felt had import for the later era.

This novel was the first of her works to express positive, clear-cut affirmations that had only been intimated previously. This note of affirmation continues in Suckow's last two volumes. It appears to be partially explained by the religious development she recounts in her Memoir. The Memoir discusses the religious experiences through which she became affiliated with the Society of American Friends.

In at least three of the stories in *Some Others and Myself,* the treatment of suffering is positive. In the interpretations of her characters, there are ennobling effects and compensations for suffering.

In the *John Wood Case* she presents an adolescent shaken from his security who, instead of retreating into the past, looks to the future.

This new affirmative note in her later fiction is of interest chiefly for its autobiographical elements and its retention of her earlier subject matter. Perhaps by contrast it intensifies one's appreciation of the totality of her previous work where the bright and the dark aspects of folk life are captured with a compelling validity and poignancy.

NOTES

NOTES TO CHAPTER I

1. Ruth Suckow, "Uprooted," *The Midland,* VII (February, 1921), 83-109.
2. *The Midland,* a journal edited by John T. Frederick. Published from 1915-1933, in Iowa City from 1915-1930 and in Chicago from 1930. From 1925 to 1933, Frank Luther Mott was co-editor.
3. Allan Nevins, "A Painter of Iowa," *The Saturday Review of Literature,* IV (March 10, 1928), 666.
4. Ibid.
5. John T. Frederick, "The Farm in Iowa Fiction," *The Palimpsest,* XXXII (March, 1951), 124-125.
6. John T. Frederick, "Town and City in Iowa Fiction," *The Palimpsest,* XXXV (February, 1954), 57.
7. Wallace Stegner, "The Trail of the Hawkeye," *The Saturday Review of Literature,* XVIII (July 30, 1938), 3-4; 16-17.
8. Frederick, "Town and City in Iowa Fiction," 67.
9. *Country People* (1924); *The Odyssey of a Nice Girl* (1925); *Iowa Interiors* (1926); *The Bonney Family* (1928); *Cora* (1929); *The Kramer Girls* (1930); *Children and Older People* (1931); *The Folks* (1934); *Carry-Over* (1936).
10. Letter from John T. Frederick, November 11, 1951.
11. Ibid.
12. Joseph E. Baker, "Regionalism in the Middlewest," *The American Review,* IV (March, 1935), 603-614.
13. John T. Frederick, "Ruth Suckow and the Middle Western Literary Movement," *The English Journal,* XX (January, 1931), 1-8; John T. Frederick, "The Farm in Iowa Fiction," *The Palimpsest,* XXXII (March, 1951), 131-134; John T. Frederick, "The Town in Iowa Fiction," *The Palimpsest,* XXXV (February, 1954), 68-74.
14. Frank Luther Mott, "Ruth Suckow," *A Book of Iowa Authors by Iowa Authors,* edited by Johnson Brigham (Des Moines, Iowa, 1930), pp. 215-224.
15. H. L. Mencken, "The Library," Review of *Iowa Interiors, The American Mercury,* IX (November, 1926), 383.
16. Mott, op. cit., p. 224.

17. Carl Van Doren, *The American Novel 1789-1939* (New York, 1940), p. 361.
18. John T. Flanagan, "From the Heartland," *America Is West* (Minneapolis, 1945), p. iv.
19. Joseph Warren Beach, *American Fiction 1920-1940 (New York, 1942), pp. 7-8.*

NOTES TO CHAPTER II

1. Ruth Suckow, *The Bonney Family,* reprinted in *Carry-Over* (New York, 1936), p. 172.
2. Ibid., p. 69.
3. Ruth Suckow, "Iowa," *The American Mercury,* IX (September, 1926), 39.
4. Allan Nevins, "A Painter of Iowa," *Saturday Review of Literature,* IV (March 10, 1928), 666.
5. *Iowa, A Guide to the Hawkeye State,* American Guide Series, Federal Writers' Project of the Works Progress Administration for the State of Iowa (New York, 1938), p. 27.
6. Ruth Suckow, "Iowa," 45.
7. *Iowa, A Guide to the Hawkeye State,* p. 27.
8. LeMars, county seat of Plymouth County; Algona, Kossuth County; Manchester, Delaware County. She is most familiar, she said, with Delaware County.
9. Ruth Suckow, "A German Grandfather," *The American Mercury,* XII (November, 1927), 280.
10. Ruth Suckow, "A Memoir," *Some Others and Myself* (New York, 1952), p. 182. In his autobiography Miss Suckow's father states that at this time the low-wheeled bicycle appeared and soon crowded their high-wheeled forerunners out of the picture. Men, women and children all took to "wheels." Bicycle clubs were organized, and "runs," tumbles, and other accidents were among the main topics of conversation.
11. Ruth Suckow, *Some Others and Myself,* p. 182.
12. Joseph E. Baker, loc. cit., 603.
13. Ruth Suckow, "Middle Western Literature," *The English Journal,* XXI (March, 1932), 176.
14. Ibid., 182.
15. Ruth Suckow, *The Folk Idea in American Life,* reprinted from *Scribner's Magazine,* September, 1930 (New York, 1930), p. 4.
16. Ruth Suckow, *Some Others and Myself,* p. 206. She writes: "In this country, they became converts to Methodism through the preaching of the famed evangelist, Peter Cartwright, and were devout German

Methodists for the rest of their lives." On page 208 she also states that her other grandparents had been converted by the same Peter Cartwright.

17. William John Suckow, "Seventy Years in Retrospect," unpublished manuscript of his autobiography ending with 1933, p. 59.
18. *Country People,* reprinted in *Carry-Over,* pp. 15-16.

19. Ibid., pp. 10-11.
20. Ibid., pp. 11-12.
21. Ibid., pp. 54-55.
22. Mary Austin, "Regionalism in American Fiction," *The English Journal,* XXI (February, 1932), 103.
23. Paul Corey, *Three Miles Square* (New York, 1939); *The Road Returns* (New York, 1940); *County Seat* (New York, 1941).
24. *Country People,* reprinted in *Carry-Over,* pp. 36-38.
25. Ibid., p. 12.
26. Ibid., p. 41.
27. Ibid., p. 46.
28. Ibid., p. 49.
29. Ibid., p. 106.
30. Ibid., p. 24.
31. *Country People,* reprinted in *Carry-Over,* p. 42.
32. Ibid., p. 143.
33. *The Odyssey of a Nice Girl,* p. 18.
34. Ibid., p. 28.
35. *The Folks* (New York, 1934), p. 720.
36. "A Start in Life," *Iowa Interiors* (New York, 1926), pp. 4-5.
37. "Mame," *Iowa Interiors,* pp. 70-71.
38. "Renters," *Iowa Interiors,* p. 129.
39. Ibid., p. 115.
40. Ibid., p. 118.
41. "Retired," *Iowa Interiors,* p. 138.
42. "A Pilgrim and a Stranger," *Iowa Interiors,* p. 143.
43. "Retired," pp. 132-133.
44. "A Rural Community," *Iowa Interiors,* pp. 159-160.
45. Ibid., pp. 180-181.
46. "Mrs. Vogel and Ollie," *Some Others and Myself* (New York, 1952), p. 52.
47. "A Homecoming," *Iowa Interiors,* p. 19.
48. "The Daughter," *Iowa Interiors,* pp. 37-38.
49. "Mame," p. 73.
50. "Uprooted," *Iowa Interiors,* p. 88.
51. "Retired," p. 137.

52. *The Kramer Girls* (New York, 1930), p. 185.
53. *Carry-Over*, p. xvii.
54. *The Bonney Family*, p. 172.
55. "A Homecoming," p. 18.
56. "Retired," p. 135.
57. *The Odyssey of a Nice Girl* (New York, 1925), p. 274.
58. Ibid., pp. 138-139.
59. *The Kramer Girls*, p. 125.
60. Ibid., p. 124.
61. *Carry-Over*, Comments and Addenda," p. xvii.
62. *Cora* (New York, 1929), p. 13.
63. Ibid., p. 49.
64. *The Folks*, p. 528.
65. William John Suckow, "Seventy Years in Retrospect," p. 125.
66. *New Hope* (New York, 1942), p. 62.
67. Ruth Suckow, *Some Others and Myself*, p. 175.
68. Ibid.
69. Mr. Suckow records the changes in church affiliation in "Seventy Years in Retrospect." In Albany the family first united with the Dutch Reformed Church; the congregation was German and services were in German. At Elkport the church was German Lutheran. It was for his family "artificially stilted, oppressively solemn, painfully ministerial." At this time they began to attend a German Methodist church.

    When he was ready to enter the ministry, after a scanty theological course at the seminary in Galena, Illinois, Mr. Suckow decided not to apply for admission to the German Conference but to the English Speaking Northwest Iowa Conference. He was appointed to a church at Sioux Rapids. Because he believed the Methodist conference "machine ruled" he decided to take a Congregational pulpit offered to him at Hawarden in 1889.
70. *New Hope*, p. 11.
71. Ibid., p. 29.
72. Ibid., p. 43.
73. Ibid., p. 227.
74. *Some Others and Myself*, p. 176.
75. Ibid. On page 175 of this book Miss Suckow writes, "I have found something of my town in Lincoln's New Salem, and in the early Springfield; in Edgar Lee Master's [*sic*] *Spoon River Anthology,* shown there in the light of contrast between the first bright beginnings and later petering out and disillusionment; in New Litchfield, Connecticut, during the childhood of Harriett [*sic*] Beacher Stowe."

76. Ibid., p. 176.
77. *New Hope*, pp. 60-61.
78. Ibid., p. 60.
79. *Some Others and Myself*, p. 184.
80. Ibid., p. 175.
81. Ruth Suckow, "A German Grandfather," p. 280.
82. *Country People,* reprinted in *Carry-Over*, p. 112.
83. *Some Others and Myself*, p. 194.
84. "A Rural Community," p. 173.
85. *Some Others and Myself*, p. 112.
86. Ibid., p. 71.

NOTES TO CHAPTER III

1. Henry Steele Commager, *The American Mind* (New Haven, 1950), p. 407.
2. Ruth Suckow, "Comments and Addenda," *Carry-Over* (New York, 1936), p. x.
3. Roy N. Horton and Herbert N. Edwards, *Backgrounds of American Literary Thought* (New York, 1952), p. 295.
4. Suckow, "Comments and Addenda," p. viii.
5. Ibid.
6. Horton and Edwards, op. cit., p. 297.
7. Ibid.
8. Walter L. Meyers, "The Novel and the Simple Soul," *Virginia Quarterly Review*, XIII (August, 1937), 507.
9. *Country People*, p. 213.
10. Ibid., p. 201.
11. *The Odyssey of a Nice Girl*, p. 344.
12. *Some Others and Myself* (New York, 1952), pp. 245-246.
13. Ibid., p. 247.
14. Ibid., p. 248.
15. *Country People*, p. 104.
16. Ibid., p. 111.
17. *The Odyssey of a Nice Girl*, p. 292.
18. Ibid., p. 297.
19. Ibid., p. 298.
20. Ibid., p. 303.
21. *The Bonney Family*, p. 216.
22. Ibid., pp. 234-235.
23. Ibid., p. 235.
24. *The Bonney Family*, p. 31.

25. Ibid., p. 172.
26. *Cora,* p. 332.
27. *The Kramer Girls,* p. 122.
28. *The Folks,* p. 301.
29. Ibid., p. 649.
30. *The Folks,* pp. 702-703.
31. Ibid., p. 708.
32. Ibid., p. 252.
33. Ibid., p. 521.
34. Ibid., p. 565.
35. Ibid., p. 725.
36. Ibid., pp. 726-727.
37. In an interview with Miss Suckow in June, 1951, she said with reference to the time of writing such a book as *New Hope* that she had not deliberately avoided social issues of the contemporary scene, but believed political, economic, and social issues were too topical for use in fiction. The publication of *New Hope* during World War II she said had nothing to do with her own attitude toward war and that the novel had been begun earlier.
38. *New Hope,* p. 40.
39. Ibid., p. 45.
40. Ibid., p. 27.
41. Ibid., p. 333.
42. Ibid., p. 342.
43. Henry Seidel Canby, "Fiction Sums up a Century," in *Literary History of the United States,* II (New York, 1948), p. 1208.

NOTES TO CHAPTER IV

1. Ruth Suckow, "Friends and Fiction," *Friends Intelligencer,* CXII, No. 7 (Second Month 12, 1955), p. 91.
2. Ibid., p. 92.
3. Ruth Suckow, unpublished manuscript. Notes prepared for publication with *Some Others and Myself.* They were not printed. p. 5.
4. Marion L. Starkey, "Ruth Suckow from Iowa to New York," *Boston Evening Transcript,* May 24, 1930, pp. 1-2.
5. Ibid.
6. B. E. Boothe, "Ruth Suckow, An Appreciation," *Diamonds Bulletin,* January 27, 1939, pp. 1-2.
7. Ruth Suckow, *The Bonney Family,* p. 285.
8. Edith Wharton, *The Writing of Fiction* (New York, 1925), p. 128.
9. Ruth Suckow, "Friends and Fiction," p. 92.

10. *New Hope,* p. 183.
11. Ibid., p. 46.
12. Ibid., p. 157.
13. Ibid., p. 271.
14. Ibid., p. 269.
15. Ibid., p. 270.
16. Richard A. Cordell, review, *Saturday Review of Literature,* XXV (February 28, 1942), p. 8.
17. *New Hope,* p. 22.
18. Ibid.
19. Edith H. Walton, review, *New York Times,* February 22, 1942, p. 6.
20. *New Hope,* p. 37.
21. Ibid., p. 99.
22. Ibid., pp. 132-133.
23. Ibid., pp. 340-341.
24. *The Odyssey of a Nice Girl,* p. 349.
25. Robert Morse Lovett, "Ideas and Fiction," *The New Republic,* XLIV (November 18, 1925), 337.
26. *The Odyssey of a Nice Girl,* p. 101.
27. Ibid., p. 140.
28. Frederick J. Hoffman, *The Twenties* (New York, 1955), p. 333 note.
29. *The Odyssey of a Nice Girl,* p. 248.
30. Ibid., p. 288.
31. Ibid., pp. 306-307.
32. Ibid., p. 317.
33. Ibid., p. 344.
34. Ibid., p. 348.
35. *The Bonney Family,* p. 200.
36. Ibid., p. 296.
37. *The Kramer Girls,* p. 68.
38. Ibid., p. 39.
39. Ibid., pp. 218-219.
40. Ibid., p. 256.
41. Ibid., p. 257.
42. Ibid., pp. 272-273.
43. *The Folks,* p. 12.
44. Ibid., p. 32.
45. Ibid., p. 318.
46. Ibid., p. 315.
47. Ibid., p. 329.
48. Ibid.

49. Ibid., p. 307.
50. Joseph E. Baker, loc. cit., 606.
51. Ibid., 607.
52. *The Folks,* pp. 355-356.
53. Ibid., p. 398.
54. Ibid., p. 411.
55. Dorothy Yost Deegan, *The Stereotype of the Single Woman in American Novels* (New York, 1951), pp. 71-72.
56. *The Folks,* pp. 223-224.
57. Ibid., p. 222.
58. *The Bonney Family,* p. 243.
59. Ibid., pp. 256-257.
60. Margaret Lawrence, *The School of Femininity* (New York, 1936), pp. 240-241.
61. *Country People,* p. 202.
62. *The Odyssey of a Nice Girl,* p. 364.
63. D. B. Woolsey, review, *New Republic,* LIV (March 7, 1928), 106.
64. *The Bonney Family,* p. 117.
65. Ibid., p. 292.
66. *The Folks,* p. 15.
67, Ibid., p. 16.
68. Ibid., p. 39.
69. Ibid., p. 50.
70. Ibid., pp. 50-51.
71. Ibid., p. 12.
72. Ibid., p. 14.
73. Ibid., pp. 15-16.
74. Ibid., p. 11.
75. Ibid., p. 529.
76. Ibid., p. 573.
77. Ibid., p. 570.
78. Ibid.
79. Ibid., p. 571.
80. Ibid., p. 649.
81. Ibid., pp. 670-671.
82. Ibid., p. 721.
83. *The Bonney Family,* p. 126.
84. Ibid., p. 292.
85. Ibid., p. 263.
86. *The Folks* p. 129.
87. Ibid., p. 141.
88. Ibid., p. 227.

89. Ibid., p. 240.
90. Ibid., p. 250.
91. *The John Wood Case* (New York, 1959), p. 4.
92. Ibid., p. 29.
93. Ibid., pp. 154-155.
94. Ibid., p. 156.
95. Ibid., p. 163.
96. Ibid., p. 180.
97. Ibid., p. 217.
98. Ibid., p. 219.
99. Ibid., p. 220.
100. Ibid., p. 233.
101. Ibid., p. 302.
102. Ibid., p. 314.
103. Ibid., p. 135.
104. *The Odyssey of a Nice Girl,* p. 331.
105. Ibid., p. 330.
106. *The Bonney Family,* p. 29.
107. Ibid., p. 30.
108. *The Folks,* p. 6.
109. Ibid., p. 568.
110. Ibid., p. 726.
111. Ibid., p. 140.
112. Philip Rahv, "Notes on the Decline of Naturalism," *Image and Idea* (Norfolk, Connecticut, 1949), p. 128.

NOTES TO CHAPTER V

1. Ruth Suckow, "The Short Story," *Saturday Review of Literature,* IV (November 19, 1927), p. 318.
2. Ibid.
3. Ibid.
4. Ruth Suckow, "I Could Write if Only–," *The Outlook,* CXLVIII (March 21, 1928), p. 478.
5. Ruth Suckow, "Development of a Story," an unpublished manuscript, p. 12.
6. Ibid., 21-22.
7. Ibid., 22.
8. Florence Haxton Britten, "Sparrows of Iowa," *New York Herald Tribune Books,* August 16, 1931, Part xi, p. 7.
9. Harold Blodgett, *The Story Survey* (New York, 1939), p. 248.
10. Britten, loc. cit.

11. H. L. Mencken, review of *Iowa Interiors, The American Mercury,* IX (November, 1926), 382-383.
12. "Uprooted," *Iowa Interiors,* p. 93.
13. Ibid., p. 90.
14. Ibid., p. 92.
15. Ibid., p. 93.
16. Ibid., p. 104.
17. Ibid., p. 87.
18. Ibid., p. 98.
19. Ibid., p. 107.
20. Ibid., p. 95.
21. Ibid., p. 106.
22. "Four Generations," *Iowa Interiors,* p. 251.
23. Ibid., p. 260.
24. "Mame," *Iowa Interiors,* p. 71.
25. Ibid., p. 73.
26. Ibid., p. 75.
27. "The Resurrection," *Iowa Interiors,* p. 199.
28. Fred T. Marsh, "Ruth Suckow, Historian of the Prairie Town," review of *Children and Older People, The New York Times Book Review* (August 23, 1931), Section IV, p. 4.
29. "A Home-coming," *Iowa Interiors,* p. 36.
30. "The Daughter," *Iowa Interiors,* p. 49.
31. Mrs. Kemper," *Children and Older People,* pp. 154-155.
32. "A Start in Life," *Iowa Interiors,* p. 2.
33. Ibid.
34. Ibid., p. 3.
35. Ibid., p. 9.
36. Ibid., p. 11.
37. Ibid., p. 16.
38. Ibid., p. 17.
39. "The Man of the Family," *Children and Older People,* p. 174.
40. Ibid.
41. Ibid.
42. "Eminence," *Children and Older People,* p. 3.
43. Ibid., p. 4.
44. Ibid., p. 8.
45. Ibid., p. 10.
46. Ibid., p. 13.
47. Ibid., p. 15.
48. Ibid., p. 18.
49. "Golden Wedding," *Iowa Interiors,* p. 281.

50. Ibid., p. 283.
51. "Midwestern Primitive," *Children and Older People*, p. 246.
52. "Auntie Bissel," *Some Others and Myself*, p. 102.
53. Ibid., p. 100.
54. Ibid., pp. 100-101.
55. "An Elegy for Alma's Aunt Amy," *Some Others and Myself*, p. 124.
56. "Mrs. Vogel and Ollie," *Some Others and Myself*, p. 36.
57. Ibid., p. 37.
58. "Merrittsville," *Some Others and Myself*, p. 71.
59. "Eltha," *Some Others and Myself*, p. 150.
60. "Merrittsville," p. 81.
61. Letter to Robert Fisher, March 21, 1951, quoted in the unpublished "Notes on Ruth Suckow's new book, *Seven Stories and a Memoir.*"

Appendix I

A BIOGRAPHICAL CHRONOLOGY

Vivian Anna Ruth Suckow (Mrs. Ferner Nuhn): 1892-1960
(The biographical information here presented was
verified by Miss Suckow in November, 1959.)

Parents: William John Suckow, son of John and Caroline
Suckow, natives of the dukedom of Mecklenburg,
Germany, and Anna Mary Kluckhohn, whose father,
Reverend Charles Kluckhohn, a Methodist minister,
came from the small city of Lippé-Detmold in the
province of Lippé.

1892   Born August 6, Hawarden, Iowa.

1894   Father accepted pastorate of Congregational Church
at LeMars, Iowa, town of 5000, which he held for one
year. During this time Ruth and her sister, Emma,
lived with an aunt in Paulina, Iowa, while their mother
was receiving medical treatment, first at Hawarden,
then at Kirksville, Missouri, and later at St. Paul.

1896   Family returned to Hawarden to live.

1898   Father accepted pastorate at Algona, Iowa. There
Ruth attended Central School.

1901   In the summer the family went to Buffalo to attend
the Pan American Exposition, to Albany to visit
relatives, and to Boston.

1902   In the spring her father accepted a church at Fort
Dodge where he stayed for three years.

During this period, Emma graduated from high school
in Fort Dodge.

Ruth attended Wabkonsa School.

197

The family spent the summer at Colorado Springs.

1906   The family moved to Manchester, Iowa, a town of 3000, and the county seat of Delaware County. This pastorate was held for one year.

1907   Father began a three-year field service for Grinnell College. The girls attended school there.

1910   Ruth graduated from high school at Grinnell. After her graduation the family moved to Davenport, where Reverend Suckow became pastor of the Edwards Congregational Church. Ruth matriculated at Grinnell College; specialized in English.

While Ruth was at Grinnell, her sister was married in Davenport, Iowa, to Edwin O. Hunting, a Grinnell College classmate. They had two children, Robert Suckow Hunting and Judith Ann Hunting.

1912   Father resigned from the ministry and took a position writing lectures for the Victor Animatograph Company, manufacturer of stereopticons and moving pictures, in Davenport, Iowa.

Father purchased forty acres of land, twenty miles west of Mobile, Alabama.

1913   Ruth left Grinnell College in June. While a student at Grinnell she spent one summer as a waitress in Yellowstone Park.

1914   Emma moved to Colorado for her health.

1915   Ruth graduated from the Curry School of Expression in Boston and came home to be with her father, who had returned to the ministry and accepted in January his second pastorate at Manchester, Iowa.

Ruth spent a month with her mother and Emma at Colorado Springs.

Enrolled in the University of Denver.

1916   Father's church building destroyed by fire on November 24, after a party.

1917   Received a B.A. degree from the University of Denver.
            While in Denver she spent one summer as waitress at
            Long's Peak Inn in Rocky Mountain National Park.

1917-18   For one year was assistant to Dr. Ida Kruse
            McFarlane, Head of the Department of English,
            University of Denver.

            Received an M.A. degree in English, University of
            Denver. After receiving degree spent one winter as
            employee of a map company in Denver. Wrote
            material for automobile guide books.

1918   First published poem, "An Old Woman in a Garden,"
            appeared in *Touchstone* in August. "Song in
            October," poem, published in *The Midland,*
            September-October.

1919   In Denver learning apiary business from Miss Delia
            Weston. Mother died and was brought to Garner,
            Iowa, for services in the Congregational Church and
            for burial.

            Father's resignation from Manchester pastorate to be
            effective in October.

            He and Ruth made a trip to Mobile, Alabama.

            Later he accepted a pastorate at Earlville, Iowa. Ruth
            moved to the parsonage with him and established her
            "Orchard Apiary" at the edge of town.

1920   Emma lost her son.

1921   First published story, "Uprooted," in *The Midland* for
            February.

            Father began pastorate at Forest City, May 1, 1921.

            "By Hill and Dale," poem, published in *Poetry,* June.

1921-22   January 25 at Cedar Falls her father married Mrs. Opal
            Swindle. She had two sons, Earl and Duane Swindle.
            During the winter of 1922-23 Ruth lived with them.

1923   Emma died of tuberculosis.

"A Part of the Institution," a short novel, published in *The Smart Set,* October.

1924   *Country People* first published serially in *The Century Magazine,* later by Knopf.

From 1924 to 1934 lived in New York in winters and kept bees in Earlville during the summer.

1925   *The Odyssey of a Nice Girl.*
1926   *Iowa Interiors.*

Ellan McIlvaine became literary agent. At Miss McIlvaine's death Marie F. Rodell, 15 East 48th Street, New York, New York, became agent.

1928   *The Bonney Family.*

Father accepted his last pastorate at Alden, Iowa.

1929   Ruth married Ferner Nuhn, son of Mr. and Mrs. Wm. C. Nuhn, Cedar Falls, Iowa.

Marriage took place in San Diego, California, March 11. Lived in Sante Fe until November, 1929.

Cora.

1930   *The Kramer Girls.*

Honorary degree awarded by Grinnell College to Ruth Suckow.

1931   *Children and Older People.*

Lived in McGregor, Iowa, part of the year.

1931-32 Lived in Cedar Falls, Iowa. While living there did some "guest instruction" and gave talks at Iowa State Teachers College, University of Iowa, and Indiana University.

1933   Spent part of winter in Des Moines and part in Altadena, California, the summer at Artists' Colony, Yaddo, Saratoga Springs, and at the MacDowell Memorial Colony at Peterborough, New Hampshire.

1934   *The Folks.* A Literary Guild selection.

1934-36   Residence in Washington, D.C.

Lived for one year in Fairfax Court House, Virginia, while her husband was connected with the Department of Agriculture, for which he wrote pamphlets and other material.

Appointed by President Roosevelt to membership on Farm Tenancy Committee of which L. C. Gray was administrator and Henry Wallace was head.

Spent summer at Robert Frost's home at Shaftsbury, Vermont.

1936-38   Lived in Cedar Falls, taking active part in community life. During this time her sister's child, Judith Ann Hunting, was married to Wells Barnett. They have one daughter, Bonnie Ruth.

1939   Father died. Buried in Cedar Falls, April 6.

Ruth and her husband traveled in Denmark, Norway, Sweden, and England.

1942   *New Hope.*

1945   Associated with the University of Wisconsin's summer Writers' Institute.

1951   Residence in Tucson, Arizona.

1952   Moved to Claremont, California. Purchased home which she retained as her permanent residence until her death January 23, 1960. After moving there spent part of one summer and early fall in Moylan, near Media, Pennsylvania. Her husband studied at Pendle Hill.

Some Others and Myself.

Affiliation with Friends Society began about this time. Interest in Friends had preceded that date. During World War II visited Civilian Public Service Camps, units in mental hospitals, fire-fighting units, starvation units under the combined sponsorship of the Service Committees of the Friends, Church of the Brethren, and the Mennonites. She spoke on literary subjects, talked with young men and read manuscripts.

1955   "Friends and Fiction," published in *Friends Intelligencer,* February, 1955.

Review of *Robert Elsmere* in *The Georgia Review,* Fall, 1955.

1958   "The Surprising Anthony Trollope," *The Georgia Review,* Winter, 1958.

1959   *The John Wood Case.*

1960   Died January 23, Claremont, California.

APPENDIX II

A Chronology of Writings by Ruth Suckow

1. *Periodical Material*

1918

"An Old Woman in a Garden: Poems," *Touchstone,* III (August, 1918), 391-392.

"Song in October," *The Midland,* IV (September-October, 1918), 216.

1921

"Uprooted," *The Midland,* VII (February, 1921), 83-109. Later in *Iowa Interiors.*

"Retired," *The Midland,* VII (April, 1921), 150-158. Later in *Iowa Interiors.*

"Resurrection," *The Midland,* VII (June, 1921), 217-222. Later in *Iowa Interiors* and in *Carry-Over.*

"By Hill and Dale," *Poetry,* XVIII (June, 1921), 142-143.

"A Home-coming," *The Smart Set,* LXVI, No. 4 (November, 1921), 39-48. Later in *Iowa Interiors.*

"The Top of the Ladder," *The Smart Set,* LXVI, No. 4 (December, 1921), 35-41. Later in *Iowa Interiors.*

"Mame," *The Smart Set,* LXVI, No. 4 (December, 1921), 107-118. Later in *Iowa Interiors.*

1922

"Just Him and Her," *The Smart Set,* LXVII, No. 1 (January, 1922), 35-40. Later in *Iowa Interiors* and *Carry-Over.*

"A Pilgrim and a Stranger," *The Smart Set,* LXVII, No. 1 (January, 1922), 11-19. Later in *Iowa Interiors* and *Carry-Over.*

"The Daughter," *The Smart Set*, LXVIII, No. 1 (May, 1922), 21-27. Later in *Iowa Interiors*.

"A Rural Community," *The Midland*, VIII (July, 1922), 217-245, Later in *Iowa Interiors*.

"Wanderers," *The Smart Set*, LXIX, No. 1 (September, 1922), 51-62. Later in *Iowa Interiors* and *Carry-Over*.

"The Best of the Lot" (a complete short novel), *the Smart Set*, LXIX, No. 3 (November, 1922), 5-36.

1923

"Other People's Ambitions," *The Smart Set*, LXX, No. 3 (March, 1923), 5-38.

"Renters" (woodcuts by J. J. Lankes), *The Century Magazine*, CVI, No. 4 (August, 1923), 599-613. Later in *Iowa Interiors* and *Carry-Over*.

"A Part of the Institution" (a complete short novel), *The Smart Set*, LXXII, No. 2 (October, 1923), 11-53.

1924

"Four Generations," *The American Mercury*, I (January, 1924), 15-21. Later in *Iowa Interiors*.

"Country People" (woodcut by Herschel C. Logan), a novel serialized in *The Century Magazine*, CVII, No. 3 (January, 1924), 406-420; (February, 1924), 536-551; (March, 1924), 731-747; (April, 1924), 908-928.

"A Start in Life," *The American Mercury*, III (September, 1924), 15-23. Later in *Iowa Interiors*.

1925

"Golden Wedding," *The American Mercury*, IV (February, 1925), 221-231. Later in *Iowa Interiors* and *Carry-Over*.

1926

"An Investment for the Future," *The American Mercury*, VII (January, 1926), 10-21. Later in *Iowa Interiors*.

"The Man of the Family," *The American Mercury*, IX (December, 1926), 412-420. Later in *Children and Older People* and *Carry-Over.*

"Literary Soubrettes," *The Bookman*, LXIII (July, 1926), 517-521.

"Iowa," *The American Mercury*, IX (September, 1926), 39-45.

1927

"Eminence," *The American Mercury*, X (March, 1927), 273-280. Later in *Children and Older People.*

"Good Pals," *The American Mercury*, XII (October, 1927), 211-221. Later in *Children and Older People* and *Carry-Over.*

"A German Grandfather," *The American Mercury*, XII (November, 1927), 280-284.

"Elsie Dinsmore: A Study in Perfection," *The Bookman*, LXVI (October, 1927), 126-133.

"The Little Girl from Town," *Harper's Monthly Magazine*, CLV (August, 1927), 327-337. Later in *Children and Older People.*

"The Short Story," *The Saturday Review of Literature*, IV (November 19, 1927), 317-318.

1928

"Midwestern Primitive," *Harper's Monthly Magazine*, CLVI (March, 1928), 432-442. Later in *Children and Older People.*

"I Could Write If Only—," *The Outlook*, CXLVIII (March 21, 1928), 461-463.

"Spinster and Cat," *Harper's Monthly Magazine*, CLVII (June, 1928), 59-68. Later in *Children and Older People* and *Carry-Over.*

1929

"The Big Kids and the Little Kids," *Good Housekeeping*, LXXXVIII (January, 1929), 50-53. Later in *Children and Older People* and *Carry-Over.*

"The Valentine Box," *Good Housekeeping,* LXXXVIII (February, 1929), 26-29. Later in *Children and Older People.*

"Strong as a Man," *Harper's Monthly Magazine,* CLVIII (April, 1929), 540-550.

"Mrs. Kemper," *The American Mercury,* XVI (April, 1929), 405-409. Later in *Children and Older People* and *Carry-Over.*

"Visiting," illustrated by C. R. Chickering, *Pictorial Review,* XXX (July, 1929), 17-19.

"A Homecoming," *Good Housekeeping,* LXXXIX (August, 1929), 54-57. Later in *Iowa Interiors.*

"Sunset Camp," *Harper's Monthly Magazine,* CLIX (November, 1929), 693-699. Later in *Children and Older People.*

"Experience," *The American Mercury,* XVIII (December, 1929), 396-402. Later in *Children and Older People.*

"Susan and the Doctor," *Harper's Monthly Magazine,* CLX (December, 1929), 20-23. Later in *Children and Older People.*

1930

"The Kramer Girls," illustrated by Maurice L. Bower, serialized in *Good Housekeeping,* LXXXIX (December, 1929), 16-19; XC (January, 1930), 36-39; XC (February, 1930), 62-65; XC (March, 1930), 78-81.

"The Folk Idea in American Life," *Scribner's Magazine,* LXXXVIII (September, 1930), 245-255. Later published as pamphlet, New York, 1934.

1931

"Three Counting the Cat," *Good Housekeeping,* XCIII (September, 1931), 30-33.

1932

"An Elegy for Alma's Aunt Amy," *Harper's Monthly Magazine,* CLXIV (May, 1932), 653-654. Later in *Some Others and Myself.*

"Middle Western Literature," *The English Journal* (College Edition), XXI (March, 1932), 175-182.

1935

"The Crick," *Good Housekeeping,* C (February, 1935), 32-35.

"Auntie Bissel," *Scribner's Magazine,* XCVIII (August, 1935), 84-92. Later in *Some Others and Myself.*

1936

"Hollywood Gods and Goddesses," *Harper's Monthly Magazine,* CLXXIII (July, 1936), 189-200.

1939

"What Have I," *Harper's Monthly Magazine,* CLXXVIII (January, 1939), 126-137.

"A Start in Life," *Scholastic,* XXXV (December 11, 1939), 11-12.

1953

"An Almost Lost American Classic," *College English,* XIV, No. 6 (March, 1953), 315-325.

1955

"Friends and Fiction," *Friends Intelligencer,* CXII, No. 7 (Second Month 12, 1955), 90-92.

"Robert Elsmere Reviewed by Ruth Suckow," *The Georgia Review,* IX, No. 3 (Fall, 1955), 345-348.

1958

"The Surprising Anthony Trollope," *The Georgia Review,* XII, No. 4 (Winter, 1958), 388-395.

2. *Books*

Country People. New York: Alfred A. Knopf, 1924.
The Odyssey of a Nice Girl. New York: Alfred A. Knopf, 1925.

Iowa Interiors. New York: Alfred A. Knopf, 1926.

The Bonney Family. New York: Alfred A. Knopf, 1928.

Cora. New York: Alfred A. Knopf, 1929.

The Kramer Girls. New York: Alfred A. Knopf, 1931.

Children and Older People. New York: Alfred A. Knopf, 1931.

The Folks. New York: Farrar & Rinehart, Inc., 1934.

Carry-Over. New York: Farrar & Rinehart, Inc., 1936.

New Hope. New York: Farrar & Rinehart, Inc., 1942.

Some Others and Myself. New York: Rinehart & Company, Inc., 1952.

The John Wood Case. New York: The Viking Press, 1959.

3. *Posthumous Works,* Edited by Ferner Nuhn

"A Little Girl's World," *Midwest,* State College of Iowa, III, No. 2 (Spring, 1960), 1.

"Cycle of the Seasons in Iowa; Unpublished Diary of Ruth Suckow," *The Iowan,* IX (October-November, 1960; December-January, 1960-61; February-March, 1961; April-May, 1961).

"Prairie Woods and Wild Flowers," *American Heritage,* XVI (April, 1965), 36-42.

4. *Anthologized Stories*

Stories by Miss Suckow have appeared in numerous anthologies. The following is not a complete list of anthologized material, but it indicates the stories most often reprinted together with the titles and editors of the collections in which they appear.

"Eminence"
Lohan, Robert and Maria. *New Christmas Treasury.* New York, 1954.

"Four Generations"
Hastings, Harry Worthington. *The College Short Story Reader.* New York, 1948.

O'Brien, R. J. *Best Short Stories.* Boston, 1924.
_____ . *Fifty Best American Short Stories. 1915-1939.* Boston, 1939.
Shaw, Henry, and Ruth Davis. *Americans One and All.* New York, 1947.
Spencer, Frances H. *American Family Album: Stories of American Family Life.* New York, 1946.

"Golden Wedding"

Becker, May Lamberton. *Golden Tales of the Prairie States.* New York, 1932.
Blodgett, Harold. *The Story Survey.* New York, 1939.
Brown, Leonard. *Modern American and British Short Stories.* New York, 1929.
_____ . *Modern Short Stories.* New York, 1937.
Kling, Samuel G. *For Better or Worse.* New York, 1947.

"Just Him and Her"

Kling, Samuel G. *For Better or Worse.* New York, 1947.
Rascoe, Burton, and Groff Conklin. *The Bachelor's Companion: A Smart Set Collection.* New York, 1944.

"The Little Girl from Town"

Burrell, John A., and Bennet A. Cerf. *Bedside Book of Famous American Stories* (also in Braille edition). New York, 1936.
Williams, Blanche C. *O. Henry Memorial Award Prize Stories.* New York, 1927.
_____ . *Short Stories for College Classes.* New York, 1929.

"The Man of the Family"

Cross, Ethan Allan. *The Book of the Short Story,* New York, 1929.
Goodman, Henry. *Creating the Short Story.* New York, 1929.
Haydrick, Benjamin A. *Americans All: Stories of American Life.* New York, 1920.
Kimball, Rodney A. *The Short Story Reader.* New York, 1946.
McDowell, Termaine. *America in Literature.* New London, Connecticut, 1944.

"A Memoir"
  Distributed by the Christian Herald Association for its Christian Herald Family Bookshelf.
"Midwestern Primitive"
  Blankenship, Russell, Winifred Nash, and Pauline Warner. *Literature We Appreciate.* New York, 1940.
  Inglis, Rewey Belle, *et al. Adventures in American Literature.* New York, 1941.
  Lucas, Harriet M. *Prose and Poetry of Today.* Morristown, New Jersey, 1941.
  O'Brien, E. J. *Best Short Stories of 1928.* New York, 1928.
  Pence, Raymond W. *Short Stories of Present-Day Authors.* New York, 1922.
"Renters"
  Fagin, Nathan B. *America Through the Short Story.* Boston, 1936.
  O'Brien, E. J. *Best Short Stories of 1923.* Boston, 1923.
  _____ . *Modern American Short Stories.* New York, 1932.
"Retired"
  Lee, Charles. *North, East, South, West: A Regional Anthology of American Writing.* Berkeley, California, 1945.
"The Resurrection"
  Frederick, John T. *Out of the Midwest.* New York, 1944.
"A Rural Community"
  Frederick, John T. *Stories from the Midland.* New York, 1924.
  Hazard, Lucy Lockwood. *In Search of America.* New York, 1930.
  Wimberly, Lowry Charles. *Mid Country: Writings from the Heart of America.* Lincoln, Nebraska, 1945.
"Spinster and Cat"
  Clarke, Frances Elizabeth. *Cats—and Cats: Great Cat Stories of Our Day.* New York, 1937.
  Palmer, Paul. *World's Best Stories of 1929.* New York, 1929.
"A Start in Life"
  Becker, May Lamberton. *Growing Up with America: An Anthology.* New York, 1941.

_____ . *Under Twenty*. New York, 1932.

Daly, Maureen. *My Favorite Stories*. New York, 1948.

Ellis, Amanda Mae. *Representative Short Stories*. New York, 1938.

Flanagan, John T. *America Is West*. Minneapolis, 1945.

Kern, John D., and Irwin Griggs. *This America*. New York, 1942.

Knickerbocker, K. L., and H. Willard Reninger. *Interpreting Literature*. New York, 1945.

Maugham, William Somerset. *Tellers of Tales*. New York, 1939.

Mirrilees, Edith Ronald. *Significant Contemporary Stories*. New York, 1929.

Taggard, Ernestine K. *Here We Are: Stories from Scholastic Magazine*. New York, 1941.

Taylor, Warner. *Varied Narratives*. New York, 1932.

"Susan and the Doctor"

Bates, Sylvia Chatfield. *Twentieth Century Stories*. Boston, 1933.

Beaty, John O., *et al. Facts and Ideas for Students of English Composition*. New London, Connecticut, 1939.

Palmer, Paul. *World's Best Short Stories of 1930*. New York, 1930.

"Uprooted"

Brewster, Dorothy. *Book of Modern Short Stories*. New York, 1928.

Ellis, Amanda Mae. *Representative Short Stories*. New York, 1928.

Frederick, John T. *Present-Day Stories*. New York, 1941.

_____ . *Stories from the Midland*. New York, 1924.

Gott, Charles, and J. A. Behnke. *Preface to College Prose,* New York, 1935.

Johnson, Ray Ivan, Esther Cowan, and Mary Peacock. *Study and Appreciation of the Short Story,* Morristown, New Jersey, 1938.

Wunsch, William Robert, and Edna Albers. *Thicker Than Water: Stories of Family Life.* edited for the Commission on Human Relations, New York, 1939.

BIBLIOGRAPHY

1. *Unpublished Material*

Fisher, Richard. "Ruth Suckow: A Study in Critical Opinion." Prepared for a seminar at the University of California at Los Angeles, May, 1951.

Frederick, John T. Letters to Margaret Stewart: November 11, 1951; July 4, 1956.

Marshall, Robert K. Letter to Margaret Stewart: December 10, 1951.

"Notes on Ruth Suckow's New Book." Unpublished notes prepared to accompany the volume published as *Some Others and Myself.*

Suckow, John William. "Seventy Years in Retrospect." An autobiography in the possession of Mrs. Opal Suckow, Earlville, Iowa.

2. *Periodicals*

Asbury, Herbert. "The American Interior," review of *Iowa Interiors, New York Herald Tribune Books* (October 3, 1926), Part VII, pp. 6-7.

Austin, Mary. "Regionalism in American Fiction," *The English Journal,* XXI (February, 1932), 97-107.

Baker, Joseph E. "Four Arguments for Regionalism," *The Saturday Review of Literature,* XV (November 28, 1936), 3-4, 14.

_____ . "Regionalism in the Middlewest," *The American Review,* IV (March, 1935), 603-614.

Beath, P. R. "Four Fallacies of Regionalism," *The Saturday Review of Literature,* XV (November 28, 1936), 3-4, 14-16.

Bessie, Alvah C. "Home-Folks in Iowa," review of *The Folks, The Saturday Review of Literature,* XI (October 6, 1934), 160.

Boothe, B. E. "Ruth Suckow, an Appreciation," *Diamonds Bulletin* (January 27, 1939), pp. 1-2.

Botkin. B. A. "Regionalism: Cult or Culture?" *The English Journal,* XXV (March, 1936), 181-184.

Britten, Florence Haxton. "Sparrows of Iowa," review of *Children and Older People, New York Herald Tribune Books* (August 16, 1931), Part XI, p. 6.

Cordell, Richard A. Review of *New Hope, The Saturday Review of Literature,* XXV (February 28, 1942), 8.

Davidson, Donald. "Regionalism and Nationalism in American Literature," *The American Review,* V (April, 1935), 48-61.

Dodd, Lee Wilson. "A Test Case," review of *Iowa Interiors, The Saturday Review of Literature,* III (November 27, 1926), 331-332.

Flanagan, John T. "A Bibliography of Middlewestern Farm Novels," *Minnesota History,* XXIII (June, 1942), 156-158.

_____ . "A Half-Century of Middlewestern Fiction," *Critique,* II (Winter, 1959), 16-34.

_____ . "The Middlewestern Farm Novel," *Minnesota History,* XXIII (June, 1942), 113-125.

_____ . Review of *Some Others and Myself, American Literature,* XXIV (January, 1953), 568-569.

Frederick, John T. "Early Iowa in Fiction," *The Palimpsest,* XXXVI (October, 1955), 389-420.

_____ . "The Farm in Iowa Fiction," *The Palimpsest,* XXXII (March, 1951), 124-152.

_____ . "Ruth Suckow and the Middle Western Literary Movement," *The English Journal,* XX (January, 1931), 1-8.

_____ . "Town and City in Iowa Fiction," *The Palimpsest,* XXXV (February, 1954), 49-96.

_____ . "The Writer's Iowa," *The Palimpsest,* XI (February, 1930), 57-60.

_____ . "The Younger School," *The Palimpsest,* XI (February, 1930), 78-86.

Gilman, Dorothy Foster. "Out of the Old Family Album," review of *The Kramer Girls, New York Herald Tribune Books* (March 30, 1930), Part XI, p. 5.

Gregory, Horace. "Back Home Among American Prairie Folks," review of *The Folks, New York Herald Tribune Books* (September 30, 1934), Part VII, p. 5.

Hamblen, Abigail Ann. "The Poetry of Place," Cornell College

Husk, XL (March, 1961), 75-79.

Haxton, Florence. "A Full-Bodied Novel," review of *Cora, New York Herald Tribune Books* (October 20, 1929), Part XII, p.10.

Hearst, Gladys Whitley. "A Cat May Look at a Queen," *Quotarian,* XXIV (April, 1947), 4-7.

Herbst, Josephine. "Iowa Takes to Literature," *The American Mercury,* VII (April, 1926), 466-470.

_____ . "Two Mid-American Novelists," *New Republic,* LXXXVIII (October 23, 1936), 318-319.

Herron, Ima Honaker. "Ruth Suckow's *The Folks,*" *Dallas Morning News Magazine Section* (September 30, 1934), p. 12.

Hill, Helen. "A Local Habitation," *The Sewanee Review,* XXXIX (October-December, 1931), 460-465.

Hutchison, Percy. "Miss Suckow Portrays Rural Iowa," review of *The Bonney Family, The New York Times Book Review* (January 22, 1928), Section IV, p. 2.

Krutch, J. W. "The Tragic Lift," review of *Country People, Nation,* CXIX (August 20, 1924), 194.

Lovett, Robert Morse. "Ideas and Fiction," review of *The Odyssey of a Nice Girl, New Republic,* XLIV (November 18, 1925), 336-337.

_____ . "Recent Fiction," review of *Iowa Interiors, New Republic,* XLIX (December 1, 1926), 50.

McDowell, Termaine. "Regionalism in American Literature," *Minnesota History,* XX (June, 1939), 105-118.

Maclead, Norman. "Regionalism: A Symposium," *The Sewanee Review,* XXXIX (October-December, 1931), 456-483.

Marsh, Fred T. "Ruth Suckow, Historian of the Prairie Town," review of *Children and Older People, The New York Times Book Review* (August 23, 1931), Section IV, p. 4.

Mencken, H. L. "The Library," review of *Country People, The American Mercury,* II (July, 1924), 382.

_____ . "The Library," review of *The Odyssey of a Nice Girl, The American Mercury,* VII (April, 1926), 506-507.

_____ . "The Library," review of *Iowa Interiors, The American Mercury,* IX (November, 1926), 382-383.

_____ . "The Library," review of *The Bonney Family, The American Mercury,* XIV (May, 1928), 127.

_____ . "The Library," review of *Cora, The American Mercury*, XIX (January, 1930), 137.

Meyers, Walter L. "The Novel and the Simple Soul," *Virginia Quarterly Review*, XIII (August, 1937), 507.

Mott, Frank Luther. "Exponents of the Pioneers," *The Palimpsest*, XI (February, 1930), 61-66.

_____ . "Iowa Looks at Ruth Suckow," *Wings* (publication of the Literary Guild), VIII (October, 1934), 25.

Nevins, Allan. 'A Painter of Iowa," *The Saturday Review of Literature*, IV (March 10, 1928), 666.

Nuhn, Ferner. "A Real Family," review of *The Bonney Family, New York Herald Tribune Books* (January 22, 1928), Part XII, p. 7.

Paluka, Frank. "Ruth Suckow: A Calendar of Letters," *Books at Iowa*, University of Iowa Libraries, Iowa City (October, 1964 and April, 1965).

Paramore, Edward E. "The New Books," review of *The Odyssey of a Nice Girl, The Saturday Review of Literature*, II (December 19, 1925), 435.

Ransom, John Crowe. "The Aesthetic of Regionalism," *The American Review*, II (January, 1934), 290-310.

Reninger, H. W. Remarks at the Memorial Service for Ruth Suckow Nuhn, *Midwest, A Literary Review*, Iowa State Teachers College, Cedar Falls, Iowa, II (Spring, 1960), 13-14; 41-42.

Sherman, Caroline B. "Farm Life Fiction Reaches Maturity," *The Sewanee Review*, XXIX (October-December, 1931), 472-483.

Sloan, Sam B. "Misrepresentative Fiction," *The Palimpsest*, XII (February, 1931), 41-56.

Starkey, Marion L. "Ruth Suckow from Iowa to New York," *Boston Evening Transcript Book Section* (May 24, 1930), pp. 1-2.

Stegner, Wallace. "The Trail of the Hawkeye," *The Saturday Review of Literature*, XVIII (July 30, 1938), 2-4, 16-17.

Walton, Edith. "An Iowa Idyll," review of *New Hope, The New York Times Book Review* (February 22, 1942), Section VI, pp. 6-7.

_____ . "The Middle Western Way of Life," review of

The Folks, The New York Times Book Review (September 30, 1934), Section V, p. 2.

Winslow, Thyra Samter. "An Interesting Picture of an Unimportant Person," review of *The Odyssey of a Nice Girl, New York Herald Tribune Books* (December 20, 1925), Part VI, p. 15.

Woolsey, D. B. "The Bonney Family," review of *The Bonney Family, New Republic,* LIV (March 7, 1928), 106.

Wright, Luella M. "Fiction in History," *The Palimpsest,* XXVIII (April, 1947), 97-111.

Yezierska, Anzia. "Seven Tales and a Fact," review of *Some Others and Myself, The New York Times Book Review* (January 6, 1952), Section VII, p. 4.

3. *Books*

Atherton, Lewis Eldon. *Main Street on the Middle Border.* Bloomington, Indiana, 1954.

Beach, Joseph Warren. *American Fiction: 1920-1940.* New York, 1942.

Bernard, Harry. *Le Roman Regionalists Aux Etats-Unis. (1913-1940),* Montreal, 1949.

Blodgett, J. B. *The Story Survey.* New York, 1939.

Boynton, Percy. *America in Contemporary Fiction.* Chicago, 1940.

Brigham, Johnson (ed.). *A Book of Iowa Authors by Iowa Authors.* Des Moines, 1930.

Brown, E. K. *Willa Cather, A Critical Biography.* New York, 1953.

Brown, Leonard. *Modern Short Stories.* New York, 1937.

Blankenship, Russell. *American Literature as an Expression of the National Mind.* New York, 1931.

Calverton, V. F. *The Liberation of American Literature.* New York, 1932.

Commager, Henry Steele. *The American Mind.* New Haven, 1950.

Cowie, Alexander. *The Rise of the American Novel.* New York, 1948.

Cowley, Malcolm. *After the Genteel Tradition.* New York, 1936.

Curti, Merle. *The Growth of American Thought*. New York, 1943.

Davidson, Donald. *The Attack of Leviathan: Regionalism and Nationalism in the United States*. Gloucester, Massachusetts: 1962.

Deegan, Dorothy Yost. *The Stereotype of the Single Woman in American Novels*. New York, 1951.

Flanagan, John T. *America Is West*. Minneapolis, 1945.

Frederick, John T. *Out of the Midwest*. New York, 1944.

Gurko, Leo. *The Angry Decade*. New York, 1947.

Hartwick, Harry. *The Foreground of American Fiction*. New York, 1934.

Hatcher, Harlan. *Creating the Modern American Novel*. New York, 1935.

Hazard, Lucy Lockwood. *The Frontier in American Literature*. New York, 1927.

Herron, Ima Honaker. *The Small Town in American Literature*. Durham, North Carolina, 1939.

Hicks, Granville. *The Great Tradition*. New York, 1933.

Hoffman, Frederick J. *The Twenties*. New York, 1955.

Hoffman, Frederick J., *et al. The Little Magazines*, Princeton, 1946.

Horton, Roy N., and Herbert N. Edwards. *Backgrounds of American Literary Thought*. New York, 1952.

Iowa, A Guide to the Hawkeye State. American Guide Series. Federal Writers' Project of the Works Progress Administration for the State of Iowa, New York, 1938.

Jensen, Merrill. *Regionalism in America*. Madison, Wisconsin, 1951.

Kissane, Leedice McAnnelly. *Ruth Suckow*. Twayne's United States Authors Series. New York: 1969.

Knight, Grant C. *The Critical Period in American Literature*. Chapel Hill, 1951.

Kunitz, Stanley J., and Howard Haycraft (eds.). *Twentieth Century Authors*. New York, 1942.

Lawrence, Margaret. *The School of Femininity*. New York, 1936.

Lewis, Sinclair. "Introductory Remarks" to *Country People,* reprinted in *The Three Readers,* edited by Clifton Fadiman (q. v.), Sinclair Lewis and Carl Van Doren, New York, 1943.

217

Lewisohn, Ludwig. *The Story of American Literature.* New York, 1939.

_____ . *Expression in America.* New York, 1932.

McWilliams, Carey. *The New Regionalism in American Literature.* Seattle, 1930.

Millett, Fred B. *Contemporary Authors.* New York, 1944.

Odum, Howard W., and Harry Estill Moore. *American Regionalism.* New York, 1938.

Rahv, Philip. *Image and Idea.* Norfolk, Connecticut, 1949.

Spiller, Robert E., *et al. Literary History of the United States.* New York, 1948.

Stong, Phil. *Hawkeyes, A Biography of the State of Iowa.* New York, 1940.

Van Doren, Carl. *The American Novel: 1789-1939.* New York, 1940.

Warfel, Harry R. *American Novelists of Today.* New York, 1951.

Wharton, Edith. *The Writing of Fiction.* New York, 1925.